KINDRED SPIRITS

Harvard Business School's
Extraordinary Class of 1949
and How They Transformed
American Business

DAVID CALLAHAN

JOHN WILEY & SONS, INC.

Published by John Wiley & Sons, Inc., Hoboken, New Jersey.
Published simultaneously in Canada.

For general information on our other products and services please contact our Customer Care Department within the U.S. at (800) 762-2974, outside the United States at (317) 572-3993 or fax (317) 572-4002.

Wiley also publishes its books in a variety of electronic formats. Some content that appears in print may not be available in electronic books.

ISBN: 0-471-41819-6

Printed in the United States of America.

10 9 8 7 6 5 4 3 2 1

Contents

Foreword

Y ou can think of this book as a morality tale for these scandal-ridden times. *Kindred Spirits* is about a disparate but closely knit group of young men, most of them veterans of World War II, who played a major role in creating the modern American economy. But for all the wealth they helped to create and for all their business accomplishments, only one of them to my knowledge ended up on the Forbes 400 list of the richest Americans—and that one through inheritance. Getting rotten rich wasn't what these people were about. The nouveau riche boorishness that led Enron's Ken Lay to own three homes in Aspen alone was not for this group. Few of them were celebrity collectors or nightspot mavens. Building successful careers and raising successful families were what most of these businesspeople were about.

The origins of *Kindred Spirits* date back to 1998. One day that summer I lunched at the Harvard Club in New York with Marvin Traub, the marketing genius who turned a humdrum department store, Bloomingdale's, into a merchandising icon. Marvin told me that his classmates from the Harvard Business School class of 1949 were planning a grand 50th reunion the next September.

I already knew a good deal about the Harvard Business School class of 1949. Its members had been in the vanguard of a new class of managers who transformed American commerce and industry in the aftermath of World War II. When they rolled up their sheepskin diplomas and entered the job market, business was evolving from a seat-of-the-pants affair into a quasi-profession; the master of business administration degree was becoming the ticket of entry to the fast track. The MBA graduates emerging from Harvard in 1949 were, for the most part, off to a running start. They held prestigious diplomas and there was plenty of opportunity in the business world, which had been starved of fresh talent during the war years and the Great Depression.

More than a third of Marvin Traub's classmates eventually rose to the rank of CEO. They and others like them laid the groundwork for the great boom of the 1990s. The Harvard Business School class profiled in David Callahan's book includes such business heroes of mine as Tom Murphy, Jim Burke, and Marvin Traub. If you were old enough to be reading the business news in the 1970s and 1980s these people would be well known to you. If the names are unfamiliar but you care about business, you will learn about—and from—them in this book.

A decade of almost unbroken prosperity is now culminating in a frighteningly volatile stock market. With revelations of corporate immorality, it is instructive to see how the executives of an earlier era dealt with sometimes overwhelming difficulties: two hot wars, Korea and Vietnam; the Cold War; an energy crisis; labor unrest; and inflation that ran as high as 14 percent annually. These young business professionals also had to deal with a mounting economic challenge from our defeated enemy, Japan, and from a resurgent Europe. The 1960s, 1970s, and 1980s may have been the best of times in some ways, but in others they were tough and trying times.

But *Kindred Spirits* is more than an exercise in nostalgia. It is the history of an economic era told through the careers of some of its leading players. The book had its beginnings in an article I wrote about the class with a former colleague, Rita Koselka. Now David Callahan has made it a gripping account of 40 dramatic years of change, progress, and turmoil in American business. Callahan, a good two generations younger than his subjects, could and did bring both objectivity and perspective to the tale.

As I write, it is midsummer 2002. The business and Wall Street people who are in the news today seem a sorry lot compared with most of the characters in this book. When I say "sorry lot," I am not just talking about the Ken Lays, the Bernie Ebbers, the Jack Grubmans. I also refer to the dozens of CEOs who destroyed corporate balance sheets during the 1990s and early 2000s. They did so by taking on short-term debt to pay for overpriced acquisitions. They went into debt to buy in their own shares at exalted prices. They showed an utter disregard for probabilities by promising an endless string of 15 percent and more annual earnings gains. And when they couldn't produce earnings, many of them claimed that earnings didn't matter; only EBIDTA mattered.

Others made their stock options pay off by gutting their corporate pay-roll, literally making themselves rich off the misfortunes of their colleagues. All this in the name of "maximizing shareholder values."

When I contemplate this sorry mess in our financial capital, I think of Harvard 49er Bill Ruane, a modest guy with a sense of humor. He will be the first to scoff if I make him sound like Mother Teresa, but I do wish there were more Wall Streeters like Bill. His Ruane & Cunniff operates the Sequoia Fund and manages money in private accounts. By current Wall Street measures, Ruane & Cunniff is small stuff. That's because Bill and his partners want it that way. By the early 1980s Sequoia's impressive performance had attracted as much money as Bill and his people felt they could handle. They closed the fund to new investors and have kept it closed for 20 years. Had they kept it open and publicized its record, I have no doubt the fund would be running $50 billion or even $100 billion instead of its current $4 billion or so.

Is Bill shortsighted? Not at all. Press him and he will tell you something Wall Street would just as soon you didn't learn: that good investment ideas are scarce—very, very scarce. If he takes on too much money he will have to lower his high investment parameters. That wouldn't be fair to his older clients.

The final moral of this particular story is that there is no need to take up a collection for Bill Ruane. He loves what he is doing and has made out handsomely doing it. As he will tell you if you praise him for his integrity, "Putting your clients first is not just good manners. It is good business." So it would seem.

Maybe that's not always true in the short run, but it certainly is true in the long run. I don't know precisely when the term *maximizing shareholder value* came into common usage, but in a way I wish it never had. Too often it means using gimmicks to get your stock up. It is rarely taken to mean building a solid business that adds value for your customers and creates exciting careers for your employees. You don't do that with financial leverage alone or by meeting and beating earnings projections. Most of the Harvard Business School 49ers knew this. Perhaps the tough times they faced and the war they lived through built their character. In any case, it is encouraging to be reminded that there is more to business than one might think after reading about the tawdry recent goings-on at Enron, WorldCom, and

Rite-Aid. *Kindred Spirits* is a pleasant antidote to today's headlines. More than that, it is an inspiring read for young people seeking to make a mark in the world of business.

James W. Michaels
Editor Emeritus, *Forbes* magazine
July, 2002

Introduction

N ineteen ninety-nine was a bad year in the stock market for Bill Ruane. It was worse, in fact, than any year he'd ever had except 1973, during the depths of a bear market. As 1999 closed, along with the century and the millennium, Ruane tallied up investment losses of an almost unfathomable scale. His legendary Sequoia Fund, which had almost consistently outperformed Standard & Poor's 500 Index over its 29-year history, had taken a staggering hit. The fund, valued at nearly $5 billion in 1998, had lost nearly a quarter of its value during 1999—lagging behind the S&P by 35 percentage points. Shareholders in the Sequoia Fund, which had long ago been closed to new investors, lost nearly a billion dollars in wealth. Among these shareholders were some of Ruane's oldest and closest friends, including buddies he had bonded with 50 years earlier at Harvard Business School.

Bill Ruane liked his privacy more than most people. Around Wall Street he had a reputation for being reclusive. Silver-haired and soft-spoken, with a youthful vitality, he maintained a remarkably low profile for a man who had built one of the most successful private investment funds in financial history and was worth tens of millions of dollars. In an industry filled with outsized egos and downright loudmouths, Ruane was unusual in his modesty and he was content with the quiet life. He lived on upper Fifth Avenue, in an apartment facing the park, and enjoyed long weekends in western Connecticut, where he and his wife Joy owned a farmhouse. Every weekday morning, Ruane dressed in a crisp, pressed shirt and an expensive suit before he headed down Fifth Avenue to his firm on the forty-fourth floor of the GM building, across from the Plaza Hotel. The firm, Ruane & Cunniff, was housed in offices with wood-paneled walls and polished antiques. It boasted soaring power views north over the green expanse of Central Park and, farther, to the George Washington Bridge.

Built up over three immensely profitable decades, the firm stood as an enduring monument to Ruane's vision and investing savvy. Several years earlier, Ruane had turned over the operational details of the business to younger people. Now, on most days, Ruane didn't spend much time in his spacious office at the firm. Instead, in a somewhat curious manner, he liked to hide out across the street, in a second office that he kept in the Sherry-Netherland Hotel. There, alone and unbothered, Ruane would do what he liked to do most, the thing that had won him his immense fortune: study companies and pick stocks. Noting his reclusive style, along with his brilliance in picking stocks, one Wall Street analyst had dubbed Ruane an "oracle."

During 1999, however, nobody thought of Bill Ruane as an oracle. Somehow Bill Ruane—Harvard Business School class of 1949, confidant of Warren Buffett, revered wise man of Wall Street—had managed to lose nearly a billion dollars during one of the hottest years in the history of the stock market. How was this possible?

The early part of the 1990s had unfolded in a fashion more fitting with Ruane's reputation, as well as that of his longtime partner Richard Cunniff. Between 1992 and 1997, the Sequoia Fund had won average returns of 27 percent a year. In early 1998, it had been ranked as one of the top three best-performing major growth stock funds on Wall Street. "Ruane and Cunniff have established themselves as two of the best investors in the world," one analyst commented in 1998. The men, said another analyst, had an "approach that works year in and year out."[1] It was in 1998 that Bill Ruane had been called an oracle—and not for the first time. Then came 1999, the year of disaster.

The felling of the mighty Sequoia Fund was, in fact, no great mystery: Bill Ruane didn't touch tech stocks, and in 1999 tech was where the money was.

Ruane's aversion to tech stocks reflected his longtime approach of "value investing." It was a simple methodology, pioneered by Columbia Business School professors Benjamin Graham and David Dodd and most famously practiced by the Omaha-based investor Warren Buffett, a close friend of Ruane's. Value investors look for profitable companies with strong, long-term prospects, but with stock undervalued by Wall Street. The strategy is to buy large holdings of the low-priced stock and then wait for common sense to prevail and for the market to eventually recognize the stock's true worth—at which point value investors sell off their shares and move on to the next bargain-basement stock pick.

For nearly three decades, value investing had worked for Bill Ruane. The Sequoia Fund had flourished, and Ruane—who'd grown up in a middle-class family in Depression-era Chicago—had become wealthy beyond his wildest dreams. This success was a vindication of the business credo held by Ruane and most of his classmates at Harvard Business School a half century earlier: Wealth is created patiently, generated by serious companies that make real things of real value. There are no shortcuts to riches, only hard work guided by strong ethics.

During the tech mania of 1999, however, shortcuts were the name of the game. Ruane's losses were due to his unwillingness to play this game. He saw tech stocks as overvalued and refused to invest in companies that made no profits. Warren Buffett, too, refused to play the game and his near-mythological status on Wall Street was tarnished as his megafund, Berkshire Hathaway, went into a downward spiral and lost billions.

In late 1999 and in the early weeks of 2000, as the full scope of losses by Ruane and Buffett was made clear, the value investors came under scathing attack. "Are these value managers in a slump or a coma?" asked an article in *TheStreet.com,* an online magazine that typified the limitless faith in a new tech-driven Wall Street. "Like Mozart flubbing 'Chopsticks' or Michael Jordan a dunk, some of the fund world's most celebrated value managers look a bit silly right now."[2] "Timber!" bellowed a headline in an *Investment News* article on Sequoia's meltdown.[3]

The revenge of Ruane and the value investors was not long in coming. In early spring 2000, Nasdaq finally crashed and huge losses swept across the entire range of tech stocks. As former Internet millionaires went broke, some moving back in with their parents, idolatrous articles on value investing would again be featured in the financial press. Once more, Bill Ruane was back to where he was used to being: on top. In 2000, the Sequoia Fund posted gains of 20 percent—29 points ahead of the S&P 500.

That fall, in September, Ruane joined a half-dozen members of the Harvard Business School class of 1949 for a lunch in Manhattan organized by Marvin Traub. Over the years, the energetic Traub had established himself as a main hub around which a vibrant 49er alumni network revolved, and when Traub sent out invitations for a get-together of class members, people responded. Just a year earlier, Traub had put together the fiftieth anniversary of the class. Several hundred class members—out of 700 or so original graduates—had shown up.

For the lunch, Ruane was dressed conservatively in a sharp suit and white shirt. It had been four months since the obliteration of Nasdaq, and Ruane nodded as his old classmates complimented him for holding tough to his philosophy during a time of utter madness on Wall Street. Many members of the class had been deeply perturbed by the hyping of the new economy and tech bull market. It was not the Internet that bothered these men; many had embraced the Web. One 49er at the lunch, Stanley Greenfield, had started an Internet company in his early 70s—"the oldest living Internet entrepreneur" he called himself—and another 49er, media powerbroker Tom Murphy, sat on the board of DoubleClick, among the hottest companies in Silicon Alley before Nasdaq tanked. Traub was also involved with the Internet, as a board member of BeautyCounter.com.

What bothered many class members were the values underlying the new economy. The business culture of the late 1990s, they felt, featured a loathsome combination of entitlement, greed, and arrogance. "There's too much belief that the ends justifies the means," complained Joe Amaturo, a 49er who had risen from poverty to centimillionaire status. Similar values also had been dominant in the business world during the go-go 1980s, and they were the precise opposite of the values that had shaped the 49ers and other businesspeople of the World War II generation. Marvin Traub once commented that the 1980s, with its leveraged buyouts and takeovers, was the "worst period in the last 50 years . . . it was the dark ages." The excesses of the 1990s were equally out of sync with the values of the 49ers. "Money is being made too easily," is how Ruane described the problem with the business world in the late 1990s. It just wasn't right.

Hard work. Sacrifice. Loyalty. Patience. Humility. These were the values that 49ers identified with. Forged by the Depression and world war, most 49ers had been able to go to Harvard only because of the GI Bill. They had arrived in Cambridge in 1947 immensely grateful for their opportunities and in June 1949 had gone out into the world with little sense of entitlement. Even years later, 49ers who commanded vast corporate empires would be remarkably humble men. In many ways,

America's hard-won victory in World War II—the seminal event for an entire generation—provided the key guiding lessons of life and business for the 49ers, nearly all of whom had served in Europe or the Pacific. They came of age believing that success grew from discipline and sacrifice, from ingenuity and building businesses that produced things of real value, from loyalty to partners and subordinates alike, and from creative risk taking. During much of their careers, they never imagined that such commonsense values could be seen as old-fashioned.

Over the decades following their graduation from Harvard, several 49ers were investigated by law enforcement officials for illegal activities. Harry Figgie, a brash conglomerate builder, was probed for insider trading and eventually fined by the federal government. Lester Crown, whose family controlled the defense giant General Dynamics, was tarnished by several scandals, including one in which he helped bribe state legislators in Illinois. Other 49ers held high-level positions at major companies like General Motors that were heavily criticized in the 1960s and early 1970s for trying to torpedo new regulations aimed at protecting consumers or the environment. But as a whole, the 49ers played by the rules of their time and led careers of exemplary integrity. And, if this earnest formula for success in business seemed quaintly anachronistic in the 1980s and 1990s there was no question that it worked wonders for the Harvard Business School class of 1949.

In the annals of American business, few distinct groups of leaders have been more successful than the class of 1949. Included among the class's alumni were some of the most successful and creative business leaders of the postwar era: James Burke, who built Johnson & Johnson into a $5 billion corporate empire with bold new marketing strategies and who won accolades for his handling of the Tylenol poisonings; Peter McColough, who turned a small and struggling company named Haloid into the legendary Xerox Corporation, helping along the way to create the personal computer and reinvent the world of office technology; Thomas Murphy, who parlayed a single failing television station in Albany, New York, into a multi-billion-dollar media empire that included ABC; Jack Davis, who wandered far off the beaten path and became one of America's leading casino entrepreneurs, first in the Bahamas and then by helping to open Atlantic City to gambling; Marvin Traub, the maestro of Bloomingdale's who forever transformed the stodgy world of department stores and, along the way, helped shape

America's consumer culture; John Shad and Bill Ruane, who both sought to maintain the integrity of Wall Street, albeit in different ways— Ruane through the antihype steadiness of value investing and Shad through the prosecution of insider trading as head of the Securities and Exchange Commission during the 1980s.

While the superstars of the class of 1949 got much of the attention, scores of other members of the class achieved impressive successes in almost every sector of American business. Near the zenith of their careers, the power of the class was staggering. A survey of 376 class members undertaken by *Fortune* magazine in 1974 found that a huge percentage were functioning as chief executives or chief operating officers. The article observed, "Collectively, they exercise command in enterprises that employed approximately 860,000 people and took in some $40 billion in revenues last year."[4] A decade later, the 49ers would have even more power, as the businesses they controlled soared to ever higher profits during the boom of the 1980s.

By the standards of today, few of the 49ers made serious money. They rose to the executive suite in an era when the compensation of CEOs still was within the bounds of reason, and few if any of them assembled fortunes in the hundreds of millions. That was fine for the 49ers. "We didn't care about money in the same way," Marvin Traub remembered. For those who did do well, the money they made was beyond anything they expected.

In the twilight of their lives, members of the class of 1949 were shocked and appalled by the corruption within the executive suites of corporate America—in companies like Enron, WorldCom, and Merrill Lynch. "There has been a dimunition of values," said Jim Burke. "Greed is a very serious problem in American business." At Johnson & Johnson, Burke had been a leader in developing a strict ethical code to guide the company known as the Credo. "I saw that value system as an asset to the business, not a constraint, but an asset." Tom Murphy, easily one of the most respected businessmen of his generation, found the rapacious behavior rampant among CEOs hard to fathom. "It's sad," he said. "We were never guilty of what corporate America does today. We were oriented toward the stockholders. . . . They've got to put some of these white collar criminals into jail." As many 49ers saw it, the bad behavior in corporate America was not just sad; it was also unnecessary. "Social responsibility—and expanding profitability—are not intrinsically at odds with one another," Roger Sonnabend believed. "Quite the contrary. They are two faces of the same coin."

As remarkable as the success of the 49ers was the enduring bond among many of them. Because of the war, most of these men never had anything like a normal college experience. This made their experience at Harvard unusual and special. Friendships were developed that spanned half a century and linked together some of the most important power centers in American business. "The best friends I've ever made in my life, I made at Harvard Business School," Bill Ruane would say, a comment echoed by many of his classmates.

As young men, straight out of business school, some of the 49ers shared apartments together in New York, along with a thirst for heavy partying. They commiserated or boasted about their first jobs, and they sought to push and pull each other to greater heights. With the passing of time, they went through life together: weddings attended, vacations shared, birthdays celebrated, deaths mourned, and personal crises managed. The friendships were never principally about career; sometimes the 49ers were in positions to help each other, other times not; always they enjoyed each others' company, and this was the glue that connected them. Yet inevitably, given who the 49ers were, there was a strong career dimension in these bonds. Swapping contacts and pooling ideas, the 49ers accelerated their rise. Over the years, as the friendships endured, the reach and influence of the 49er network increased. By the late 1970s and early 1980s, this web of quiet personal bonds constituted one of the most important power networks in American business.

If the story of the class of 1949 were simply about the careers and friendships of one of the most gifted groups of business leaders in American history, this itself would be a tale worth telling. To follow the journey of the class through the second half of the twentieth century is to understand just how vast has been the shift in the value systems that pervade American business culture. The story of the class reveals how the values forged by the Great Depression and World War II powerfully shaped the postwar business elite and how those values began to vanish by the 1980s as a different business elite—one driven more by greed and infused with a far greater sense of entitlement—came to positions of leadership.

But there is another reason to tell the story of the 49ers: to understand the dramatic rise of wealth in American society over the past half century. That the United States has become spectacularly wealthier since World War II is a fact obvious to older generations but little understood by many younger Americans. The America of the 1940s was not an impoverished country, but it was a place where millionaires were rare, where the ranks of the poor were vast, and where middle-class people had few assets and often a tenuous grasp on their economic position. Before the great postwar boom, millions of Americans still lived without indoor plumbing or central heating, two-thirds of young people didn't graduate from high school, and going to college was still considered a rare privilege, one that most families could not afford for their children.

The Harvard Business School class of 1949 was largely drawn from the ranks of a middle-class America, and many were the first in their families to go to college. Most of the 49ers never expected to make any real money and aspired mainly to a secure livelihood. During the late 1940s, in an America with so little wealth overall, it simply did not seem that easy to make a fortune in business. And, in any case, the imperative to make a fortune was not so great. Living standards were lower, as were expectations. "It was a far more serious time," observed Roger Sonnabend. "We were happy with much less." The spread of luxury fever among Americans was many years away.

The 49ers played key roles in creating a new kind of American business economy, one that generated unprecedented amounts of wealth. The boom economy of the postwar period rested in large part on three major pillars that emerged over several decades: first, a vast domestic consumer market for goods and services that, by the 1980s, was one of the greatest drivers of economic activity in America; second, rapid technological innovation that produced major productivity gains and spawned endless new products; and third, an ever more sophisticated financial services sector that was able to greatly leverage and amplify both personal and corporate wealth.

To follow the journey of the class of 1949 is to see and understand the rise of each of these pillars of the postwar boom economy. While 49ers like Marvin Traub, Jim Burke, Peter McColough, John Shad, and

Jack Davis played important roles in developing this new economy, many other 49ers were important supporting actors in the spectacular enrichment of America that occurred in the decades following World War II.

The immense wealth produced by the 49ers and others of their generation profoundly affected American society and culture. It dramatically raised the living standards of all Americans, even the poorest, and it produced one of the most highly educated societies in the world. It underwrote the cost of a greatly expanded social safety net, a space program, an interstate highway system, and a huge investment in medical research and health care that boosted the life expectancy of Americans by nearly a decade during the second half of the twentieth century. The new wealth paved the way for the great social upheavals of the 1960s, the self-absorption of the 1970s, the materialism of the 1980s, and the technology revolution of the 1990s. The juggernaut of postwar economic growth—exploding in tandem with population growth—also transformed America's physical landscape, often in profoundly negative ways, as homogenized sprawl spread to every corner of the country.

The tidal wave of new wealth in the postwar era changed the way Americans lived and how they thought, in good ways and in bad.

The story of the 49ers is the story of how today's America came to be.

BEGINNINGS

T hey came to Harvard in 1947 from towns and cities across an America that still lived with the legacy of the Great Depression and a half decade of war. They were middle class mostly, but at a time when that stratum of Americans lived within far more limited means than today. The vast majority had served on the battlefields of Asia and Europe and had been shaped by the Spartan, class-leveling nature of that experience.

To be sure, several members of the Harvard Business School class of 1949 constituted a corporate aristocracy in waiting. There was Lester Crown, a tall and quiet student who kept a low profile around campus, but whose father, Henry Crown, was among the wealthiest industrialists in Chicago. Daniel Parker, of Parker Pen, showed up on a campus where few students could afford cars in a shiny new Oldsmobile convertible with whitewall tires. Other scions included Ernest Henderson III, whose family ran the Sheraton Hotel chain, and Roger Sonnabend, who came from a wealthy real estate family in Boston and had been groomed for an elite life since his childhood. The class also included an Indian prince who lived off campus in the entire top floor of a Boston hotel and who strode to classes followed by a servant who carried his books.

But overall, the 49ers were average Americans who reflected their times. And modest times they were. In 1947, the United States had an annual gross domestic product (GDP) of under $300 billion—less than a third of the wealth in inflation-adjusted terms that the country has today. The median income of an American family was less than a sixth of what it would be five decades later. The term *upper middle class* was not yet in widespread use and the ranks of the truly rich in America remained small. World War II had helped to lift the United States from the Depression, but the burdens of both the Depression and the war would not disappear over night. The Depression had been an economic meltdown unlike any seen before. Wealth built up by families over generations had been either liquidated by the stock market crash or slowly bled away during long years where employment rates had hovered at 25 percent.

Most of the 49ers expected to earn only modest wealth in the future, despite the fancy credentials they were getting from Harvard. "The idea that you might make $100,000 some day was inconceivable to most of us," Bill Ruane would say later. "Nobody knew anybody who made $100,000. The idea of making a lot of money never occurred to us because we had no memory of anybody making a lot of money." During the first years after the 49ers left Harvard, these modest expectations were widely confirmed. Most of the class members would cash in their freshly minted MBAs for jobs earning under $75 a week (less than $28,000 a year in 2001 dollars), and they would be thankful for these jobs in an America where the minimum wage had just been raised to $.75 an hour. But for the members of the class of 1949, it was not too long after graduation before the modest salaries and entry-level positions gave way to serious opportunities. By the end of the 1950s, class members such as Tom Murphy, Jim Burke, Marvin Traub, and Peter McColough would already be on the fast track to corporate stardom.

Even in this first decade out of Harvard, the class of 1949 distinguished itself as being different from other classes. This was not a group content to just climb corporate ladders and respond to the business environment of the day. A good number of them had far bigger ideas. Perhaps it was the brashness of a generation forged by war and mature beyond its years, but many 49ers were unusually determined to reshape the business world in which they lived and to rise, as fast as they could, to positions that would give them the power to achieve these dreams. To reshape American business in the 1950s meant looking beyond the usual sources of wealth generation and profit such as manufacturing and petroleum refining and mining and steel and construction. It meant imagining a different kind of America, in which unprecedented wealth was generated by the consumer demand of the largest middle class in the history of the world; by innovations in technology and the productivity gains they spawned; by new kinds of financial services that put the savings of Americans to work in the stock market and leveraged corporate wealth; and by sustained high levels of government spending on defense, education, space exploration, and infrastructure—an unprecedented activist state all justified by the exigencies of the Cold War.

Not every graduate of the class of 1949 saw the coming of this new economy. Those who imagined a radically different era of American business were actually a tiny minority. Many stumbled upon the opportunities of the new era purely by accident. But whether by luck, smarts, or drive, the 49ers had an unprecedented chance to change the world in which they lived.

Generation GI

T he story was so good that Vince Gregory came to be known at Harvard as "Parachute Man." Around campus, during the first months of business school, Gregory would tell his story all the time.

A working-class kid from Oil City, Pennsylvania, Gregory had flown P-51s in combat against the Luftwaffe during the war. After the Germans surrendered, he stayed in Europe and became engaged to an English woman named Margie. But with wartime rationing still in effect, his bride-to-be couldn't find materials for a wedding dress. Gregory solved the problem by taking his parachute to a German dressmaker, who made a gown from the white nylon. "Beautiful DuPont nylon," Gregory recalled. "It was gorgeous." The only problem was that Gregory was now a pilot without a parachute, and getting a new one would require explaining to the Air Force what had happened to the old one.

Shortly after the wedding, Gregory found himself flying a C-64 Norseman over mountains at night through a terrible storm. The Norseman was a small, light plane, and it shook wildly from the wind. The radio went out, and it seemed that the plane might plunge into a mountainside at any minute. Gregory and the man he was flying with made the decision that their best chance of surviving was to bail out— to cast themselves into the rainy darkness and hope they made it safely to earth. They were all ready to jump when Gregory remembered that he didn't have a parachute. Gregory urged his passenger to bail out without him and at least save his own life. But the man refused to jump alone. Left with no alternatives, Gregory stayed at the controls of the plane and managed to coax it to a safe landing.

Gregory's parachute story may have been the most popular around campus, but Paul Ames and James Chalmers, both of whom had served as navigators on B-24 Liberator Bombers, also had dramatic parachute stories. Ames had been a navigator on bombing raids over the German-held oil fields of Rumania. "It was sort of like suicide," he would tell people. On one raid, the Liberator—a mammoth plane with four propellers and a crew of 10 that dropped bombs from five miles up—got hit by flak. Everybody bailed out of the crippled plane in a terrifying rush. When Ames went to pull the rip cord on his parachute, nothing happened. Hurtling downward through the air at over 100 miles an hour, Ames began grabbing at his parachute, trying to get it open with his bare hands. The ground below grew ever closer, buildings and roads clearly visible. Finally, Ames got the chute out and it popped open. Safely reaching the earth, he quickly found himself surrounded by German soldiers. They trained their rifles at him and told him to stand up. Ames thought he was about to be shot. Instead, he was taken off to a POW camp.

James Chalmers also experienced the terror of dodging flak during the 35 bombing missions he flew over Germany. On one mission, a piece of flak ripped into his plane, bounced around the cabin, and landed on his maps. Decades later, Chalmers still kept the piece of flak as a momento of his near-death experience. On another mission, flak knocked out the hydraulics of Chalmers's B-24, which made the breaks on the landing gear inoperable, as well as the wing flaps. Chalmers and the other members of the plane's crew were stumped about how to safely land, since without breaks and wing flaps, it would be impossible to stop the plane once it set down on the runway. Then somebody had an idea: They could use their parachutes as a brake, opening them behind the plane when it landed. The scheme was risky in the extreme, but it worked—the white parachutes billowing out behind the plane on cue—and the landing went off without a hitch.

In fall 1947, as the Harvard Business School class of 1949 got settled in on campus, the war was still a dominant theme in American culture, and it would remain so for several years. War movies were in the theaters, and in 1948 everyone would be reading and talking about Norman Mailer's haunting tale of the Pacific war, *The Naked and the Dead*. Almost all the 49ers had a war story, because nearly all of the class members had served. Jim Burke had commanded a landing craft during the brutal island war in the Pacific. Jack Alexander was part of the great campaigns through Africa and Italy before taking part in D-Day. Marvin Traub saw heavy action in France after the Normandy landing and dropped out of the war when he took machine gun fire in the leg. James Calvert was a "hump pilot," one of the courageous airmen who carried supplies to China over the snow-covered Himalayan peaks through some of the worst weather in the world. Howard Davis had commanded a bombing group of 28 B-24s, flying the lead plane in huge raids over Germany from bases in Italy and encountering swarms of German fighter planes, along with heavy flak. Some 227 flight officers started out as part of Davis's group; less than 20 made it back to the United States alive. George Wilkerson had gone into Iwo Jima with the 21st Marine Regiment on the third day of the U.S. assault of the Japanese-held island. The regiment suffered 50 percent casualties in the bloodiest battle of the Pacific War, and Wilkerson himself was evacuated from the island after being wounded in action.

All told, 91 percent of the new students had served in the armed forces during the war, 70 percent as commissioned officers.[1] Most of the class members were born in the early or mid-1920s, which meant they reached the draft age of 18 at the height of the war. Few young able-bodied men of the time avoided military service; many who could have avoided it chose not to in an era of stirring patriotism. The call to service had interrupted undergraduate education for most of the 49ers, resulting in a higher-than-average median age for the group. "Most of us never had a normal college education," Bill Ruane observed. And their maturity transcended their age, reflecting the experience of World War II. "We had a lot of responsibility thrust upon us at a young age," Jim Burke would later say. Many of the new students, like Burke, had had men under their command and all the responsibility that came with this duty. More than one-third of the class was already married.

In the wake of World War II, professors at overflowing universities across America were encountering an unusual kind of student: the confident military veteran, mature beyond his years. In 1947, the class entering Harvard Business School was filled with some of the cockiest men who had ever walked through its doors. Paul Ames described his approach to school and work after surviving being shot down over Rumania: "Nothing scares you after that."[2] Other 49ers would say the same thing. Compared to Japanese machine gunners or German Luft-waffe pilots, the professors at Harvard Business School—and the business world beyond—did not seem all that intimidating to the 49ers. Many 49ers were glad just to be alive. Many were also determined to make the most of the lives they had been granted. Surviving history's most destructive war had impressed them with the importance of seizing the day. "We learned to take risks," Burke commented.

These young men were survivors, too, of another formative event of the twentieth century: the Great Depression. "We were all children of the Depression," as Vince Gregory put it. "Everybody had this work ethic imbued in them from the very fact that they liked to eat and that their families eat." Jack Davis grew up outside New York City in a family that was prosperous and secure—only to be financially wiped out in the 1930s. His father, too proud to declare bankruptcy, was saddled with impossible debts and never recovered. "It was a very devastating thing," Davis recalled. Stanley Greenfield also watched his father clobbered by the Depression, with the result that he disappeared from family life into long hours of toil to try to put food on the table. Ned Dewey's father was an educated man, a Harvard graduate and an economist, but when he got fired, things went downhill for the family. "We were always the poor, poor people on the lot, on the block." Jack Muller had watched as his father had been forced to abandon his construction business and knuckle under in a drab job selling insurance. He remembers a day when his father, at home with pneumonia, had risen from his bed and trekked out to make a faraway sales call that he couldn't afford to miss. Gray Garland remembered his father losing all of his money and the family selling their house and moving in with his grandmother. Other 49ers had grown up in families struck by far worse calamities in a decade in which high unemployment rates destroyed the spirit of an entire generation of workers.

The experience of war may have encouraged risk taking, but the legacy of the Depression had the opposite effect. Although many risk takers in the class would eventually emerge, most 49ers would gravitate toward the safest, most secure jobs in business after graduating from Harvard. "It made me put money number one on my list for life," Davis later said of the impact of the Depression. The conflicting influences of the Depression and war that shaped the 49ers—a drive for security coupled with an appetite for risk—were reflected in America's business culture in the early postwar period. It was at once a culture that was notorious for its corporate conformity and yet spawned many revolutionary innovations.

Only through the GI Bill was Harvard in reach for the most of the 49ers. "I'm sure that the overwhelming majority of us would not have gone to Harvard without the GI Bill," said Stanley Greenfield. One of the most sweeping social programs ever passed, the GI Bill offered a cornucopia of benefits to Americans who had fought in the war. There were home loans and job training and, of course, education assistance. The Servicemen's Readjustment Act of 1944, as it was officially known, entitled anyone with 90 days of service to a minimum of one year of higher education. For each additional month of active duty, a person earned a month of schooling, up to a maximum of four years. The law set a $500 per year limit for tuition, fees, and supplies—this at a time when the cost of even the best schools was $350 to $450 a year. Unmarried veterans got a stipend of $50 per month, and those who were married drew $75. (In 2001 dollars, the stipends would be worth $436 and $654, respectively). These generous provisions of the GI Bill made both college and graduate school available for Americans who could never have afforded it otherwise, bringing unprecedented social mobility to U.S. society. And, in contrast to later generations of students, few members of the Harvard Business School class of 1949 had any debt upon graduation.

In 1947, the school year at Harvard Business School began relatively late, in early October. When the entering class arrived in Cambridge for registration, dressed in suits and ties, hair cropped close, they didn't head to Harvard's main campus—with its hallmark brick buildings and old, leafy oak trees—but instead found themselves reporting to a separate business school campus across the river known as Soldiers Field. The campus was a peaceful, almost idyllic setting, very different from the bustling quads of Harvard's main campus. It was designed with low-lying buildings and grassy lawns and dogwood trees and a wide asphalt footpath that ran down the center of the campus like Main Street in middle America.

The entering Harvard Business School class in 1947 was huge, some 700 students. They were a homogenous group in terms of race and gender. No women were in the class. Although "Rosie the Riveter"—the archetype woman who worked in an armaments factory—had become a symbol of the new female worker of the 1940s and the second great wave of American feminism was just beginning, Harvard's MBA program would not admit women until the 1960s. Blacks were allowed at Harvard, but were very few in number. The class had a single black member who soon dropped out. Nearly all of the Asians in the class came from overseas. One of the few Asians in the class was Frank Chen, who was born in Beijing and grew up in the north China port city of Tianjin, amid a civil war and the invasion by Japan.

The few other nonwhites also were mainly from overseas. Mahesh Chandra came from Bombay, where he had been a junior executive at a steel company before deciding to leave India for a business school 10,000 miles from home. Another Indian, Hemendra Prasad Barooah, came from Calcutta and had been sent to Harvard to be groomed to some day take over the family tea business. Five other class members were also from India. Although most 49ers were drawn from the major Christian denominations, the school did have its fair share of Jews. Indeed, the success of Jews, mostly immigrants, in getting their children into elite educational institutions in the middle part of the twentieth century was among the great, if quiet, civil rights advances of the time.

But what was markedly new and different about the class was its diversity in terms of wealth and background. A later survey of more than half the class members revealed that 10 percent or more came from blue-collar backgrounds—men like Fred Hilbish, who had grown up the son of a coal miner in the backwoods of Washington state. A quarter had fathers who owned a business, but only a small percentage of 49ers had fathers who were presidents of large companies. The majority of class members had fathers who worked in middle management or professional jobs. As a whole, the entering horde of 49ers could be described as middle-class kids. There were a few rich kids and a few poor kids.

Lester Crown was one of the rich kids. He was born in Chicago on June 7, 1925, the second of three boys, and grew up in Evanston, right outside of Chicago. His parents were the children of immigrants, Eastern

European Jews who were no strangers to hunger and fear. "My dad started at long below zero," Crown would say later about his father, Henry Crown, born Henry Krinsky. But by the time Lester was born, his father had already begun a white-knuckled ascent to wealth and power. Henry Crown started a building supplies firm called Material Service Corporation, which soon commanded a major share of the Chicago-area construction market. Its success was the Crown family's chief preoccupation. "We ate and slept business," Lester recalled. "There wasn't any separation between the family and the business."[3] Lester grew up going down to the plants with his father and brothers on the weekends. He had his first job with the company when he was 12, working as an office boy. As a teenager, he spent most of his summers working in the quarries and yards alongside the laboring men. Shoveling gravel and sand, Lester and his brothers lived out the gritty underside of the American dream even as they were being groomed to become corporate princes.

For those who met Lester Crown around campus in the fall of 1947, there was nothing to make him stand out as the heir to a growing industrial fortune. Crown was tall and a bit on the gangly side, with heavy eyebrows and dark hair parted far to the left. He was neither outwardly dynamic nor prepossessing. Instead, Crown had a quiet style that reflected his father's very humble manner: Be rich, be successful, but don't flaunt it. At the age of 22 and beginning Harvard Business School, Lester Crown just wanted to work hard and prove himself.

Roger P. Sonnabend was another of the privileged young men entering Harvard. He was born on September 17, 1925, in Boston and raised in Brookline, a leafy suburb with mansions and ancient oak trees. Like Lester Crown, he was Jewish and grew up in a striving family with two brothers. His parents, Abraham (called "A.M." or "Sonny") and Ester Sonnabend, raised Roger, Paul, and Stephen in the elegant tradition of the local elite, though the family's Jewish heritage meant that they would never take their place among Boston's Brahmin establishment. Abraham Sonnabend, one of the first Jewish aviators during World War I, had been educated at Harvard and then had built a successful real estate company that included a number of hotels. The elder Sonnabend first owned hotels in Palm Beach and then expanded to cities such as Chicago and Cleveland. Roger grew up amid wealth and expectation, a handsome and athletic boy. He was never sent to religious school because his father thought it was more important that Roger play tennis with him on weekend mornings. As a student at the prestigious Philips Exeter Academy and later as a member of the Algonquin Club and other restrictive societies, Sonnabend learned to be a "good Jew," as he put it later, grateful for his own inclusion and willing to overlook examples of institutionalized bigotry.[4]

Sonnabend learned about his father's business firsthand, working summer jobs in the hotels from the age of 12 on. He went to MIT, served in the navy at the tail end of World War II, and then joined the family real estate business after graduating from college. "My father believed in starting his sons at the top," Sonnabend recalled.[5] The challenge, however, was that Roger and his brothers "had to prove on a daily basis that we could stay there."[6] At 21, his father made Roger general manager of Sonnabend property in New York, the Nautilus Hotel and Beach Club in Atlantic Beach, Long Island. Filled with energy, Sonnabend enrolled as a full-time student in the business school at Harvard, even as he tried to turn around the rundown Nautilus. He would spend the next two years commuting between Cambridge and Long Island.

Sonnabend's grueling routine in business school meant that he wasn't around a lot to party with his classmates. But those who did get to know him in the fall of 1947 encountered an easygoing young man with close-cropped wavy brown hair and a great deal of confidence about his place in the world—someone who saw Harvard Business School as a stopping place, not a turning point. "Since I was going into a family business that was successful, I knew I'd get whatever I wanted out of it and it would become my business," Sonnabend said later of his attitude. "And if I wanted to be a millionaire, I'd be a millionaire."

James Burke didn't have any such sense of entitlement. He came of age far away from the power and glamour that some of his Harvard Business School classmates took for granted as young men. Born on February 28, 1925, in Rutland, Vermont, Burke grew up near Albany, New York, in the small town of Slingerlands. He remembered his childhood as idyllic, and also small-town life as "an enabling existence." The people of Slingerlands had "good values, the values of a small town. It couldn't have been a better way to grow up." Even as a child, Burke was immensely entrepreneurial. He operated various roadside stands, selling things like cider and daffodils. During the winter he sold Christmas trees that he bought for 12 cents each and hawked to village residents at a healthy markup. "I was always selling something." Proceeds from Burke's various ventures financed a new cigarette habit and a 1931 Ford that he bought for $15 and kept hidden in the woods—since Burke was too young to have a license.

Burke's parents encouraged their three children to be outspoken and to learn how to argue with one another in support of their opinions. "The dinner table was always a stimulating place to be," Burke remembered.[7] The good-natured sense of engagement that Burke would learn at the dinner table shaped his personality. He was dubbed the "Happy Warrior" in his high school yearbook and brought enthusiastic engagement to everything he did. But he also saw himself as a very measured young man—despite the smoking and illegal car. He was a devout Catholic who never missed church on Sundays and went to Holy Cross for college. Burke's father, an insurance salesman, "had strict ethical standards," Burke recalled.[8] It was not enough to just do well. One had to always do the right thing. Like many of his classmates, Burke had interrupted his undergraduate studies to serve in World War II as a U.S. Navy ensign. In 1947, he was yet another veteran who showed up for class at Harvard. With a direct, plainspoken manner and a keen intelligence, Burke was immediately popular with his classmates.

Marvin Traub arrived at Harvard Business School via Harvard College, the battlefields of France, and a long, agonizing stay in a military hospital. He was born in the Bronx on April 14, 1925. Before he was five years old, he moved with his parents to Manhattan's Upper West Side and the stylish milieu that helped to shape his future tastes and ambitions. His parents, Sam and Bea Traub, aspired to the glamorous life that they came to know intimately as retailers to New York's fashionable set. As a salesman and manager for the lingerie firm Lily of France, Sam dressed models, actresses, and dancers with the famous Ziegfeld Follies. He conveyed his show-business sensibilities in his personal style, wearing a fresh flower on the lapel of his hand-tailored suit, visiting elite barbers, and spending hours at home tanning under a sunlamp. He also had a mistress whom he didn't try very hard to hide. Bea Traub was employed by Bonwit Teller as a personal shopper for the department store's most famous customers, including Mamie Eisenhower, Mrs. Ed Sullivan, and Flor d'Oro Trujillo, the fashion-plate daughter of a Caribbean dictator. From an early age, Marvin imbibed the heady atmosphere of his parents' chic associations: backstage with his father among half-clad starlets or at Sardi's for a late-night dinner with local merchant impresarios. His parents wanted their son to grow up to be a doctor, but Marvin loved the excitement of retail, and he chose his mother's friend Stanley Marcus, chairman of the famous Neiman Marcus department store of Houston, Texas, as his idol. Traub would say later about his mother and father that "they were not the warmest or most doting parents but they did bring me up to appreciate retail."

A recommendation from Marcus helped Marvin Traub secure admission to Harvard College in 1942, but his education was soon interrupted by the war.

As a member of the 379th Infantry division, Traub landed at Utah Beach in Normandy in July 1944, six weeks after the D-Day invasion of France. In November, Traub took machine-gun fire in a raid on fortified German positions in western France. The bullets shattered his body. Traub remembers gaping at a bone protruding from his leg even as he tried to attend to this wound. Evacuated to Tilton General Hospital in Fort Dix, New Jersey, the 19-year-old Traub spent over a year in traction and body casts, undergoing seven operations to save his leg. It was a dark period; Traub's closest friend in the military had been killed the same day he was shot, and memories of that fateful time in France haunted him in the hospital. "Yet for all the horror, I felt good about my war experience," Traub would say later. "I had been challenged, met the test, and come out a different person, more mature and with greater self-confidence." He returned to Harvard on crutches in January 1946.[9]

Speeded by Harvard's decision to give college credit for wartime service and training, Traub completed the requirements for a degree in government the following spring. He graduated magna cum laude in June 1947. After participating in an executive training program at Macy's during the summer of 1947, Traub enrolled in Harvard's graduate school of business.

Showing up on the business school campus in the fall, Traub was as confident as any man in his class. He had survived the battlefield and, worse, the long painful months in the hospital. He knew Harvard inside and out. He knew who he was and had a pretty good sense of who he wanted to be: somebody like his father, but way, way bigger.

Thomas Sawyer Murphy grew up a few miles and a world away from the flamboyant Traub household. Murphy was born on May 31, 1925, in Brooklyn, New York. He attended a Jesuit high school and was a devout Catholic.[10]

Murphy's early years fitted him with two great advantages for a career in business. The first was a penetrating intelligence and drive. Though his college grades were barely sufficient to gain admission to the Harvard Business School, Murphy would come to awe his classmates with his clever intellect, so much so that he was widely regarded as the 49er most likely to succeed.[11] The second advantage was an honor roll of family connections. Murphy's father, a state supreme court justice, had friends among the elite of the New York Republican Party, including Governor Thomas E. Dewey and presidential nominee Al Smith Jr. As a kid, Murphy was once introduced to President Franklin Delano Roosevelt by his father.

At their summer home in the Quaker Hill section of Pawling, New York, the Murphys rubbed elbows with such notables as journalists Edward R. Murrow and Lowell Thomas. Growing up, Tom Murphy played golf and kept counsel with daring and ambitious men—family friends who helped to shape Murphy's values and goals. Murphy went to Cornell University, powering his way through college in two and a half years. Even with the war winding down, Cornell was suffused with military discipline. "We marched at breakfast and we marched at lunch," Murphy remembered. Entering Harvard Business School at the age of 22, Murphy was younger than most of the men at the school, but he didn't seem that way. He had a fast-receding hairline that made him look older this his age, and he projected a powerful sense of self-confidence. Murphy commanded the immediate respect of his classmates.

Unlike Murphy, William J. Ruane had no family connections to speak of. He was born on October 24, 1925, and grew up in a middle-class neighborhood of Chicago, where his father owned a few trucks. Both his parents were warm and loving, and he had one sister. "I really had a very happy family," Ruane recalled. "I revered my father and I loved my mother." Ruane went to Catholic schools growing up, barely pulling Cs. "I was never a serious student. Didn't take anything very seriously." Still, he managed to get into St. Mary's College, although he never finished there. Instead, he enlisted in the United States Navy in 1943 and served for three years.

Ruane first tried to get into Harvard Business School in 1946. He was just getting out of the navy and was at the University of Minnesota, where the navy had sent him for training in engineering. Ruane's initial bid to enter Harvard was quixotic. He hitchhiked from New York to Boston in August 1946 and filled out an application in late August. He typed it up neatly and took it to the admissions office. A secretary laughed at him. She said that school started in a week, the entering class had already been admitted, and there were 3,000 other people on the waiting list. "You don't have a prayer," Ruane was told. Still, Ruane managed to finagle an interview and things went well. His application was put on file for the next year. In the meantime, Ruane decided he'd try to get a job at General Electric. Again, his strategy was to show up in person. He traveled to GE's headquarters and walked into the office of the vice president for personnel. Ruane soon had a job as a trainee in GE's electronics park in Fort Wayne, Florida, making $49 a week. In this position Ruane realized he was "a mechanical idiot" and was in the wrong line of work. He pushed hard to get into Harvard for the following year, pestering the admissions office. Finally, the acceptance letter came through.

John Shad easily gave Marvin Traub a run for his money as the 49er most destined for a life of glamour. Shad was born deep in Mormon country, in Brigham City, Utah. But his family moved to Hollywood when he was very young. For young John, the move to Hollywood meant a radically different—and more fun—youth. By the time he was a teenager, Shad styled himself as a beachcomber and zoot-suiter, at ease with celebrity classmates at Hollywood High. He left home at age 16, found work as a riveter, and imagined a lifestyle that centered on swing music and fast living.

The news that he could earn more money as a college graduate struck Shad as a revelation. His grandmother in Utah, he later explained, had urged him to spend "the first third of my life learning, the second third earning, and the third part serving."[12] The maxim made little sense to the young rebel until some Hollywood friends gave him a chart that showed earnings increasing along with education levels. Shad set out to better his income with a sense of resolution that became a personal hallmark. Keeping his job as a riveter on the night shift, he attended the University of Southern California during the day. The routine was punishing, but it turned out that Shad had unusual endurance for hard work and sleep deprivation. Shad's education was interrupted by a stint of service in the navy. When he returned from the military, he graduated and then headed off to Harvard Business School. It was the beginning of a journey that would lead to unimaginable wealth.

Peter McColough was anything but a rebel. He was born on August 1, 1922, in Halifax, Nova Scotia. His father had served as a deputy minister of Public Works for the government of Canada and had four children. Like others of his generation, McColough served in the military during World War II. As a pilot for the British Royal Navy, the five-foot seven-inch Canadian saw his share of action.

Before and after the war, McColough studied law, first at Dalhousie University Law School in Halifax. He received his LL.B. from Osgoode Hall Law School in Toronto in 1947. Though he passed the Canadian bar, McColough had already decided that law was a business and that he would be more successful in the corporate world than as an attorney. "I went to get my papers admitting me to the bar in Canada at noon and returned right to my job as a concrete inspector to make some money to go on to Harvard Graduate School of Business Administration," he remembered.[13] If he was going into business, McColough reasoned, he was going to do it with the best credentials in the field.

McColough enjoyed some advantages over his business school classmates. He already possessed an advanced degree and, like Tom Murphy, his prematurely receding hairline gave him an air of authority. His voice—resonant and deep—and his Canadian background added to his mystique. But McColough's easygoing nature and appreciation for a good gag would make him one of the boys.

The admissions office at Harvard Business School had done an extremely thorough job in selecting the class of 1949. It had sifted through over 10,000 pieces of correspondence and considered some 2,300 formal applications in order to come up with a list of some 700 selectees. Ninety-five percent of those admitted had college degrees, a figure that was high for an era in which many men had seen their college educations interrupted, but reflected lower standards than those enforced subsequently. In later years, 49ers would often say about Harvard Business School, as one class member put it, that "we were glad we went then because we're not sure we could get in now." Still, many in the entering class had impeccable Ivy League credentials: 101 had been undergrads at Harvard; 31 had graduated from Yale; and another 23 had gone to Princeton. Others came from Cornell, MIT, and Notre Dame.

An admissions officer scanning over a list of the men starting Harvard Business School in the fall of 1947 would have no reason to imagine that the class of 1949 would be remarkable. Yes, the vast majority of the class were worldly veterans of war. They had commanded men in battle; they had grown used to risk. But this was typical of students of the day in universities crowded with beneficiaries of the GI Bill. And yes, there were many men entering the school in 1947 who had already distinguished themselves as among the smartest young men in all America. But this caliber of student was typical of the Ivy League, particularly of Harvard.

No, there was nothing about the entering class of 1949 that was, at first glance, so extraordinary. Yet in the fall of 1947, a class of young men entered Harvard Business School who—as a group—would end up having a greater impact on the American economy than any class of any business school before or since.

Kindred Spirits

Harvard Business School would be easy for Joe Amaturo.

It was easy for the reason that Amaturo had the luxury of being a full-time student. This was a completely new experience. "I had never been to day school," Amaturo remembered. Amaturo was the son of Italian immigrants who had grown up in the Bronx, with his father eking out a living with small businesses. He was a compact young man full of energy who had always had to work. He had held two paper routes while attending Morris High School and took a clerk job at a law firm after graduating. By day, he worked downtown at the firm for $11 a week. By night, he was a student at Fordham University, attending classes from 6 P.M. to 10 P.M. It was an exhausting routine. War interrupted his education, and Amaturo spent four years commanding a landing craft tank in the Pacific. He'd seen action in Okinawa, one of the bloodiest battles during the entire war, and on other islands. After all this, being at Harvard Business School as a full-time student on a generous GI stipend was almost like being on vacation.

A relaxing experience, of course, was not the idea of Harvard Business School. It was a boot camp for future business leaders. That was the essence of the school, but it was a concept that didn't much faze an entering class that had been through a war. Grueling hard work was famously part of the business school routine—known around campus as the "Ulcer Derby"—only it didn't seem so grueling to the entering class of 1949. Like Amaturo, most of them were used to hard work and a

Harvard Business School degree, many believed, was worth just about any amount of deprivation.

The prestige of a Harvard business degree came in part from the rarity of MBAs in the early postwar era. In 1949, there were less than 50,000 people alive who held advanced business degrees, and each year saw only 3,000 new MBAs; four decades later, some 60,000 such degrees would be granted in 1985 alone. In 1949, only 100 U.S. institutions conferred MBAs. That number would grow to over 700 by the 1990s.

A Harvard MBA was not valuable just because it was rare. It was also coveted because it came from the most respected university in the world and the very institution that had helped invent the MBA.

Asked to consider opening a school of business at the nation's oldest university in 1907, Harvard president Charles William Eliot initially declined. "There's no market for it," he demurred.[1] Business education remained on the fringes of the academic establishment in the early twentieth century. Though a handful of programs at major universities offered business instruction and undergraduate business majors, scholars and business leaders alike expressed skepticism about the enterprise. Academic critics saw the business curriculum as a diluted version of existing offerings in economics, engineering, and mathematics, and the captains of industry continued to endorse the value of hands-on experience for future executives. A persuasive contingent of Harvard alums and professors, however, eventually persuaded Eliot and others to support the establishment of a new kind of business program at Harvard. The decision led to the creation of the Graduate School of Business Administration at Harvard, which not only became the most distinguished institute of business education in the United States, but one of the most successful academic experiments of all time. The business school opened in 1908 with 33 students.[2]

The founders of the Harvard Business School accepted the premise that the study of railroads and other complex business organizations constituted an emerging science. They also endorsed the concept of executive leadership as an art. This dual focus determined in part the structure of the business program at Harvard, which became the first in the country to offer instruction at the graduate level only. No other business school in the United States required a bachelor's degree for admission, though the practice was standard for law and medical schools.

Harvard's insistence on placing business education on the level with law and medical studies reflected a self-conscious effort to secure professional status for business managers. It was a considerable challenge. Rapid change and the fledgling state of scholarship about business limited the number of useful lectures and texts on business topics. The university dealt with this problem creatively by adopting a case study approach to teaching business that quickly became the school's signature contribution to business education.

Faculty liked to joke that the case method was a "pedestrian approach" to learning the problems of management: Cases walked students through the decision-making process.[3] For students schooled in the strictly formal setting of secondary education of the time, the Harvard approach could prove baffling. Rather than textbooks, instructors assigned one or more cases as preparation for a class meeting; in class, the instructors held back and asked students to take the lead in discussing the case. The free-form discussions that ensued often left students grasping for the "correct" answer, and many objected that the "absence of professorial dicta" made it difficult to gauge their standing vis-à-vis the other members of the class.[4]

The Harvard Business School rapidly became the premier institution of its kind. In 1924, the school received a $5 million donation from George Fisher Baker, president of the First National Bank of New York, to build a new campus across the river from Cambridge at Soldiers Field in Boston. Soon, its graduates were ascending to the top ranks of the new managerial elite in U.S. corporations. By the 1930s, when the Depression had sapped the material and morale conditions at business schools everywhere, enrollment in Harvard's two-year program had reached 1,200 students from all over the world.[5]

World War II projected the Harvard Business School's influence well beyond the academy and the boardrooms of top corporations.[6] As the nation's top business school, Harvard took the lead in contributing business expertise to the defense effort. In 1943, the faculty voted to suspend all regular instruction and concentrate the business school's resources on helping win the war. The most influential of these wartime programs, the U.S. Air Force's Statistical Control Unit training, instructed 15,000 personnel in the emerging science of cost accounting. Championed by Robert S. McNamara, a young Harvard Business

School professor who became an influential advocate of quantitative analysis at the Ford Motor Company and later the Pentagon, the "Harvard Method" rationalized the incredibly complex processes of managing the 230,000 new aircraft produced for the war effort.[7]

The urgency and energy of the war years kept intellectual ferment alive at Harvard after the victories of 1945. A committee on educational policy proposed major changes in the first-year course lineup at the school, and the faculty endorsed new objectives for the kinds of business leaders they hoped to produce. New MBAs would not only possess a "considerable knowledge of business techniques in one or more areas," their education should promote an "[u]nderstanding of ethical considerations" and "the beginnings of an integrated social and economic philosophy." Harvard students in the future would exhibit the "spirit of vigorous and courageous enterprise" that had demonstrated such power during the war.[8]

Postwar political exigencies sharpened the business school's sense of its historic mission. As the contest for influence between America and the Soviet Union hardened into Cold War, observers saw the success of the postwar economic conversion in the United States as a critical step in the defense of freedom. Dean Donald K. David saw the school engaged in fighting a "war of ideals against communism," in which the resourcefulness and morality of business professionals would prevail against the foe.[9] "A good case could be made," observed a Harvard Business School professor in 1949, "that the welfare and even the freedom of all Americans depend on how well we, as a nation, do in turning out an adequate number of properly equipped business leaders during the next ten years."[10]

The professor's preoccupation with the "adequate number" of trained business professionals reflected the pressures of extraordinarily high enrollments at Harvard Business School after the war. The resumption of regular instruction in 1946 ensued amid an avalanche of applications for admission—5,500 applicants for only 300 available spaces.[11] To meet Harvard's urgent obligations to provide instruction for would-be business leaders, the overworked but enthusiastic faculty agreed to stagger admissions on behalf of high enrollment; 1946 and 1947 saw not two but four MBA classes matriculate. And even though the business school increased class size by 50 percent, it continued to turn away hundreds of qualified applicants.[12]

Nobody could question that the class of 1949 was filled with high-quality students, but to Joe Amaturo the men of Section G, his section, were the real superstars.

Section G was one of more than a half dozen different sections that divided the class of 1949 into manageable groups. Students in the different sections were expected to collaborate on projects and to support each other in their class work. The section system was meant to ensure that students didn't get lost and that they could bond with each other. Inevitably, it engendered friendly competition with other sections. Forty years later, the 49ers would still be ribbing each other about whose section was the best. "That was a good section," Thomas Graves would say about Section G in 1994, "but not as good as Section C."

Amaturo would argue the merits of Section G without quarter. For Amaturo—or "Joe-Joe," as he was known—Section G became something of an extended family. "They were the greatest group of guys you could ever hope to meet," Amaturo said. The men of Section G spent extraordinary amounts of time together, working through the difficult case studies thrown their way by the faculty. When they weren't working, they were partying. Tight friendships were forged that lasted decades. Amaturo became particularly close with the soft-spoken Bill Ruane. The two men clicked from the start. Other Section G pals of Amaturo's included Gray Garland and George Berman.

Amaturo was among the small number of students who had a car, and he led many a mission out to local Boston hot spots. And the hot spots were hotter than they had been in years. Fresh music was coming onto the scene, as the big-band era gave way to bebop and rhythm and blues. Crafting the emerging sound was a new breed of musicians: Charlie Parker, Dizzy Gillespie, Billie Holiday. "Boston isn't San Francisco or Paris but there is fun to be had," declared an article in the Harvard Business School campus paper, the *Harbus News,* that appeared as the 49ers arrived to start school. Boston didn't have the most hopping club scene—New York held that distinction—but there was still plenty going on.

There was also action to be found in Boston's suburbs. One of the favorite hangouts of the 49ers was a nightclub called The Meadows, out in Framingham, about 30 minutes from campus. The Meadows featured big bands, along with local women who loved to dance. To avoid the cover charge, 49ers would show up early in the evening, before the bands started, and drink at the bar waiting for the revelry to get under way. Sometimes a group of 49ers headed out to The Meadows as often as two or three times a week.

A night on the town or at The Meadows beat a night in the hushed library at Soldiers Field. It also beat sitting in the main lounge of the student club in front of a big, heavy, walnut-sided box that cast a blue glow, the television. To some of the 49ers, there was nothing more fun than watching Milton Berle's slapstick comedy show, *Texaco Star Theater,* or Ed Sullivan's *Toast of the Town.* Not Amaturo. He wanted action. When he couldn't recruit fellow revelers, Amaturo went out by himself, cruising Boston's downtown and scouting for some company, which often wasn't hard to come by. "Local female philosophy has switched from specialization on men who have money to men who are going to make money and you won't find it hard to get a date," explained a wag writing in *Harbus News.* With his New York Italian charm, Amaturo cleaned up. "For me, it was a substitute college experience," Amaturo said later of business school.

George Berman also believed he had a mandate to have some serious fun while at Harvard, and he never lacked for company in this endeavor. "We were not noted for intellectual accomplishment," Berman said about the class of 1949. "We were a noisy, exciting, friendly, go class. I mean Friday afternoons we'd get bombed on beer and everybody's in downtown Boston and we'd go to all the strip shows and so on. It was that kind of class." For more staid nights on the town, there were the movies of Gary Cooper, Cary Grant, Jimmy Stewart, Humphrey Bogart, and Marlene Dietrich. Boston also had a number of theaters. *A Streetcar Named Desire,* with a young actor named Marlon Brando, came through in fall 1947, playing at the Wilbur Theater for a few weeks before it opened in New York. One of the 49ers, Bernard Siegel, translated his interest in Boston's nightlife into cash by teaching the rhumba one night a week downtown. It was an edgy, sexy dance, with much moving of the hips, that made the jitterbug look tame.

Not everyone in the class was into the nightlife or carousing. Tom Murphy and Jim Burke were deeply religious Catholics who went to church regularly. Murphy was always up for a good time, and he had many friends, but he didn't drink because of a stomach condition, nor did he smoke. Other class members like Fred Hilbish, the son of a coal miner, didn't have enough money to party downtown with the likes of Amaturo and found it enough of a treat just to eat out occasionally in Harvard Square.

Military discipline helped the 49ers adjust to the rigors of the Ulcer Derby. The students occupied dormitories or, if married, military-surplus Quonset huts just off campus. Housing arrangements kept wartime camaraderie alive despite the competitiveness of the new environment. "It was a very close community," Amaturo recalled. In the dormitories, the men were right on top of each other, sharing bathrooms and pooling toiletries like shampoo and toothpaste. For decades later, Sumner Feldberg would think of Jim Burke and Tom Murphy as his "bathroom buddies"—a moniker that seemed more amusing to him as both men became titans of the business world. To be sure, the tight quarters and the common academic challenges helped create community, but even more important was the shared mission. "You fight a war and all that means in terms of maturity," recalled Burke. "You come back and go to a school with kindred spirits, not kindred in background but in what we wanted to do with our lives. We talked things through, business, you wanted to live your life, your family."[13]

The intensity of the workload may have reminded many of wartime sacrifices. Augustus Minton, one of the class's handful of military officers, would recall Harvard as requiring a greater effort than anything he had ever experienced in the military. The 49ers were "lean and mean from military service under the worst conditions," Minton said, and they were "working more hours per week than ever before—or since." With a course load that demanded an average of six hours of reading each day—and the most ambitious among them asking professors to recommend more—the class hit the books with the same ferocity and drive that helped them storm the beaches of Normandy and Okinawa. Written case studies, due each Saturday before 9 P.M., cut weekends in half and required students to master the nuances of the case method. Although the hours could be grueling, the case study method made the studies seem more tangible and interesting. "You go through the kind of thinking that you do in real life," Brewster Kopp said about the case study. "In real life, life is complicated. You've got to marshal out your information, analyze it, strategize." Same, too, with the Harvard Business School case studies, which could make an all-night studying session a lively undertaking.

Basic training for the 49ers featured the revised first-year curriculum adopted by the faculty at war's end. In addition to the course in Written Analysis of Cases that dominated the weekend's work, MBA candidates at Harvard completed six courses during the first year: Production, Marketing, Finance, Control, Administrative Practices, and Public Relationships and Responsibilities. Students in Production, for example, learned to enhance profitability by lowering the cost of component parts or ingredients of the finished product.[14] Marketing professor Melvin T. Copeland, a pioneer of the case method, used examples from industry to teach students how to seek out niche markets and to find commercial applications for military technologies developed during the war.[15] In Finance, instructors focused on the financial transactions required to initiate, operate, and expand various businesses, as well as general aspects of banking and financial markets. The course Control emphasized the *active,* or wise, use of accounting data to make administrative decisions.[16] Equipped with slide rules and a portfolio of mathematical formulas for estimating costs and returns, the class of 1949 and subsequent graduates of Control set out to replace the old intuitive model of administration with the latest scientific management strategies. For their generation, numbers became "the one true moral compass" of business decision making.[17]

Another innovative course appeared under the ordinary-sounding title Administrative Practices. In fact, the name was "purposefully vague," according to its faculty sponsor, designed to incorporate several different approaches to the emerging study of human relations in business.[18] Administrative Practices emphasized different strategies of human relations in each of its seven sections, and the 49ers took home different lessons from each. Herb Shayne, who went on to make his career at Lever Brothers, one of the country's largest manufacturing concerns, remembered the class as "how to make the contented-cow syndrome work for you."[19] Others joked that the course title should have been Machiavelli for Beginners. One of the class's most flamboyant characters, the future conglomerate-builder Harry Figgie, described "Ad Prac" as "how to saw the legs out of someone's ladder without him knowing it."[20] Noting that his outlook on the workplace was completely different from Harry Figgie's, 49er Clarence Brown, a member of the U.S. House of

Representatives, observed, "What I learned is that you don't go in and start hacking away until you know the landscape."[21] However they remembered it, the members of the class considered Administrative Practices a terrific contribution to their business education. "It was a first step in understanding how to work with other people and motivate other people," Joe Amaturo recalled. In a survey taken before graduation, more than 90 percent described it as one of the most important courses in their curriculum.[22]

While electives in the various specialized fields—accounting, finance, retail, and the like—made up the heart of the second-year curriculum, the class of 1949 scrambled to find spaces in Manufacturing, the business school's most popular course. As in the case of Administrative Practices, the course title revealed little of its content and failed to convey the sense of excitement that students took away from the class. Since 1926, the second-year manufacturing course had been the exclusive domain of Professor Georges Frederic Doriot, a 1922 graduate of the Harvard Business School. A naturalized American citizen, the French-born Doriot had earned the rank of brigadier general during World War II for his service in the research and development program of the U.S. War Department. In 1946, Doriot founded the American Research and Development Corporation, the first publicly funded venture capital firm in the United States and an early model of entrepreneurial investing. Doriot was a dapper man with a cropped mustache and French accent. His entrepreneurship, distinguished military record, and charismatic classroom style made him a campus legend. Many in the class of 1949 considered his course the most memorable and its instructor the most remarkable of their tenure at Harvard.[23]

Doriot's prestige gave him wide latitude in the subjects and methods employed in the class. Unlike other Harvard business courses, Manufacturing did not employ the case method. Instead of using prepared cases, Doriot sent his students into the field to do their own research and sometimes brought captains of industry into the classroom for questions and answers. "I want my students to get the feel of making a real contribution to industry," Doriot explained.[24] The approach paid off admirably for students who already had career plans after graduation. Doriot's report, one graduate remembered, "gave me the opportunity as a student to study all the competition."[25] Another practical advantage stemmed from the opportunity to maintain close contacts between the business school and corporations, arrangements also reinforced by Doriot's active duties as a venture capitalist.

Some of Doriot's most memorable lessons diverged entirely from the everyday problems of business management, focusing instead on the character of business managers. Doriot offered his manufacturing students a profile of the responsible executive, both in his personal example and in his pronouncements on behavior, comportment, and values. The general, an ardent defender of what he called "the free enterprise system," partook fully in the strident anticommunism of the era.[26] Effective business leaders, in Doriot's view, embodied the virtues of the system in their character as well as their work. Doriot's vision embraced the extreme conformity of the early postwar years: business leaders were men (invariably) who dressed and acted like businessmen (conservatively); businessmen stayed abreast of the going trends by immersing themselves in mass culture (as suburbanites and readers of the largest-circulation newspapers); businessmen were upright family types who depended on the support and encouragement of their wives (whom Professor Doriot invited into his classroom to learn their proper place and gain an appreciation of their husbands' responsibilities).[27] Doriot's formula for success emphasized the importance of hard work, follow-through, and a realistic worldview. "A creative man merely has ideas," he observed. "[A] resourceful man makes them practical."[28]

At the beginning of each semester, Doriot would urge new students to come to come to his class wearing suits and polished shoes. Many 49ers eager to please the professor followed this edict. Others in the class made it a point, as James Craig recalled, to wear "the dirtiest chinos we could find."

Doriot's conventional, masculine ideal of business leadership resonated throughout the curriculum at Harvard Business School during the late 1940s. A respected professor of marketing, Malcolm P. McNair, a stern bald man with heavy dark glasses, exhorted students to become more "tough-minded" in their approach to business, life, and politics. The call echoed the veneration of toughness in popular culture during the early Cold War, in which traditional masculine virtues were held up as crucial elements of the survival of the free world. "It is the instructor's job," McNair observed, "to see that the men in the class settle down to a tough-minded analysis of facts and issues, following logical paths of reasoning and judgment to appropriate decisions and conclusions."[29]

Not all the faculty shared the dominant vision of the business leader. Fritz Roethlisberger—who saw his work as "the more monkey business, nonlogical, and feelings side" of business education, as opposed to "the more serious, masculine, and logical part"—denounced as "mumbo jumbo" the Harvard stereotype of the business executive.

In the spring of 1949, with their time at Harvard winding down, the class of 1949 started to wax nostalgic. "I'd never known as many really nice people," George McManmon said later, in a comment that summed up the way a lot of 49ers felt about each other. People had a sense that they were in a very special time and place, and they were saddened to see it fading. In May, Jack O'Connell was approached by a group of classmates that include Jim Burke, Tom Murphy, and Bill Ruane, who urged him to make a film about the class. O'Connell was among the most creative members of the class of 1949. As an undergrad at Princeton, he had been a member of the exclusive Triangle Club, which was the oldest collegiate musical-comedy troupe in the nation. At Harvard, O'Connell wrote regular comedy columns for the *Harbus News,* and he helped put together various skits that the 49ers put on for each other and the faculty. O'Connell had never made a movie, but that didn't stop him from jumping on the suggestion of his classmates.

Stanley Greenfield and Paul Ames chipped in help on the "screenplay," even though the film had no dialogue. Facetiously entitled *Tomorrow's Leaders Today,* the film captured the essence of life on Soldiers Field in the spring of 1949: breakfast at Cowie Hall, where serious students began their day with the *Wall Street Journal;* faculty members like Professor Neil Borden lecturing in a three-piece suit, waving his reading glasses to make a point; 49ers smoking cigarettes at the student club; Joe Amaturo in a bow tie heading off to cruise for women; Stanley Greenfield arriving at the women's college of Wellesley with a guitar and flowers; Jim Burke and Tom Murphy at a dinner dance.

A few weeks after *Tomorrow's Leaders Today* was filmed, the class of 1949 picked up their degrees in a June graduation ceremony and dispersed across America.

Heading out into the world, the 49ers were uncertain about what they would encounter. Life in America had been so unstable for so long, with the Depression and the war, that it was too early to say what normal times might look like or how such times would affect business. Many 49ers were also unclear about what, exactly, they had learned at Harvard that might be useful in the real world. During the spring of 1949, the school sponsored a series of career counseling lectures that featured Harvard Business School grads who had done splendidly in the business world. At regular evening lectures in Baker Hall, a steady stream of grads—including bona fide tycoons who arrived in limos—talked of how they had parlayed their MBAs into success and fabulous wealth. The talks were reassuring to the hundreds of 49ers facing the unknown.

At some level, most 49ers would come to believe that the basic skills they had picked up at Soldiers Field were useful. "Prior to going to business school, I had never encountered a balance sheet," said Joe Amaturo. "I had zero experience in business." After business school, Amaturo at least felt that he had mechanical knowledge about business. Conrad Jones would say later that he went out in the world with "supreme, if unwarranted confidence" in his own abilities, plus "a hell of a lot of practice in making decisions with a limited number of facts, under deadlines." Others also felt that the case study method and the pressures attached to the work prepared them for business life. "You learn what it's like to have a complex thing chucked at you," said Dan Parker. More grandiosely, one 49er would later say that Harvard Business School "converted me from a drifting cynic to an enthusiastic supporter of American capitalism."

However, not everyone was high on Harvard Business School. Many saw the school as nothing more than a training ground for big business, and they resented being shaped in that mold. Students were treated more as future managers in large organizations than as independent businessmen. " 'Entrepreneurship' was a word in a French dictionary," Jack Muller said of the attitude there. "Nobody knew what it meant." Roger Sonnabend would say that business school had given him "confidence in myself" and that "the case study method introduced me to a lot more ways of looking at things. . . . That I didn't need to do things the way they'd always been done." But he also felt that the experience was antithetical to any kind of personal growth. "I didn't learn about myself. There was nothing at the business school to compel me to look at my own needs, to find what kind of person I was. There was nothing to develop my creativity."[30] James Craig put his criticisms of the school more bluntly: "I learned later that we were taught a whole lot of nonsense."

Whatever the concrete value of their education, many 49ers would later come to believe that learning business skills was only part of what they did at Harvard. For many, the time spent at Soldiers Field was far more personal and emotional. "Something happened in our lives at the business school that made us very important to each other," Burke observed 25 years after graduation, noting that his friends from the class of 1949 were still "the best friends I ever made in my life."[31] Joe Amaturo, Bill Ruane, and many other 49ers felt the same way: that the friendships they made in business school were tighter than any that came later. Ruane would attribute the friendships to the pressure of business school. "There's a bonding to that. And we'd all had similar experiences."

Another thing that drew the 49ers so close together was the heady sense of optimism that they shared. "It was obvious to us when we came back from the war that the country was going to boom," Burke recalled. They would not only build a stronger economy, Burke believed, but like America itself, would help to build a better world. "After the war," Burke said, "we all believed that good can prevail."[32]

The notion that good could prevail would be tested again and again in the America of the postwar era. It would be tested by foreign wars in Asia and by social upheaval at home. It would be tested by recession and oil shocks. And it would be tested by the rapacious greed that swept the corporate world during the merger mania of the 1980s.

The first tests for the 49ers would begin almost immediately upon graduation.

3

A Taste of Success

T|he seal of the Harvard University proclaims a simple word: *veritas,* or "truth" in Latin. It is a rather pretentious seal and not one that conveyed the dreams of the class of 1949. Before they left Harvard, the class members came up with an emblem of their own: a miner on his way to the gold rush.

Not everybody in the class believed that the emblem was a true compass of their future. Most 49ers just wanted to make a decent living and avoid the economic meltdown of their parents' generation. Yet the hope was there for many that they had a real chance at the big time: power, authority, and riches.

During the early 1950s, the unofficial headquarters in New York City for grads of the Harvard Business School class of 1949 was 21 East 11th Street, a brownstone on a tree-lined street right off of Fifth Avenue. A group of 49ers, including Bill Ruane, rented the apartment for $300 a month. Ruane was on Wall Street, working at Kidder, Peabody. Joe Amaturo was a rep for radio and TV advertising deals. Herb Shayne and Hal Lackman lived in the brownstone at one point or another. One 49er even slept on the couch for six months.

Jack Lanahan's apartment on 32nd Street was another center of action. Lanahan was one of the few 49ers with a television, and so friends like Tom Murphy, who lived on the Upper East Side, would come over some nights to watch hit programs like *Your Show of Shows,* starring Sid Caesar.

All told, over 100 members of the class of 1949 had moved to New York City after graduation. They were there to milk the tremendous opportunities that existed in the epicenter of global capitalism—and to have fun. Most of the men were still unmarried, and they would remain so for several years, taking advantage of New York's fabled nightlife to date and party. There was a thriving music scene in midtown—if you had the cash, you could catch Nat King Cole or Thelonious Monk or Ella Fitzgerald—and new bars and cafés were springing up around Greenwich Village. Broadway was thriving, with classics like *South Pacific* and *Death of a Salesman*. The Yankees dominated baseball, rivaled occasionally by the Brooklyn Dodgers, which had one of the few black men in professional sports, Jackie Robinson. For a dime, New York's fabled subway could take you to either of New York's baseball stadiums—or anywhere in the city.

New York's women were another major attraction of the city for 49ers. World War II marked the beginning of a new wave of women's lib, and one manifestation of this was a growing number of young professional women moving away from home to take jobs in big cities. In their dress, the New York women of the early 1950s tended to follow the conservative fashions of the time, wearing dresses pinched in at the waist and high heels and hair pulled back. But the attitudes of New York's swarms of single women were hardly conservative. Joe Amaturo felt that he had been transported to heaven. "New York was great for a young bachelor," he'd say later, an understatement accompanied by a wistful nod. Amaturo's buddy, Jack O'Connell, lived on West 12th Street, near St. Vincent's Hospital, in an apartment strategically located next door to a nursing school. O'Connell and his roommates found it was easy to make friends in the neighborhood.

The apartment on East 11th Street was the scene of endless parties put on by the 49ers. During weekend nights, the place would be jammed with scores of 49ers anxious to live it up with other young and ambitious class members who had moved to Manhattan. During summers, there were occasional house parties out in a sleepy, undiscovered part of Long Island called the Hamptons. It was a spirited group, grateful for the opportunities that lay before them. "We were all happy to have a job," Ruane said.

The rhythm of a steady job was essential to calm the nerves of those who lived in the 1950s, a decade of turbulence at home and abroad. Six months into 1950, in late June, North Korean forces launched a surprise attack down the Korean peninsula. A number of 49ers, fresh out of school and in their first jobs, would find themselves called back to military service to fight yet again overseas.

George Wilkerson had just begun a job as an accountant in Chicago and was looking forward to a calm life after two years of combat with the marines in World War II and two years in the boot camp of Harvard Business School. It wasn't to be. On August 4, less than two months after the North Korean invasion, Wilkerson received an order from the U.S. Marines to report for duty at Camp Pendleton. He drove down from Chicago with his wife Frances, who then was nursing their infant child.

Wilkerson imagined that he would remain at Camp Pendleton as a trainer. But the situation on the Korean Peninsula was dire, and Wilkerson was shipped straight to Asia and into the maelstrom of war. He landed with General MacArthur at Inchon and saw heavy action in the Battle of Seoul. He served as an artillery forward observer as the marines battled their way up the Korean peninsula. The war was going in the United States' favor, until the Chinese entered the action with hundreds of thousands of troops. Wilkerson found himself among U.S. forces trapped near the frozen Chosin Reservoir in December 1950 as wave after wave of Chinese soldiers attacked. "Our chances didn't look good," he recalled. "You'd look out at enemy lines and it seemed like there were millions of them, like ants. . . . It was a scary, brutal business; a kill-or-be-killed situation." Wilkerson survived the heavy fighting, but the terrible cold would take its toll on him. He caught pneumonia and frostbite and was shipped back down the peninsula, and then onward to Japan. Later, Wilkerson won a Bronze Star for his valor in the war.

Other class members also found themselves in the thick of the war effort. Clarence "Bud" Brown, who had returned to his hometown in Ohio after Harvard to run his family's newspaper, became a military journalist in Korea. Jack Alexander and James Dunn were called back to active duty in the air force to train pilots. Frank Chen also supported the air war in Korea by going to General Electric's complex in Evandale and working on crash schedules to help produce the J-47 engines that powered air force Sabre jets. The U.S. Army shipped Bill Davis to Korea, where he worked with American artillery forces. Over a dozen 49ers served in the navy during the war, including Hal Edwards, John Horgan, John Miller, and Frank Stevens.

William Henschel was another 49er drawn into America's clash with communism right after graduation when he was recruited by the CIA. Henschel was trained in covert operations by the Agency, then still only a few years old, before being sent to Europe. The 1950s was the heyday of CIA covert operations, as the United States worked actively to destabilize the new communist governments in Eastern Europe. Henschel found himself in the center of the action. He quickly rose to become a senior intelligence agent and ran numerous covert operations.

The outbreak of the Korean War was just the beginning of a tumultuous decade. The coming years saw detonations of H-bombs by the United States and Soviet Union that signaled a mounting arms race; a wave of anticommunist hysteria unleashed by Senator Joseph McCarthy; civil rights showdowns in Montgomery and Little Rock; and the launching of *Sputnik* in 1957, a Soviet satellite whose beeps in the darkness of space shook American confidence to its core. During nearly every year of the 1950s, public opinion polls would show that issues of war and peace were the number one concern of Americans.

But even though the 1950s was a dangerous time, it also seemed extremely sunny to young professionals—especially those with a Harvard MBA and a regular invitation to the swinging parties put on by the 49ers on East 11th Street. "Basically, business hadn't hired anybody new for executive positions for a long, long time, and so we were there," explained Stephen Jarislowsky, who took a top job at Alcan Aluminum. "We were Johnny-on-the spot, and we had an enormous choice of jobs."

Though 1949 was a recession year as the result of the military demobilization, the 49ers quickly took up prestigious positions in a wide variety of firms. On the job, they were earmarked as future general managers, whose training had focused on the broad responsibilities of top executives. One graduate, asked to describe the aspect of the real world that surprised him most, said he was shocked "to find that there are human beings below the rank of assistant vice president—for at Harvard we never looked at anybody lower than that."[1]

Most graduates of the class took jobs making less than $4,000 a year—good pay in an era in which the average salary of an American man was under $1,500 a year. But it was nothing in comparison to what freshly minted Harvard MBAs would be paid in the future, in a far wealthier

America. (To make $4,000 a year in 1949 would be the equivalent of making $28,000 a year in 2001. In 2001, the average starting salary of a Harvard Business School graduate was just under $100,000.)

Corporate recruiters had been frequent visitors to the Harvard Business School in 1948–1949, trolling for fresh troops to fill their management ranks. By 1949, competition for graduates of the top business schools had become intense, and corporate recruiters sought Harvard graduates with a special determination. Stories of CEOs staffing the tables at job fairs and limousine rides for prospective hires were the stuff of legend.[2] "The world was our oyster," Jim Burke recalled. The big manufacturing companies were the most visible and persistent recruiters, and their efforts paid off. Almost half the class of 1949 would go into the manufacturing sector. Less than 10 percent went into retailing. Less than 5 percent went into banking, and a comparably small number went to Wall Street. As they embarked on their futures, the 49ers mainly dispersed into three kinds of business organizations: Many went into major corporations with thousands of employees. Others went into well-established midsize companies. And a significant number—heirs to family businesses like Lester Crown, Ernie Henderson, and Roger Sonnabend—went to work for companies started by their fathers or grandfathers.

Very few 49ers struck out on their own and forged an entrepreneurial course right after business school. Established organizations seemed a better bet. "One of the experiences of growing up in the Depression was that it paid to work for somebody big enough to weather financial downturns," Jack Muller recalled. Muller took the safe route, going to Macy's and then General Foods—career choices that would soon bore him. Ned Dewey recalls a lot of guys talking about starting their own businesses and then not following through:

> But when push came to shove, most of us either didn't have the nerve to go it alone or couldn't come up with an idea that seemed worth chasing. And those of us that did found out that the School hadn't prepared us at all for the day-to-day mucking around with a start-up business. We liked to think of ourselves as adventurers, but come on— we were a bunch of twenty-five-year-olds out of the Army, full of bluster but mainly just wanting a paycheck. And Harvard liked to

think of itself as where the action was, a breeding ground for people who'd really make a difference, but come on again—in fact it was a finishing school for GM.[3]

Of course, for a group of young men with vivid memories of the Depression, the GMs of the world looked pretty attractive. "The idea of working for a big company was like getting a home," recalled Joe Amaturo. "Your income was more secure in a big company. There was less risk." Amaturo's first job was working for a big ad representative company in New York selling advertising for radio stations. The pay certainly beat the $11 a week he'd made back in his office clerk days, but life in a big firm didn't fit his personality; he was desperate to get out within a year.

For those 49ers with other dreams, it was hard to see ready alternatives to the staid companies that dominated the business world of the early 1950s. Even those graduates most in a hurry and even those who had gotten used to risk in the battle zones of Europe and the Pacific did not easily imagine themselves as daring entrepreneurs. "There was no possibility of getting rich quick or starting your entrepreneurial business that would be a rousing success," Roger Sonnabend commented. "We had no role models of that kind." Venture capital was scarce, reflecting the larger limits on the overall wealth of American society in 1949. Also, because Harvard Business School did not train its students for the entrepreneurial life, there was little sense that one could go it alone. Beyond Georges Frederic Doriot and his famous course, Manufacturing, the business school was not a place that inspired entrepreneurs. It was a place that trained managers and leaders for corporate America. "They [the faculty] wanted us to go to work for big companies and end up as chief executives," Muller recalled.

By and large, the class of 1949 chose staid paths after leaving Harvard. But that didn't mean all stayed on these paths. During the 1950s, many 49ers had surprisingly similar experiences: They went to work for established companies only to soon be bucking the system and insisting on doing things a different way. These personal journeys paralleled an emerging uneasiness in the 1950s with America's culture of bureaucratization conformity. Best-selling books like David Riesman's *The Lonely Crowd* and William H. Whyte's *The Organization Man* critiqued the conformity, and the 49ers had to choose to either accept a numbing life "in the gray flannel suit" or struggle for something different.

Most 49ers—products of their times and culture—chose the gray flannel suit. For the minority of 49ers who wanted to find a more original path, opportunities came in the form of a changing American economy. These changes included the emergence of new technologies that promised novel ways of generating greater productivity and wealth; the increasing size and fast-moving nature of the domestic consumer market; and the revival of financial services sector on Wall Street, as the stock market came to play a larger role in financing business expansion and multiplying the wealth of individuals.

In the early 1950s, tectonic forces were at work in the American economy, slowly shifting the basis of wealth production and economic power. Those who sensed the magnitude of these shifts would be among the most successful and influential business leaders of their generation. What was remarkable about the class of 1949 was *how many* such visionaries emerged within its ranks.

Peter McColough was typical among his classmates in that he ended up at a large, old-economy company after Harvard. He started as a salesman at Lehigh Navigation Coal Company in Philadelphia. There was little in this beginning to suggest that McColough would become one of the great technology innovators of his day.

McColough's serious manner, his air of gravitas, and his academic credentials speeded his rise through the executive ranks at his first job. He didn't mind starting near the bottom of the company ladder, despite his MBA. "There seems to be a prejudice against persons spending so many years in college and then becoming salesmen," he observed later. "But I've never regretted it." McColough noted that his work in sales gave him intimate knowledge of products and clients that was invaluable to him as an executive decision maker. Besides, he said, "A man doesn't have to spend his whole career as a salesman."[4] McColough's upward trajectory during his brief tenure at Lehigh provided ample confirmation of that claim. Within four years, he was vice president for sales.

Despite his rapid advancement, McColough was restless in Philadelphia. "I knew for me there was really no future in coal or railroads," he remembered. Like many of his Harvard classmates, McColough had gravitated toward an established industry in which he could refine his skills and establish credibility within an "old reputable company."[5] McColough wanted to use his education and experience to "get in on an interesting company" where he could make a bigger difference.[6] His plan was to leap from Lehigh to a more promising organization, one directed toward the future of industry rather than the past.

Like Peter McColough, the Haloid Company of Rochester, New York, had its eye on the next big thing. In the mid-1940s, the company had obtained the rights to market an experimental electrophotographic process for duplicating office documents, which had been developed by Chester Carlson, a struggling inventor. The *xerographic* process—which derived its name from the Greek words for "dry" and "writing"—aimed to make better and less-expensive copies than those produced on the chemical copiers of the day. Haloid's president, Joseph C. Wilson, committed virtually all of Haloid's earnings and everything he could borrow toward research and development.

Haloid's profile, accordingly, was less than stellar when McColough arrived for a job interview in 1954. The corporate headquarters, which doubled as a factory and laboratory, was squat and windowless. White-collar employees were being asked to provide their own desks.[7] McColough met with Haloid's vice president for sales, John B. Hartnett, in an office where orange crates served as bookcases. The Harvard MBA was shocked to see that his Haloid counterpart had brought his dinner in a lunch box.[8] "My God," he thought, "what am I doing here?"[9]

McColough got a compelling answer to that question when Hartnett introduced him to Joe Wilson. McColough was taken by Wilson's visionary talk of a revolution in copying and, by the end of their conversation, was ready to join Haloid. The job offer came through a few days after McColough's visit. The position paid $5,000 less than what he earned at Lehigh, but McColough accepted, convinced that Haloid's potential for success was worth the gamble. His low salary was offset by compensation in the form of stock.

McColough's friends from Harvard Business School were not quite sure what to make of the move. Jack Muller had lunch with McColough the day before he started on the job and couldn't grasp how Haloid might succeed. "It sounded so off the wall. It was a really a new kind of thing, and it was hard to figure out whether it would work."

McColough started out as the general manager of Haloid's reproduction service center in Chicago and began a rapid ascent up the corporate ladder. By 1957, McColough was the marketing manager at the corporate headquarters in Rochester, and he almost single-handedly put into place a new national sales force for Haloid. The xerographic duplicating machine, however, was still two years away from production. McColough and Haloid soldiered on with the conviction of true believers. When IBM, a company already famous in the 1950s for its marketing savvy and taste for innovation, refused Haloid's offer to collaborate on the release of the first xerographic copier, naysayers concluded that the technology would never make it to the market. The future of Haloid itself was in doubt.

McColough was undeterred. The prototype machines were big, heavy, expensive, and—above all—an unknown entry into the competitive market for office duplicators. But McColough's experience in sales had taught him enough about customers' needs and priorities to overcome some of the initial objections. Given a chance, he was confident that the superior results of the xerographic technique would earn Haloid's copiers a (large) place in American offices.

McColough's classmate, Tom Murphy, also had his eye on new technology and a different kind of American economy. As with McColough, the entrepreneurial spirit burned hot for Murphy even as he toiled away in a conservative corporation. Five years out of business school, he was working his way up in the organization as a marketing manager for Lever Brothers manufacturers. He helped to sell soap, among other things. It was hardly inspiring work and Murphy didn't have much real responsibility. "All the decisions were being made at a higher level than I was," he recalled. New York was exciting, with the parties and many close friends, but Murphy was ready for something else. "I was bored with what I was doing."

Murphy's big break came on Labor Day weekend 1954. Still a bachelor, he went to visit his parents at their summer home in Pawling, New York, for the weekend. He tagged along when they went to a cocktail party at a friend of theirs, Lowell Thomas. At the party, Murphy sipped only soda as usual; he still didn't drink or smoke—and never would. One of the other guests that day was small, balding man named Frank Smith, an investment manager who sometimes played golf with Murphy's father.

"Tom, perhaps you can help me," said Smith whose diminutive stature and Tennessee accent gave him a distinctive flair.

"How's that?" Murphy replied. He towered over Smith by more than half a foot.

Smith wondered whether Murphy knew of anyone who could help him run an Albany television station that he had just bought. The station had a feeble UHF signal and was called WROW.

Smith didn't ask Murphy that day if he would be interested in the job, and Murphy's first reaction was to suggest his Harvard classmate, Jim Burke.

Later, though, it became clear that Smith wanted Murphy to be the one to run the television station. When the two men talked further, Smith made a direct pitch to Murphy. He was honest about the situation. It was a great opportunity for a young fellow, Smith said. "If we do well, you can make a quarter-million dollars in five years. If we go broke, you've got great experience."[10]

Murphy was 29 years old. Almost completely bald by this time, direct and calm in his manner, he had the demeanor of someone far older. Murphy didn't know much about the television industry or the technology behind it. But one didn't have to be a genius to sense that television was a vast and exciting business frontier. Smith's talk of riches did not seem entirely far-fetched. Still, the mission Smith was proposing to Murphy was filled with risk. To be sure, by 1954, television was well established. Hit shows like *The Honeymooners* and *I Love Lucy* drew tens of millions of avid fans, and the popular soap opera, *The Guiding Light,* had premiered in 1952. Color television broadcasts had just become possible, and news programs increasingly carried live feeds that showed pictures of events as they occurred. The rise of television in the 1950s changed more than the leisure habits of Americans; it also accelerated the homogenization of America's consumer culture, with national product brands and chain stores becoming more dominant.

Yet UHF was the speculative frontier of the burgeoning television industry, an untested technology with uncertain commercial applications. A handful of VHS broadcasters, licensed in the years before World

War II, dominated the airwaves. Few if any American television sets were equipped to receive UHF signals in the early 1950s.[11] But the Federal Communications Commission (FCC) was promoting UHF and assured franchises of its efforts to speed the necessary conversion in television manufacturing and to expand its UHF licensing and research programs. The challenge for stations like WROW was to survive the wait.[12]

Could the venture succeed? "It's a crapshoot," Smith admitted. They all could get rich, or young Murphy could find himself back in New York City with empty pockets, looking for a new job.[13] Murphy decided to take the risk.

After saying yes to Smith, Murphy went to see a friend in charge of media for Lever Brothers. Murphy asked, "What's a UHF television station?" The friend said, "UHF television is bad news."

"A lot of people thought I was nuts," Murphy remembered. Murphy took the risk because of Smith's reputation. "I was betting on a man who my father thought was smart," Murphy said later. "Smitty was a charismatic, charming man. . . . I had great great confidence in Smitty. I never had any second thoughts. Not ever. Maybe I should have, but I was too young and too dumb to know any better."[14]

Smitty seemed to have all the winning tricks up his sleeve. Smith had bought into the television station on an inside tip from a Quaker Hill comrade, former governor Thomas E. Dewey, and another personal friend, chief executive of the Columbia Broadcasting System (CBS), Frank Staunton. The Albany UHF station broadcast to an area designated to receive VHF signals on Channel 10 as soon as the FCC began issuing new licenses. WROW-TV would be in a position to offer a competitive bid for the local franchise.[15] And Smith had experience in the entertainment industry as a pioneer radio businessman and a leading developer of three-dimensional moving photography.[16] He had the cash, with investors who anted up admirably and had the resources to meet future emergencies. Chief among them was the adventurer and radio personality Lowell Thomas (the man who first publicized the exploits of Lawrence of Arabia), who attracted potential investors aware of Thomas's reputation for making waves and getting rich. "When you're a small company starting out," Murphy observed later, "one of the greatest things that can happen to you is to be able to say, 'Well, our major stockholder is Lowell Thomas.' "[17]

Perhaps most important among Murphy's considerations when he made the decision to hire on was Smitty himself, a kind of confidence man who inspired real confidence. Thomas described his friend and business manager as a "two-way genius: a genius in financial matters and a man with a genius for friendship."[18] The combination mirrored Murphy's own business strengths. Years later, Murphy offered career advice for young people that showed his enduring admiration for his mentor. "[I]f they're lucky enough to find a boss who is smart . . . go work for them," he urged. "Because that doesn't always happen to you."[19]

The television station was outside Albany. Hudson Valley Broadcasting occupied a drafty house that had previously served as home for retired nuns. Dozens of tiny rooms dominated the upstairs floors, conjuring images of quiet lives devoted to faith. The house, its paint peeling, stood at the end of a dirt road that crossed the property of a cantankerous farmer who had been known to confront trespassers with a shotgun. Murphy arrived, took in the lay of the land, and thanked God for his rich investors. Appearances were important in television, and Murphy had his new staff paint the two sides of the building that could be seen from the road.[20]

Murphy took enthusiastically to the challenge of his new job. Still single when he moved to Albany, he focused obsessively on work. "I worked all the time. I couldn't wait to get to the office in the morning." With Smitty concentrating on the big picture, dealing with the FCC and investors, Murphy built the station and did whatever he could to "meet next week's payroll."

Filling the many hours of airtime at WROW-TV was a major challenge. In the mid-1950s, the networks themselves offered only a limited number of programming hours. Many network programs were broadcast live, and taping technology remained primitive. Without reruns of popular shows to fill daytime, late-night, and weekend slots, television stations relied on old movies, often cut to accommodate network broadcasting schedules and locally produced programming. Commercial spots were also produced locally and live. The studio at the big house in Albany was a show business workshop, complete with one camera, a news desk, and a unisex bathroom.

Aggressive business management complemented the efforts of WROW's programmers. Smith continued to build up the ranks of investors, raising an impressive $1 million to meet the station's expenses in the first three years.[21]

A steady flow of money was essential for survival, since by 1956 the station would be $700,000 in the red and it perpetually tottered on bankruptcy during those early days. To increase the audience, the business staff organized marketing drives to educate viewers on antenna placement and promote the sale of UHF converters. Lobbying at the FCC and a series of lawsuits paid off in 1957, when Hudson Valley Broadcasters obtained the rights to VHF Channel 10. Also in 1957, the company adopted a new name—Capital Cities Television Corporation—and an ambitious new goal. With Capital Cities, Murphy and Smith would make their bid for the national television market.

Murphy's personal life moved forward along with his business fortunes. In 1955, after many arid months of bachelor life in Albany, he became engaged to his future wife, Suzanne. They were married that November at a wedding attended by many of Murphy's friends from Harvard Business School. "It was the best thing that ever happened to me." Soon, Murphy was a father, settling into a comfortable family life in Albany, which he and Suzanne found to be a great place to raise children.

Even in the difficult early days, local television broadcasting that served a sufficient audience generated tremendous revenues. Spending on television advertising increased from 3 percent of the total for all media in 1950 to more than 13 percent in 1959, as companies competed to promote their wares on hit shows like *Lassie* and *Father Knows Best*.[22] The booming postwar consumer economy invigorated the advertising industry and advertising-supported businesses like television and radio, which collected what Murphy called a kind of "royalty on the gross national product."[23] Television operators benefited from their position as a limited-access business, in which a handful of licensees profited from the most dynamic new economic sector. "If you had the access for it," Murphy later observed, "you were in a wonderful business."[24]

Not yet 35, Tom Murphy was on his way to the big time.

Like Tom Murphy, Roger Sonnabend's first decade out of Harvard was marked by major opportunity. Fit and energetic in his 20s, Sonnabend plunged headlong into the family hotel business. He moved into the hospitality industry at a time when Americans had more money than ever to burn on travel and leisure. "When I got out of Harvard Business School, the hotel business was most noteworthy for the disaster that had occurred throughout the Thirties—when eighty percent of all hotels went bankrupt," Sonnabend recalled. In the postwar era, everything was different. A consumer spending binge, the likes of which America had never seen, got under way as the economy began to wake up after years of depression and war. The Sonnabend family, which had bought many of their hotels at cut rates in the 1930s and 1940s, was positioned to prosper.

Roger had spent his Harvard years commuting between Cambridge and Long Island, where his father had given him his first opportunity—serving as general manager of the Nautilus Hotel and Beach Club in Atlantic Beach. Sonnabend's drive to meticulously restore "this relic" would test his mettle as an aspiring hotelier. "I knew I had to spend money to make money," Sonnabend said, and he spared no expense.[25] By the time Roger had graduated from Harvard, the once-derelict property was turning a profit and Roger was on his way to the next challenge in the family business. After Nautilus, he ran the Whitehall Hotel in Palm Beach, Florida, the Somerset Hotel in Boston, and the Samoset Resort in Rockland, Maine. With his father increasingly focused on business ventures outside of the hotel world, Roger gained more responsibility. "He more and more turned things over to me on the hotel end of it. . . . So I had the unique opportunity to take a group of individual investments and mold them into a company."

In 1954, Sonnabend got some badly needed backup from James Craig, who had been a roommate of his at both MIT and Harvard. Craig came to the fledging Sonnabend hotel empire from a job in the defense industry, at Raytheon, that had begun to wear on him. Like Murphy and other 49ers, Craig rebelled against the stifling rigidity of a huge company. "I wasn't a fan of the corporate culture at Raytheon." Sonnabend lobbied Craig to join him in the hotel business. He went to work with his old roommate with some misgivings—"I was worried I would lose a friend"—but soon found himself fascinated by the business challenges of his new job. Together, he and Sonnabend set out to implement a blueprint for transforming a number of disparate hotel properties into a cohesive chain with highly professionalized operations. "It was a very dynamic time. . . . We literally revolutionized the way hotels were organized and operated *as businesses*," Craig would say later.

In 1956, the Sonnabend Operated Hotels merged with the Childs Restaurant Company to form the Hotel Corporation of America. At the time, HCA was the third-largest hotel chain in the world, and A. M. Sonnabend dreamed incessantly of catching up with number one. Driven by "the shrewdness of an operator and the mania of an empire builder" as *Forbes* would write in 1958, the elder Sonnabend even entertained the idea of adding Disneyland to HCA's list of properties.[26] The three Sonnabend brothers served as Sonny's lieutenants in his restless push for expansion, managing a chain that grew to include 10 hotels and 17 motor hotels in the United States, Europe, and the Caribbean, as well as a long list of manufacturing and distribution firms. Roger took a leading role as president of the company's hotel and motor hotel division and corporate vice president.

By the late 1950s, the hotel business was strong and getting stronger. One factor driving the boom was that the World War II veterans were becoming more prosperous as the postwar era progressed. These men had seen a lot of the world during their years in service, and they were interested in travel. As their incomes grew, travel was one thing they spent it on. In fact, nearly all Americans were spending more on travel—or could be persuaded to through advertising. Sonnabend became a keen student of changing American traveling habits as he moved deeply into the hotel world. "We began seeing in places like Bermuda, a tremendous increase in blue collar customers, who became familiar with travel and said, 'Well, why don't we go to Bermuda,' or 'Why don't we do something more exciting than just getting in the car and driving to Oklahoma?' " For those Americans who couldn't afford the trip to Bermuda, the Sonnabends and other hoteliers tried to provide a sense of getaway at new roadside hotels and motels. The first Holiday Inn opened in 1952. Howard Johnson hotels were also proliferating. Accommodations like these served an America in which historically unprecedented rates of car ownership (70 million cars on the road by 1955) and a developing interstate highway system made people more mobile than ever before. Cheap room rates lured in many Americans who had seldom experienced overnight stays in a hotel. "And the more people began to travel," Sonnabend said, "the more they began to discover how much they liked it."

Even as Sonnabend saw the long-term boom in roadside hotel chains, he came to decide that this business was too generic for him. Sonnabend was a man interested in refined things. He had a strong interest in art and architecture and the high ideals of hospitality. He had taken pleasure in restoring the faded elegance of the Nautilus Hotel while still in business school. He aspired to provide a unique, high-quality experience to hotel guests. "The idea of just providing a room wasn't very interesting, exciting for us personally," Sonnabend later said. Those who built the sterile, overnight warehouses next to the interstates were not really hotel people, as Sonnabend saw it. They were providing a service, not an experience. Sonnabend decided that he'd rather "get a full-scale hotel, particularly a resort hotel, where we could provide the excitement, and the glamour."

It would take some years for Sonnabend and his brothers to fully shift gears, moving away from empire building for its own sake and toward exclusively upscale hotels.

The Fast Track

 ew York City was home for Marvin Traub.

Returning to the city after Harvard, Traub was back at the scene of his youth, and it suited him. He liked the action of New York, the glamour, the casual high fashion that was everywhere. New steel and glass towers, built in the international style with sheer, smooth surfaces, were rising in midtown, casting long shadows in the day but twinkling brightly in the evening sky. And late at night, when every restaurant in Boston would have been long closed, New York had nightspots like Sherman Billingsley's famous Stork Club where people were just *arriving* for dinner.

Along with his young artistic wife, Lee, Traub took in the city's culture. For two years, from their arrival in New York in summer 1949 to 1952 when their first son, Andrew, was born, the couple could do what they wanted. Like his parents, Sam and Bea, Traub gravitated toward New York's sophisticated set. Not yet 25, with thick dark hair and a taste for snappy suits, Traub wanted to live large.

During the days, Traub pursued his first love in business: retailing. He did so with great seriousness, feeling that he had lost time in life because of the war and his long months in the hospital. To keep himself on track, Traub began a lifetime habit of making five-year plans for himself, and he exemplified the can-do mentality that author Norman Peale proselytized in his 1952 best-seller, *The Power of Positive Thinking*. Wealth was a natural part of Traub's plan, but only part of it. "I cared more about being successful as a businessman than about money," he said later.

Success in department stores was his goal, and nothing else. Following his brief experiences at Macy's before Harvard Business School, Traub remained keenly focused on department stores. In business school, he had enrolled in a retailing course taught by Professor Malcolm P. McNair, who insisted that department stores had reached "the maturity stage of their life cycle" and would not be a vital economic sector in the future. Traub disagreed, and in later years he recalled McNair's prediction as the first of many warnings about the imminent demise of the department store. He did learn from McNair, however, about the potential benefits of creating an atmosphere of prestige that sparked the desires of the customer. This idea had natural appeal to Traub.

Traub had worked as a trainee at Abraham & Strauss during the summer of 1948. After graduation from Harvard, he became an associate buyer at Alexanders. In 1950, he took his first job at Bloomingdale's. Neither his position as an assistant to the manager of the basement store nor the store itself bespoke an aura of prestige. Bloomingdale's was on the Upper East Side of Manhattan, with a branch store out in Queens. In 1950, the Upper East Side was unfashionable. An elevated train ran up Third Avenue, a blight on a neighborhood that was home to many dreary tenement buildings with fire escapes zigzagging down their facades. Bloomingdale's reflected the area. It was the fifth-ranking department store in the city, known for its selection of uniforms for household domestics. In the retailing world, Bloomingdale's had long had the reputation of being the "poor man's Macy's." That reputation had only slowly begun to change in the late 1940s, as the store focused on becoming more upscale and dropping much of its lower-end merchandise.

Traub's new domain in the basement store at Bloomingdale's was drab and unpromising. It was the old Bloomingdale's, not the aspiring new one. In addition to discounted merchandise and other goods unfit for the upstairs, the downstairs store at Bloomingdale's housed a post office. Traub was not put off by appearances. Instead, he was excited. As a separate business within the department store, the downstairs division provided an opportunity to experiment with merchandising strategies— Traub called it a "merchandising laboratory." The downstairs store was where Marvin Traub would discover the retailing arts that would eventually make him wealthy and famous: the magic of drawing a crowd, the marketing of exclusive products, and the identification of high-fashion suppliers abroad.[1]

Traub's early career at Bloomingdale's revealed the interdependence of his professional responsibilities and a glamorous personal lifestyle. He became a store buyer in 1953, assigned to update Bloomingdale's rug department as part of a storewide effort to offer more upscale merchandise. Bloomingdale's CEO, Jed Davidson, the champion of the transition, urged Traub to take his wife Lee along for a five-week tour of rug and furniture factories in Denmark, Sweden, and Spain. Bankrolled by the store, Marvin and Lee swept into remote villages and urban studios in pursuit of distinctive merchandise, with instructions to absorb a sense of the setting and use of the household objects they discovered. This unique merchandise increased revenues in the rug department and also earned the more intangible benefits of offering something special that appealed to a customer's higher taste.

By 1956, in addition to rugs, Traub's responsibilities included furniture, curtains, draperies, cameras, stationery, and toys. He contributed to the makeover of Bloomingdale's image as leader of a home furnishings team that not only identified the finest modern and traditional European goods, but arranged and marketed the materials in dramatic model room settings that attracted sightseers as well as potential buyers. Learning by seeing, Traub developed an appreciation for European comforts in a series of fruitful purchasing tours. By the late 1950s, Traub was known at Bloomingdale's as a rising young star with more pizzazz than most of the young men climbing up through the ranks. Bloomingdale's itself remained a staid company. But as Traub moved higher at the store, he was maneuvering himself into a position where he could change all that.

Jim Burke was another restless entrepreneur in the consumer product world of the 1950s. Burke had gone to Cincinnati after business school, taking a position at the Procter & Gamble Corporation. The job at the giant firm didn't thrill him. "The bureaucratic apparatus at the company bothered me," Burke remembered. "I found it very constraining. I didn't feel I was where I ought to be." After three years in Cincinnati, Burke quit the job and moved to New York City to search for something else. After a few months in New York, Burke accepted a position in 1953 as product director at Johnson & Johnson in New Brunswick,

New Jersey. His portfolio was Band-Aids, one of the company's most hallowed products.

Johnson & Johnson had been founded by brothers James and Edward Mead Johnson in 1885 to make medical products. A third brother, Robert, joined the company a year later. By the 1920s, J&J had established itself in American consumer culture with both Band-Aid and with Johnson's baby powder. Robert Johnson Jr. took over the company in 1932, leaving it only briefly during World War II to serve in the war effort in Washington (managing to earn the rank of brigadier general). "General" Johnson, who would remain the company chairman until 1963, believed in decentralization and in giving his managers substantial freedom. Johnson was also a strong believer in social responsibility, and he emphasized the importance of good working conditions and wages at the company. The year that Burke joined J&J was the same year it introduced what would quickly become its famous Johnson's baby shampoo. One reason the product took off so quickly was because J&J poured the staggering sum of $1 million into promoting the shampoo—the most that it had ever spent promoting a new product. The cornerstone of the campaign was a catchy slogan: "No More Tears."

Burke was unimpressed by J&J's alleged dynamism. Managing the Band-Aid portfolio put Burke in charge of one of the company's most sacred and successful products. But Burke quickly discovered a dark truth about Band-Aid: It was losing its dominant market share. Burke began to look for ways to halt the slide, only to encounter corporate bureaucracy and obstinacy. Nobody at J&J was particularly interested in any of the ideas Burke had for innovation at the company, either in the Band-Aid portfolio or elsewhere.

Burke quit after only a year. "I was bored," he recalled, complaining that the company was too centralized, too conservative, and too indifferent to developing and marketing new products.[2] J&J was "stifling," Burke would say later. As he saw it, the revenues from Johnson & Johnson's successful baby products line had lulled the company into a false sense of security. Of course, the baby products leaders were doing good business in the 1950s, riding the crest of the baby boom. But Band-Aid and other product lines were less secure. Burke feared that demographic trends meant that the company would shrink substantially in the long term. Without a commitment to developing new products, he told his superiors, Johnson & Johnson would watch its market disappear.

Within three weeks of announcing his resignation, Burke was persuaded to stay on with J&J. Initially, the offer was a temporary one. Burke was asked to evaluate how J&J might approach opportunities for new products—the challenge that fascinated him most. That position soon turned into a full-time arrangement. Burke suggested creating a new-products division, and the company's high command bought the idea. Burke landed the job of leading the new division. The incident revealed some of the better qualities of both the man and the corporation. Burke was a practical idealist, willing to risk his own position on behalf of sound business principles. Johnson & Johnson prided itself on being an enormously flexible and dynamic organization. When a manager quit because of a lack of autonomy and support, General Johnson didn't take it personally: He tried to get that person back. Burke was willing to give J&J another try.

Fired up by a sense of possibility, Burke set about marketing his first new product: a children's chest rub for colds. The product failed. It was a stinging setback. Burke had sought to buck the established system and carve out an entrepreneurial role for himself only to have his first major effort flop.

Burke was summoned to the General's office for an accounting. Strangely, he wasn't dreading the encounter at all. "I was actually excited," Burke remembered, "that the CEO was going to personally fire someone at my level."[3]

Burke walked into Johnson's office ready to get the ax. The office was vast, and the desk seemed as though it was "a mile and a half from the door."

Initially, the General didn't even look up. He was giving dictation and continued on for a few minutes, letting Burke wait. Finally, when he was done, Johnson picked up a piece of paper. It was a report saying that J&J had spent a total of $865,000 on the failed children's chest rub product. Johnson fixed his eyes on Burke. "Are you the one who just cost us all that money?"

Burke nodded.

"Well, I just want to congratulate you," Johnson said. "If you are making mistakes, that means you are making decisions and taking risks. And we won't grow unless you take risks."[4]

Burke breathed a sigh of relief, although Johnson did add that if Burke made the same mistake again, he would be fired.

Intelligent risk taking became a hallmark of Burke's career and emerged as a dominant feature of the corporate culture at Johnson & Johnson. Burke remained as director of new products through 1957. His hard-driving style and risk taking continued to win the approval of Johnson, who promoted him in 1958 to the critical position of director of advertising and merchandising.

Jim Burke was a man on the fast track.

Jack Davis's career after Harvard started out with few surprises and little promise of surprises in the future. He steered a conservative course in the first years after Harvard, initially taking a job with a small consulting firm at $60 a week. Then he took a position as director of planning for the Rheem Manufacturing Company. Davis, a child of the Depression, was a buttoned-down kind of guy who wanted security above all else and had modest expectations. Soon after graduating from Harvard, when somebody asked him how much money he hoped to be making when he was 35, Davis said, "Gee, it would be great to be making $10,000 a year."

Money, though, was not Davis's only goal. He always wanted to make things happen. "I wanted to be an operating person." To friends, Davis complained about his job at Rheem. The real decisions were being made at the top of the company, and he was working in the middle. "It was frustrating always being an advisor." Davis' lament was a familiar one among 49ers.

Davis got a chance to finally run something in the late 1950s. Attending the wedding of his good friend Tom Murphy in November 1955, Davis met the man who would offer him a life-altering career opportunity.

James Crosby was Murphy's new brother-in-law, a Midwestern businessman with a burning ambition to build a financial empire. Family ties would be the basis of Crosby's new enterprise, which included James Crosby's brother William, Tom Murphy's brother, Charles, and a Murphy cousin, Henry Murphy. Jack Davis, an outsider, obviously struck a chord with the Crosby and Murphy clans. He was asked to sign on as president of Mary Carter Paint Company in 1958, a company that James

Crosby had recently bought, backed by major investors like former presidential candidate Thomas Dewey and radio commentator Lowell Thomas. Davis didn't know anything about paint, but that didn't matter to Crosby and the others. "To them, it was most important to have somebody they could trust," Davis recalled. The downside of Davis's new position was that the existing management and staff of the paint company were very mediocre, and Davis's first order of business was to fire almost 150 people as a part of a reorganization. Soon Mary Carter Paint was making serious money. In 1959, only 10 years out of Harvard Business School, Jack Davis was making a lot more than $10,000.

A paint company. It was hard to imagine a tamer and more all-American kind of business. There was nothing risky or fancy in producing cans of paint, and with America in a housing boom, it seemed that steady profits were a sure bet. Jack Davis had found a job that offered the perfect combination of predictability and profitability.

What Davis could not have imagined in 1959 was that Mary Carter Paint Company would eventually metamorphose into one of the largest casino gambling companies in the world—and that he would stay with the company every step of the way.

In time, the glamour and intrigue that surrounded Jack Davis's long tenure with Mary Carter, which eventually took the name Resorts International, would come to distinguish Davis as one of the savviest and most controversial members of his class.

Bill Ruane liked numbers. This was the most important thing he learned about himself by the time he finished Harvard Business School. A practical young Midwesterner, straightforward in his manner and his thinking, Ruane was attracted to the solid truth of numbers. Just as he learned during his time at GE that he was a "mechanical idiot," Ruane left Harvard convinced that he'd excel in a position involving quantitative analysis. The financial investing world struck him as an obvious career track.

Ruane's sense that his future lay on Wall Street was deepened when he experienced an intellectual revelation upon reading a book at Harvard called *Security Analysis,* by Benjamin Graham and David L. Dodd about *value investing.* Using research and mathematical calculations to identify good bargains, value investors eschewed the erratic psychology of the stock market in favor of quantitative measures of corporate health, including the price-to-earnings ratio, cash flow, personnel, and market placement. "It just seemed so logical," Ruane thought. "It isn't about stock market moves. It isn't about a momentum." It was about looking "at a stock as a business, instead of a piece of paper that moves up and down in price."[5] The approach gave an air of respectability to the stock market, which remained the object of popular suspicions among survivors of the Great Depression and World War II.[6] Instead of spinning profits out of straw, like the stereotype of the despised speculator, the value investor contributed capital to the potentially productive enterprises that needed it most. "I just thought that this is the answer and I liked it," Ruane said later. Value investing was a vision that brought Midwestern values to Wall Street and convinced Bill Ruane that New York City was the place to be.

Ruane hitchhiked down to New York from Cambridge to try to find a Wall Street job. Outside Hartford, he caught a ride and told the driver about his plans. When Ruane said he was heading to Wall Street, the man almost put him out of the car. He explained that he himself had gone into the field in 1928, that he had lost everything, and that he didn't want to be part of ruining a young man's life. Ultimately, however, the driver turned out to be a nice guy. He recommended the firm of Kidder, Peabody, which he said was a good one because it was diversified and there would be lots of opportunities to learn.

Ruane followed this advice and did, in fact, end up with a job at Kidder. It proved to be a good choice. The firm was a small and warm place, where everyone knew each other. Because of the market slump, there had been virtually no new hires since the 1920s, so there were lots of old-timers. Ruane had the opportunity to work with the legendary Al Gordon, a Harvard Business School grad himself (class of 1925) who had become famous for saving Kidder from bankruptcy in 1931. Signing on as a trainee, Ruane went through all the various departments—securities, municipals, underwriting—even though he was already pretty sure he wanted to work with stocks.

As he explored the different aspects of investing, Ruane was also enjoying New York City. The apartment on East 11th Street in Greenwich Village was his base of operations, and the place seemed to get more chaotic all the time. Initially, Ruane had rented the apartment with two other 49ers, splitting the $300 rent between them. Soon they took in another roommate and then one more. The five guys threw parties constantly, jamming the place with friends on weekend nights. On Saturday and Sunday mornings there would often be a 49er crashed on the couch in the living room and empty beer bottles littering the room. Stan Greenfield was among those 49ers who used the 11th Street apartment as an emergency crash pad on those nights when he couldn't get home to his place in Riverdale. Because the apartment was on the parlor floor of the town house, it was possible to walk up the stoop and lean across to throw open one of the tall windows to get in.

Beyond the parties, there were also plenty of nights out on the town. Joe Amaturo was one of Ruane's roommates and carousing partners, and the two began to deepen a friendship in New York that would last for 50 years. Like Ruane, Amaturo was unmarried during his early New York days and always up for adventure. Amaturo knew the city well, and he delighted in showing the Midwestern Ruane around.

Something was always happening on Friday and Saturday nights, usually a party, but there was also no shortage of exciting clubs and bars. On summer weekends, Ruane, Amaturo, and other 49ers got out of town. Jack O'Connell, who lived on 12th Street and made good money in advertising, was one of the few 49ers who owned a car in Manhattan. O'Connell became the chauffer in the crowd, and for several summers in a row, Ruane, Amaturo, and he rented a house out in Westhampton, not far from miles and miles of unspoiled beaches.

Ruane's job at Kidder was great, even though initially not very lucrative. His compensation arrangement was a base salary that was supplemented by commission after he had grossed a certain amount. But he made so few transactions in the early years that he earned only his base salary for years. The good news was that Ruane was under no pressure to earn his pay. He didn't have to buy and sell much and had time to study specific companies and investing practices in general. To learn more about his new world, Ruane sought out a seat at the feet of the master. In 1951, he signed on for Ben Graham's seminar at Columbia University's business school. Graham's lectures expounded on theories about the psychology of the stock market, which he considered vulnerable to emotional extremes of optimism and pessimism that had little to do with the underlying productive capacity of the companies listed. "You are neither right nor wrong because people agree with you," Graham liked to say.[7] The professor taught techniques for calculating the difference between a company's price and its intrinsic value. Given the capriciousness of the market pricing mechanism, the value investor who stuck with the margin of safety would find opportunities to buy "dollar bills for 40 cents."[8]

The Columbia seminar introduced Ruane to a cadre of Graham disciples led by Warren Buffett, a Columbia Business School student from Omaha, Nebraska, who became a lifelong friend of Ruane's. Buffett quickly established himself as Graham's intellectual equal. "Sparks were flying" between the professor and his best student, Ruane remembered. "You could tell then that [Buffett] was someone who was very unusual."[9] Young Buffett's enthusiasm for value investing set a standard for commitment that few of his Columbia classmates were willing to emulate. Instead of remaining in New York to build a base of support for value investing within established brokerage firms, Buffett husbanded his resources by moving back to his parents' house in Omaha right after graduation. He would put every penny in the stock market. Ruane followed the more established course with his position at Kidder. For the next 17 years, while Buffett pioneered value stocks as an independent investment adviser, Ruane worked to win converts to the new technique on Wall Street.

"When I first came into this business back in 1949, the banks were dominating the market," Ruane recalled later. "They did the safe thing then, they bought blue-chip stocks."[10] The young stockbroker worked hard to square Kidder, Peabody's offerings to the investment philosophy he had imbibed at Harvard and Columbia. It was not an easy balancing act. For camaraderie, Ruane teamed up with Rick Cunniff, another young guy at Kidder, and the two men pursued their own value-investing activities within the company that scored impressive successes. Eventually, in 1956, they were allowed to establish an investment advisory department at Kidder, Peabody "to seek out unusual values."[11]

By the late 1950s, Bill Ruane effectively had his own investment firm on Wall Street. And he was doing things his way.

During his early days on Wall Street, Bill Ruane often spent time with a classmate who had also gone into financial services: his friend John

Shad. Flat broke after graduation from Harvard, Shad moved to New York City with $500 from the Harvard Business School student loan fund and took an apartment in Greenwich Village, not far from where Ruane lived.[12] He was starting from scratch, but Shad had always been coming from behind. At Harvard, even as he put in killer hours, he felt underworked in comparison to the days when he had combined college with the graveyard shift as a riveter. In New York, anxious to make his fortune, Shad was primed for almost any sacrifice.

Shad set out to build a career on Wall Street with fierce determination. He chose the securities industry, a rarified niche in the postwar economy.[13] His first job was as a securities analyst with Value Line, the market advisory service. The job required lots of fast learning and long hours. But in typical fashion, John Shad set out to work harder with the hope of reaping greater returns. He decided that becoming a lawyer on top of having a business degree would give him a huge competitive advantage in an industry so closely chaperoned by federal regulators. He and his wife Patricia enrolled at New York University, where they took night classes together. The new routine was akin to Shad's old days as a riveter, leaving very little time for leisure activities in New York. Within several years, Shad and Patricia both passed the New York bar exam.

Shad's law degree gave him precisely the edge he wanted in his new career. Since the turn of the twentieth century, a growing body of laws and government agencies had grown up around corporate and municipal finance. Committees of Congress, the Interstate Commerce Commission, the Justice Department, and above all, the Securities and Exchange Commission (established in 1934), had incrementally added additional layers of arcane details to the obscure procedures of bond issues, mergers, and acquisitions. Securities lawyers such as Shad were equipped to advise investors on how to maximize returns within this complex system. As the servant of two masters—the profit principle and the sanctity of law—Shad would rapidly assume his rank in the high courts of American finance. During his early years in New York, Shad rapidly acquired a personal fortune, another crucial attribute of stature on the Street. As a securities analyst for *Value Line,* Shad was part of a team that evaluated the financial data of more than 1,000 publicly traded stocks. One of Shad's Value Line clients, Associated Transport, struck Shad as a likely bargain. Associated Transport had failed to meet its dividend obligations in recent quarters, and its stock price had declined to a low $2.50. Shad's analysis of the company's books and discussions with Associated Transport officials, however, revealed potential strengths in the corporate portfolio. He recommended the stock in his Value Line analysis and borrowed $5,000 to purchase shares for himself. Six months later, with the price of Associated Transport stock at $9, Shad sold his shares and pocketed a profit of $13,000.[14]

The windfall affirmed the acuity of Shad's research, but it also straddled the boundary between the ethical and inappropriate use of his influence as a market analyst for the public. Even as chairman of the Securities and Exchange Commission in the 1980s, however, Shad told the story as an example of the money waiting to be made by playing the stock market. Throughout the 1950s, Shad continued to bet on the properties he evaluated as a securities analyst for Value Line and later Shearson, Hammill & Company, compounding his personal investment portfolio by 30 percent a year. The dramatic accumulation of wealth, which Shad himself described as "extraordinary," added to his mystique among his Wall Street peers.[15]

John Shad was on his way.

In June 1949, graduates of the Harvard Business School had gone to work in a sluggish economy and many worried that hard times might again return to the United States. By the mid-1950s, these fears were long forgotten. "Everybody thought the economy wasn't going to be that good," recalled Jim Burke. "But of course, we got lucky. The economy went through the roof." A boom was under way in the 1950s, with economic growth rates averaging over 3 percent a year. New skyscrapers soared in the cities, and vast tracts of homes were being built in suburban areas that had been opened by freshly constructed highways. Armies of engineers and construction workers built factories, oil refineries, chemical plants, and electrical power stations and dams.

Perhaps nowhere was the bustle and haste of this quintessential American boom more frenetic than in Chicago, the city where Lester Crown moved after business school to join his family's flourishing company.

Crown was comfortable working for his father, Henry, and alongside his elder brother Robert and other family members. Crown considered his father to be an absolute genius and viewed him with awe. He admired the way his father had built a business empire from nothing, the way he took risks to get bigger, and the humility the elder Crown always showed. Coming into the family company, Material Service Corporation, Lester saw himself walking in the footsteps of greatness. He felt privileged to work at Marblehead Lime Company, one of the subsidiaries of MSC. Business thrived amid the Chicago construction boom of the 1950s.

Henry Crown taught Lester and his brothers to do business the Chicago way. The family firm managed to keep a reasonably clean record, attracting the attention of the Internal Revenue Service, but otherwise steering clear of controversy and legal trouble. Material Service, however, made its fortune in the most convoluted and corrupt construction market in the country, where city officials routinely sold building permits and the mafia demanded its cut of the juiciest contracts. "Henry played by the rules, such as the rules were," a company official noted, years later.[16] The firm's success is the best evidence of its complicity. Launched on a $50 investment in 1915, Material Service made its first $1 million in 1924, earned $10 million in 1940, and brought in $20 million in 1950.[17] By 1958, the firm's net worth exceeded $72 million. "We were getting to be a bank," Henry Crown said.[18] Two years later, Crown bought into an aerospace company called General Dynamics Corporation, trading the family business for $125 million in convertible stock.[19]

"We believed, we built," Henry Crown would say later, of the dynamic 1950s:

> Whatever was going on, we were going to bet on it in a big way—bigger than the Harvard Business School would have called prudent, I expect. Aerospace was booming, and GD looked golden at the time. Construction—forget it; you barely had time to overhaul the trucks before they had to be out on another job. People were starting to fly like crazy and the hotel business was phenomenal. Freight was moving, and even the railroads were hanging in. The banks and insurance companies couldn't make a bad investment. Everything was working and everything was fitting together. It was a dream time, believe me.[20]

At the close of the 1950s, Lester Crown finally realized his destiny and became president of the Material Service Corporation. He ended the decade with five children as well. Two more would eventually follow. At 35, Crown's life was intensely full, and he easily ranked among the stars of his Harvard class—as could well be expected from the position he glided into after school.

Decades later, a mantra of those who graduated from the Harvard Business School in 1949 was that they were the "luckiest guys alive." Entering the business world at the beginning of the 1950s was the single greatest stroke of good fortune for the 49ers—except, that is, surviving World War II. In a survey taken in 1999, a majority of class members would point to their timing in entering the business world as having more influence over the course of their careers than any other factor or experience. In the late spring of 1949, this great fortune was not manifestly obvious to many graduates as they headed off to jobs that often paid less than $75 a week. As the engine of the postwar American economy revved up during the 1950s, the ideal historical positioning of the class became ever more obvious. The fast ascent of many class members in the business world was testament to the remarkable opportunities of the day. "It was hard to fail in that period," Burke said.

It was not just upward movement that was defining the 49ers. It was also their fierce determination to shape the business environment of the times rather than operate quietly within the status quo. This determination reflected both a fresh vision of the American economy and the energy needed to redirect major organizations. Men like Jim Burke and Marvin Traub not only understood the changing nature of the domestic consumer market and the vast new opportunities this market offered, they had the patience to educate their bosses and colleagues about these changes. Likewise, 49ers on Wall Street and in the technology world showed their capacity to both think ahead of the curve and position their organizations to profit from new trends. Even second-generation business leaders like Roger Sonnabend and Lester Crown—wealthy before they ever got to Harvard—brought tremendous drive to the work of building America's new postwar economy.

That work was not always easy. After years of depression and war, the U.S. economy of the 1950s struggled just to meet the demands of ordinary Americans. By the end of the decade, up to a quarter of all

Americans still lived in poverty, with the elderly and minorities impoverished at far higher rates. Many American households lacked such basic amenities as indoor plumbing. Public schools were woefully underfunded. Some of the blame for these shortcomings lay with the caretaker policies of the Eisenhower administration, which did little to address social and economic inequities during the 1950s. But it is also true that the American economy was not yet producing the level of wealth that Americans would later come to take for granted.

The 1960s would change that. And at the center of major new trends pushing forward wealth creation in the decade's boom economy would be 49ers.

LAND OF
OPPORTUNITY

Bill Ruane struck it rich on Wall Street. Marvin Traub became a star in the retailing world. Jim Burke soared at Johnson & Johnson, becoming a millionaire along the way. Joe Amaturo made a huge fortune buying and running radio and TV stations. Peter McColough not only became a multimillionaire from his Xerox stock options, he also became a legend in the business world.

The 1960s was a golden age for American business, and opportunity was everywhere for the 49ers. During the last year of Dwight D. Eisenhower's tenure, 1960, America's gross domestic product stood at $500 billion. Within 10 years, U.S. annual GDP had doubled to $1 trillion[1] (nearly $6 trillion today, adjusted for inflation). During the course of the decade, over $5 trillion in new wealth would be generated by the boom of the 1960s. Beyond a minor recession in 1961 and creeping inflation in 1968 and 1969, the decade was largely free of economic bad news.

Overseas, economic giants like Germany and Japan awoke in the 1960s but were not yet in a position to challenge the global hegemony of American business. The phrase "Japanese imports" was still synonymous with cheaply made goods. Hong Kong, South Korea, and Taiwan were only beginning to industrialize. At home, the environmental and consumerist movements were still in their infancy. The American public still trusted major corporations during the 1960s—just as they still trusted government and the news media. The age of American innocence endured, even as the seeds were planted for its demise.

To be in business in the America of the 1960s was to live in a land of opportunity. New sectors of the economy—television, early computers, fast food, jet travel—were emerging, and old sectors were still thriving. Traditional manufacturing remained robust, and vast new wealth was being generated through service sector businesses that barely existed a few decades earlier. A bull market on Wall Street—the Dow would hit 1,000 for the first time in 1966—made it possible for businesses to raise cash as never before.

The Harvard Business School 49ers were uniquely positioned to reap the bounties of this amazing decade. In 1965, the average class graduate was 40 years old and hitting the prime of his career. Many 49ers thrived during the 1960s in traditional sectors of the economy. Some 40 percent of class graduates went into manufacturing. Several 49ers became rising stars in the auto industry, helping to bring new production techniques to the huge car plants. Others went into steel and mining and oil refining— industries that boomed along with the rest of the economy. Of course, not every 49er soared during the 1960s. There were numerous class members who just got by, finding themselves trapped in the anonymous ranks of middle management at drab and conformist corporations.

Nor did all class members spend the 1960s in the business world. Augustus Minton, one of the handful of military officers who'd been in the class of 1949, spent much of the decade far away from corporate suites in the thick of the war in Vietnam. After graduating from Harvard, Minton climbed through the ranks in the U.S. Air Force. He became chief of staff for the Pacific wing of the U.S. Air Force in the 1960s, a position from which he helped orchestrate an air war in Vietnam that included massive bombing campaigns along the Ho Chi Minh trail and attacks on key targets in North Vietnam. Minton witnessed firsthand the limits of America's massive, high-tech arsenal against communist forces that needed few supplies to sustain their war effort in South Vietnam.

Clarence "Bud" Brown was another 49er who didn't go into the business world. During the 1950s, Brown had developed a career as a newspaperman in Ohio. In 1965, Brown decided to run for Congress to replace his recently deceased father—a longtime Republican member of Congress. He won by a landslide in a special election and went to Washington at a time of mounting political turmoil. Brown would struggle tremendously with his position on the Vietnam war. A reluctant supporter of the war, he often found himself making speeches at cemeteries, as one by one, sons of his district returned from Vietnam in flag-draped coffins.

Many of the Harvard Business School 49ers who did make a true mark in business during the decade did so by helping American business realize the promise of three new powerful drivers of economic growth and wealth creation: an exploding domestic consumer market, advances in high technology, and the new wizardry of financial services. None of these business trends was entirely new in the 1960s. What changed in the 1960s was the scale of wealth generated by them. Increasingly, these elements of the economy drove large sectors of the business world. Key members of the Harvard Business School class of 1949 understood this better than most people. By the end of the 1960s, 49ers like Peter McColough of Xerox, John Shad of E.F. Hutton, and Marvin Traub of Bloomingdale's were already on their way to helping to reshape not just the American economy, but American society as well.

5

Consumer Fever

J im Burke was not the kind of guy to gloat. But during the 1960s, Burke and his classmate Marvin Traub liked to occasionally remind their classmates just how wise they had been to pick career tracks related to consumer products. After years in a sector of the economy often overshadowed by other areas, both men were suddenly in the right place at the right time.

The 1960s witnessed the greatest consumer spending spree the United States had ever seen. The spree was driven by the fact that Americans had more cash to spend than ever, but the baby boom generation—with its 70 million young people—and rising leisure time were other key factors driving the spree. Nearly half the U.S. population was under the age of 18 in 1960. More children meant the need for larger houses with more furnishings, more clothing and shoes, and more personal care products like shampoo, toothpaste, and toilet paper. Leisure time increased due to the unprecedented power of unions and to rising wages. Saturday workdays, once common for millions of workers, became rarer, and Americans had more time to develop hobbies, to shop, and to take travel excursions—in short, more time to spend money.

And there was no shortage of things to spend on. To step into one of the glittering big department stores of the early 1960s was to discover a world of wonders unavailable to previous generations. Technological advances during the 1950s, both large and small, had introduced a range of new consumer items, from portable televisions to coffeemakers to electric razors to dishwashers to new kinds of stereos and cameras. The 1960s saw these items become more affordable to everyday Americans, who were more focused on nesting than ever before. In 1960, 61 percent of Americans owned their homes, many in suburbs that expanded even faster in the 1960s than in the 1950s. Meanwhile, wide-body passenger jets opened up many new travel destinations, and advances in pharmaceutical drugs (Valium was introduced in 1963) gave Americans a parade of new options for self-medication.

For class members like Marvin Traub and Jim Burke, consumer developments in the 1960s would launch superstar careers. Others, like Mel Taft, who joined Milton Bradley straight out of school, labored in relative obscurity. Taft entered the toy company near the beginning of the baby boom and would remain there for 35 years, helping Milton Bradley develop increasingly sophisticated—and expensive—toys and games. Once a tiny market, the toy business was exactly the kind of area that saw phenomenal growth during the 1960s. Parents had more children than ever and more money to spend on toys. America's children, exposed to advertising on television and the new acquisitions of their playmates, demanded toys as never before. They wanted G.I. Joes and Barbie dolls, slot cars and skateboards. Taft would eventually run Milton Bradley's research and development department, and he loved the "excitement and the challenges" of trying to keep one step ahead of millions of pint-sized consumers.[1]

While class members like Taft were in the business of meeting consumer demands, others were in the business of driving them. In New York, at Ziff-Davis Publishing, Stanley Greenfield found himself involved in one of the most innovative new approaches to romancing American consumers: specialized magazines that focused on hobbies and consumers products. These magazines armed Americans with information on how to outdo the Joneses. As Greenfield would say later, "Once you made the cut in your middle or upper middle class social group, the question at cocktail parties was no longer, 'What is your job?' but rather how you spend your leisure time and discretionary dollars—your ability as a golfer, boatman, private pilot, your sports car, your camera, your high-fi equipment, your tennis, spring skiing." Specialized magazines helped competitive consumers answer these questions with greater authority and spend more money with confidence. In 1954, when Greenfield was hired as the first executive at Ziff-Davis, the fledging media company was worth $5 million. In the coming years, specialized magazines helped turn Ziff-Davis into a $1.2 billion company. Greenfield had an endless stream of ideas for specialized magazines, helping to develop such publications as *Popular Photography, Flying, Car & Driver, Popular Boating,* and *Stereo Review.*

In the 1960s, as in decades past, American consumers spent most of their money in three areas: (1) food, beverages, and tobacco; (2) housing and home needs; and (3) transportation. Yet even as these pillars of the domestic consumer market held steady through the 1960s, new areas of personal spending increased rapidly. Leading 49ers would respond to changes in the domestic consumer market with some of the most dazzling business moves of the 1960s. In the process, they would make a major mark on American culture.

Jim Burke liked a good argument. When he was young, Burke had been encouraged to voice his opinions at the family dinner table and not be afraid to tussle over differences. As a manager, rising fast through the ranks of Johnson & Johnson, he took the view that conflict was good. In dissecting the wants and needs of the American consumer, as well as the pros and cons of various products, obvious facts were often elusive and a dialectical process was essential for solid decisions. "By putting a lot of contention into our system we get better results," Burke would say. "Certainly it makes us more honest with each other. I don't think it bruises people to argue and to debate."[2] Burke believed that the best way to test an idea was to put it up against opposition—to probe and prod it and to put its proponent on the hot seat.

Burke had the perfect personality to put this philosophy into action. He had an insatiable curiosity and loved to ask questions and see where a line of logic led. With a ready smile and a crooked front tooth, he could be blunt and direct without being threatening. His manner to subordinates was challenging, but never hostile—like a boxing coach who kicks the butts of his students while making them feel loved and protected. As Burke would explain it, he created a "contentious environment, but it is not an ulcer-producing one. Most of us have a hell of a good time, and most people would probably say that they can tell me whatever they want to tell me, and they often do."[3]

Burke's restless energy and probing mind ensured that he rose rapidly in the Johnson & Johnson organization of the 1960s. At the dawn of the 1960s, Johnson & Johnson was an aggressive company willing to take risks. One area of major growth was in pain relievers, and Johnson & Johnson sought to compete with a new product called Tylenol. Another new frontier was oral contraception—"the pill." In 1960, amid much fanfare, the federal government authorized the sale of oral contraceptives, a move that boosted the profile and profits of J&J's contraception division, the Ortho Corporation. Burke, a devout Catholic, was never thrilled by this line of J&J's work, but business was business. By 1970, 80 percent of American women would be using some kind of contraception.

As Jim Burke shot upward through the management ranks of Johnson & Johnson during the 1960s, he put his own stamp on the company. Burke was a fierce believer in the power of marketing, and it was his advocacy of new marketing techniques in the early 1960s that established his reputation as the corporation's rising star. As the director of advertising and marketing from 1958 to 1962, Burke employed new media and targeted new audiences to increase the visibility of J&J products. Burke was fascinated by the marketing potential of television, still a quickly evolving venue for advertising. At the beginning of the 1960s, the percentage of Americans owning televisions was increasing rapidly and would do so through the decade until nearly 95 percent of American households had a television in 1970.[4] Americans were glued to their sets as never before in the 1960s, transfixed by hit shows like *I Dream of Jeannie, Bewitched, Beverly Hillbillies,* and *The Twilight Zone.*

The demographic range of viewers, along with the amount of programming and quantity of advertising also increased rapidly. Young children were watching more television, pulled in by cartoons like *The Jetsons* and *The Flintstones* and *Mr. Magoo.* Daytime viewing skyrocketed, as new soap operas premiered and captured a huge female audience. It was a marketing gold mine, and the 1960s witnessed the transformation of advertising media for J&J's products. Newspaper ads for drugs and toiletries were deeply slashed, while television ads increased dramatically.

Demonstrating brave outspokenness within J&J's councils of power, Burke insisted that television was an appropriate venue for advertising health care products, even those that had long been considered too controversial for public airing. Burke used television to market Carefree and Stayfree feminine products, shaking off the exaggerated delicacy that had relegated the line to the pages of women's magazines.[5] Burke's willingness to take risks in marketing broadened the appeal of J&J products and helped to make Johnson & Johnson one of the most familiar brand names in the United States by 1970.

Johnson & Johnson's products not only became better known during the 1960s, there were also more of them. One of the big changes at J&J during the decade would be the huge increase in the range of products that the company made. Diversification resulted from two innovations championed by Burke: research and development and the acquisition of promising companies.

Acquiring new companies was the easiest way to add new products to J&J's portfolio, and Burke was a strong believer in J&J's decentralized approach to business. Robert Wood Johnson, the "General," insisted that Johnson & Johnson's decentralized corporate structure was the company's best asset in promoting innovation and product diversification. The corporate offices in New Brunswick where Burke made his start constituted a relatively small part of the health care conglomerate. Johnson & Johnson went into the 1960s with its operations divided among wholly owned subsidiaries, each with its own facilities and corporate infrastructure. Ethicon made surgical sutures; Surikos made surgical packs and gowns; Modess (later the Personal Products Company) sold J&J's line of feminine hygiene products, including Carefree and Stayfree sanitary napkins. The largest division, Johnson Home Products, marketed the famous baby powder and baby oil as well as the hallowed Band-Aid and an array of other consumer products. Ortho Pharmaceutical Corporation produced contraceptives. Over the course of the 1950s and early 1960s, Johnson & Johnson purchased other pharmaceutical companies, including the Swiss firm Cilag-Chemie, the Belgium-based Janssen Pharmaceuticals, and the successful U.S. firm McNeil Laboratories.

By the early 1970s, there would be 88 companies in the J&J fold. All were largely autonomous, except in regard to their finances. Each had its own president and board of directors, and each did its own research— although ideas were shared freely among the different subsidiaries. The decentralized business model allowed companies within Johnson &

Johnson to remain focused on a specialized series of products, concentrating their resources and their talents. In an era notable for centralized organizations—in both the public and private sector—the Johnson & Johnson corporate model raised eyebrows. In a 1972 *Forbes* article, Burke defended the model against the conventional wisdom of the time that such fragmentation sacrificed economies of scale. "We have periodically studied the economics of consolidation," Burke told *Forbes*. But these thoughts had been rejected "because we believe that if the manager of a business can control all aspects of his business, it will run a lot better. And we believe that a lot of the efficiencies you are supposed to get from economies of scale are not real at all. They are elusive."[6] Sixteen years later, Burke would be making the same arguments. "Decentralization equals creativity," he told a reporter in 1988 when he stepped down as chairman of Johnson & Johnson. "And creativity equals real productivity."[7]

Not every Johnson & Johnson product was a success. For every J&J product that was a hit, several failed. This was fine with the top management of J&J, which encouraged an atmosphere of risk taking. And if Jim Burke had been discouraged by J&J's conservative atmosphere in the 1950s, the adventuresome and decentralized J&J of the 1960s was a company he could commit to unequivocally.

Burke's ascendancy at Johnson & Johnson during the 1960s would make him a wealthy man. While the executive salaries of the decade were tiny compared to what they would balloon to in later decades, Burke was nonetheless very well paid. By 1970, at the age of 45, he would be a millionaire, with the promise of more riches—and greater influence—to come.

Most important, as the 1960s ended, Burke fully grasped the enormous power that advertising had to change the buying habits of an American public that, more than ever, belonged to a single national community tied together by television. While a new breed of critical social commentators of the late 1960s pointed out the troubling ways that corporations manipulated the American psyche through advertising, and decried how consumerism was replacing community, Burke wasn't bothered by any of this. He believed that the products of Johnson & Johnson improved people's lives. And he was determined that these products reign in the marketplace as never before.

Like Burke, Marvin Traub began the decade of the 1960s as an entre-preneurial junior exec who fully grasped the consumer revolution sweeping America. By the start of the 1970s, he would be a wealthy man in a position of growing power and influence. Traub understood that American consumers in the 1960s had both greater needs and greater wants. Their greater needs grew out of basic demographic facts. Larger American families during the baby boom meant more houses and larger houses.[8] This, in turn, meant the need for more furniture, curtains, rugs, kitchen items, and decorations. The baby boom also created a huge new market for clothing, as the largest generation in U.S. history matured from childhood to adolescence to young adulthood—buying new clothes every step of the way.

The wants of Americans grew just as fast. People wanted better clothes, better home furnishings—better everything. And it wasn't just higher incomes that drove these desires. Two predominant new social facts shaped the world of Marvin Traub and the business of retailing during the 1960s: Americans were becoming better educated, and they were being exposed to more media and advertising. Through television and travel, they encountered new cultural ideas and tastes. As media and technology accelerated the general tempo of American life, fashion tastes evolved ever more rapidly. Consumers who wanted to keep up with cosmopolitan trends had to shop more and spend more. Credit cards, newly introduced in the 1950s, made this easier than ever. Traub had endless ideas during the 1960s about how to tap into—and shape—the psyche of the American consumer.

Traub's rise through the management ranks coincided with Bloomingdale's commitment to the large-scale promotion that aimed to draw customers in pursuit of a specific look and generate interest in the store as a cultural institution. These promotions were Marvin Traub's kind of undertakings: risky, flashy, and new.

In 1960, Traub's home furnishings department played a key role in organizing a big promotion, "Casa Bella," that showcased Italian goods at Bloomingdale's. The promotion came at a time when Americans were getting tired of the staid Eisenhower era and a new hipness was beginning to affect the culture. Casa Bella was a major success, and it helped to establish Bloomingdale's as the home of fabulous themed extravaganzas. Casa Bella was followed in 1961 by "L'Esprit de France." The promotions created a market for exclusive products such as specially packaged French perfumes, as well as more common goods like black berets. A series of shopping bags featuring French tarot cards produced for L'Esprit de France became a status item, giving rise to Bloomingdale's signature self-promotion technique.[9] Annual themes—"Tradition," "Romance," "Symphony in B"—flooded Bloomingdale's with new products throughout the 1960s and later provided the opportunity to showcase more exotic merchandise in the India, Israel, and China promotions of the 1980s. Above all, the promotions answered Traub's early calls for more excitement in Bloomingdale's merchandising and helped to establish the store as something akin to a museum.

Bloomingdale's was not the first store to use elaborate promotions. Neiman Marcus had been doing major promotions in its Dallas store. But Bloomingdale's took the concept to a new level, and Traub felt that it could take credit for the way this changed the department store world. "I would like to think that we were one of the first stores really to use retailing as theatre and harness that excitement as marketing concept," Traub would say later.[10]

With his refined tastes and background, Marvin Traub was the perfect person to bring more pizzazz and culture to Bloomingdale's. The world his parents had created on Manhattan's Upper West Side had been rich with foreign influences and people. Traub was drawn to the chic and the exotic, and he took naturally to the task of broadening the tastes of the American consumer. Promoted to merchandising manager in 1962 at the age of 37, Traub committed the store to the pursuit of excitement. It was an effort grounded in sound marketing strategies. Years later, Traub observed the connection between retail sales and emotion, observing that people don't really need another suit or tie. A good retailer, Traub said, "creates the feeling that you've got to have this, even though you may have enough."[11] Traub and his associates set out to create an image for Bloomingdale's that would sell itself, a festive atmosphere that would loosen the purse strings of affluent customers.

Promotions and model rooms were part of this effort. Bloomingdale's sought to educate consumers about the cosmopolitan lifestyles that the store could help them achieve through shopping. The store as culture became a Bloomingdale's trademark. Traub observed that Bloomingdale's was competing with local institutions such as the Guggenheim and the Metropolitan Museum of Art as much as it was with other department stores.[12] Cooking demonstrations, fashion workshops, and adult education courses in bonsai and macramé fit into the program. A branch store customer once joked that she felt like a graduate of "Bloomingdale U."[13] Presiding over this cultural institution for the upscale shopper was merchandising manager Marvin Traub, whose impresario role would later be compared by the *New York Times* to that of "merchants, curators, and social philosophers."[14] And Traub himself fit the image of fashion guide to the discriminating shopper, making sure that he was always immaculately attired in the latest men's fashions.

Traub's new responsibilities as merchandising manager required that he bring the same level of refinement and spark to Bloomingdale's clothing sales that he had to home furnishings. With help from fashion coordinator Katherine Murphy Grout, Traub set out to transform the appeal of the women's apparel department. He added high-fashion clothing to the store's traditional offerings of matronly, conservative clothes that were increasingly passé in the America of Jackie Kennedy. Grout and Traub tapped into the French ready-to-wear women's fashion market, becoming regular fixtures at the annual *Prêt-a-Porter* show.

Ready-to-wear, unlike the more rarified haute couture featured in fashion shows, was a new concept for U.S. department stores. It was mass-produced designer clothing that appeared seasonally as part of a coordinated collection. The prices were high and the focus was on sportswear rather than on evening clothes and suits. The more casual sportswear styles suited the emerging youth market of the 1960s, coordinating Bloomingdale's merchandising strategy with the demographics of the baby boomers. Just as the model rooms had promoted a unified household style, the display of women's apparel aimed to create a "total fashion look," complete with expensive accessories.[15] Distinct shops, with names like the Mic Mac boutique and Paradox, allowed merchandisers to group products that seemed to reflect a theme and to experiment with unusual or unusually expensive selections. Sales—and the requisite sense of excitement about shopping—increased commensurately. Traub summed up his philosophy this way: "It was my belief that what makes a great store, much like what makes a great restaurant, is the total experience; how you are greeted when you arrive, the decor and the ambience, the selection and the presentation, the service."

The promotion of individual designers dovetailed with Bloomingdale's new fashion image. On his annual pilgrimages to *Prêt-a-Porter,* Traub persuaded designers to give Bloomingdale's buyers a preview of that year's collection. Soon European designers such as Emanuel Ungaro, Missoni, and Sonia Rykiel offered exclusive Bloomingdale's lines. The establishment of designer boutiques, set apart from the store by decor and architectural features, benefited the designers as well as Bloomingdale's, helping to create a new class of celebrity in U.S. culture. Traub himself claims credit for the discovery of soon-to-be famous designers such as Halston, who came to Bloomingdale's as a disgruntled hat designer, and Calvin Klein, a coat designer for whom Traub proposed diversification into womenswear.[16]

Bloomingdale's most famous rags-to-riches story featured Bronx-born Ralph Lauren, a Beau Brummell tie designer who became fixated on the prospect of selling his own line of wide ties at Bloomingdale's. Initially, the store offered Lauren a spot on the condition that he narrow his ties by an inch and include a Bloomingdale's label on them. At the time, Bloomingdale's was still hesitant about promoting designers; Christian Dior's clothes were the only ones in the store with their own label. Lauren refused this offer, but persisted. Eventually, the future fashion giant succeeded in winning a single display cabinet at the 59th Street store, which he showed up on Saturdays to polish himself.[17] In time, Lauren developed a line of men's clothing for Bloomingdale's that carried the label "Polo by Ralph Lauren." Bloomingdale's promoted Lauren's fashions and his own stylish image in advertisements (including a full-page photo of a female model wearing nothing but a Ralph Lauren tie), created a specially designed Ralph Lauren shop, and even paid in advance for Lauren products during the lean early years. The relationship launched the career of the most famous American-born designer of his generation and burnished Bloomingdale's image as a fashion broker.

In turn, Traub's own star continued to rise. By the late 1960s, Traub was the company president, second in command to the CEO, the soft-spoken Lawrence Lachman. In his early 40s, Traub himself met the profile of Bloomingdale's target customer: young, affluent, and a resident of the Upper East Side. Traub's lifestyle did not include a strong countercultural sensibility. He kept his hair neatly trimmed and never wore a beard or mustache. His horn-rimmed glasses made him look square. "I wasn't into the 1960s," Traub would say later. "It wasn't my bag." Traub was deeply opposed to the Vietnam War, and he understood the causes of social rebellion, but he was turned off by the excesses of the times—acid-dropping hippies and Black Panthers and student radicals taking over university buildings.

Bloomingdale's ventures with Ralph Lauren indicated yet another Traub innovation in fashion merchandising—*men's* ready-to-wear. The idea of enhancing men's fashions came naturally to Traub and the Bloomingdale's high command. Prior to the 1960s, men's fashions evolved almost imperceptibly. Business suits and tourist clothes with few variations dominated the market. Ralph Lauren's designer ties signaled a change: Not only were the cuts wide and the fabrics outlandish, the ties carried the eye-popping price tag of $10 to $15 at a time when typical ties sold for as little as $2. The style was infectious, however, remembered Traub, who was an early convert. "Once you had a wide tie . . . all your other ties were dated. And you needed a new shirt, and a new suit to go with it."[18] Traub worked with Lauren to develop a full line of high-priced men's designer clothing, featuring natural fibers and tailored looks that had long been out of fashion. When Lauren won a Coty award, fashion's equivalent of an Oscar, in 1969, the store's investment in his talent was vindicated and the future of men's fashions at Bloomingdale's solidified. The Bloomingdale's look was not just for women any more.

In a single decade, Marvin Traub had completely transformed one of the most important department stores in America. And yet, even as he was increasingly celebrated as a star of the retailing world at the end of the 1960s, Traub's greatest period of influence still lay before him.

Jack Davis and Roger Sonnabend were two other class members who strode into the 1960s with grand ambitions for capturing the new disposable income of Americans. Davis, as president of Mary Carter Paint, would be part of a bold bid to expand the company into resorts and gambling. Sonnabend sought to turn his family's hotel business into a national empire. Both would be in for a wild ride during the 1960s.

In 1958, when he joined Mary Carter Paint Company, Jack Davis thought he was signing up for a relatively predictable job. Things didn't turn out that way in the 1960s. The great ambition of Davis's boss, James Crosby, the CEO of Mary Carter Paint, was to make a fortune. He was interested in the paint company as a stepping-stone to that end, not as the end itself.

The chance to turn Mary Carter Paint into a springboard to great riches came when Crosby and Davis learned that Paradise Island, a fledgling resort island in the Bahamas near Nassau, was available for sale. The island was about three miles long and a half mile wide. Although it was reachable only by boat, the island (previously known as Hog Island) did have some development—a chic hotel called the Ocean Club with 50 rooms, along with a golf course and a restaurant. The remainder of Paradise Island was relatively unspoiled, with beautiful white sand beaches and palm trees that swayed in the sea breeze.

Paradise Island was for sale thanks to the bad business decisions of Huntington Hartford, a playboy heir to the A&P fortune who had spent millions developing the Ocean Club and the island's other amenities. Hartford was a dilettante businessman of the first order who hadn't realized that a hotel with only 50 rooms could not possibly bring in enough revenue to sustain his lavish new resort. Worse, Hartford liked to keep himself surrounded by a bevy of young women, some still in their teens, and many of the rooms of the Ocean Club were regularly filled by non-paying members of his entourage. With his original inherited fortune of $400 million fast draining away—not just on Paradise Island, but on other bad investments that would eventually leave him nearly penniless—Hartford was ready to sell the resort.

Crosby and Davis jumped at the chance to purchase Bahamas Developers, Ltd., which included the resort and about 80 percent of the island. The investment looked to be a wise one. Rising disposable income and the advent of jet travel combined in the early 1960s to boost the popularity of sunny resort destinations like Miami, Las Vegas, and spots in the Caribbean. The Bahamas became the focus of much attention in the leisure and gaming industries in the early 1960s, as hoteliers and casino operators desperately sought to develop a substitute for the paradise lost in Cuba after Fidel Castro's revolution. The Bahamas enjoyed the same advantages of ocean, climate, and proximity to the United States as Cuba. Nassau was no glittering metropolis, like Havana, but the coziness of the archipelago's colonial relationship with Great Britain and its English-speaking population was reassuring during an era of revolutionary ferment in Latin America.

Crosby and Davis were soon hatching big plans to turn Paradise Island into something much bigger than the resort property they had bought. A centerpiece of their investment scheme was a new casino. This idea came about out of necessity. As Davis said later, "The reason we wanted to go into the business was because without that, the income from the casino, the resort was not financially viable. It couldn't support itself. The casino provides the ability to support the rest of the resort. I mean we had to build sewer plants. We had to build roads. We had to build all kinds of things." Davis and other company execs imagined their new resort and casino being a magnet for the same kinds of American high rollers who had once flocked to Havana.

To help manage the casino, Mary Carter Paint turned to U.S.-born entrepreneur Wallace Groves, a latter-day pirate who wore cufflinks made from shipwrecked Spanish dubloons and who presided over a private city, Freeport, on Grand Bahama island.[19] Groves's Bahamas Amusements, Ltd., ran the first casino opened in the Bahamas, the Lucayan Beach Casino. The Bahamian government strongly recommended Groves to Crosby and Davis as the best person to manage their new casino under a lease arrangement. What the Bahamian government didn't mention was that Groves also coordinated his operations with Meyer Lansky, the notorious head of the Lansky organized crime syndicate.[20]

The new venture opened for business in 1966, the second casino in the Bahamas. All of this was new terrain for Jack Davis. Gambling and glittering resorts were not the typical milieu for a button-down businessman born in staid Westchester County and schooled at Williams and Harvard. "Nobody talked about the casino business at Harvard," Davis would say later. In the mid-1960s, there were not yet any publicly held companies in the casino business. "It was all private, and all mob."

Jack Davis took well to his new world—and the troubles that came with it. The partnership with Groves was the biggest source of trouble. When Crosby and Davis learned of Groves's organized crime connection, they "freaked," Davis recalled. They quickly bought out their lease with Groves and suddenly found themselves without a guide in the dangerous and unfamiliar world of casino gambling. For advice on how to proceed, Davis and Crosby visited the Justice Department in Washington. U.S.

attorney Robert Peloquin, who headed the Organized Crime Division, explained that every casino he knew of was controlled by the mob, and therefore Mary Carter Paint would have a difficult time finding anyone it could trust to run its gambling operation on Paradise Island. Because no experienced and aboveboard players were available, Peloquin recommended that Mary Carter Paint should manage its own casino operations.[21] Convinced that they had no alternative, Jack Davis and other key officers of Mary Carter Paint transformed themselves into casino operators.

The first order of business was to establish a security force that could keep the American wise guys at bay. Crosby and Davis turned to Peloquin, whose expertise in organized crime and connections in government agencies had impressed them during their Washington meeting. For a salary of $60,000, Peloquin left government and agreed to assemble a private police force that drew its members from the ranks of the FBI, CIA, the National Security Agency, Scotland Yard, Interpol, and the Canadian Mounted Police.[22] By 1970, Peloquin's organization, which called itself Intertel, or International Intelligence, Inc., was nearly as feared as the mobsters it was designed to thwart. While Intertel could not offer complete independence from the mafia, which continued to demand a cut of the proceeds from group tours to the Bahamas and other kickbacks, the agency gave Mary Carter Paint sufficient muscle to manage its own casinos.[23] Over time, Intertel emerged as an independent security agency with a top-secret list of more than 200 clients, generating additional profits for the parent company.

Jack Davis himself stepped into the role of casino boss with astonishing sangfroid. In addition to managing Peloquin's security force, he proved himself willing to dirty his hands in a manner that was not typical for a Harvard Business School graduate. The success of Paradise Island and other gambling operations in the Bahamas depended on the goodwill and participation of local officials, who dispensed operations licenses, building permits, and other services for the casinos and hotels. Davis personally supervised the greasing of wheels. He arranged all-expenses-paid junkets to Las Vegas and Acapulco and provided wristwatches and prostitutes for Bahamian customs officers and other bureaucrats.[24] He established an unrecorded slush fund for making under-the-table payments in cash.[25] Other bribes came in the form of "political contributions" to the party of Lynden Pindling, who served as

prime minister during the early years at Paradise Island. Pindling himself once received a thank-you gift of a $40,000 Rolls-Royce from
Mary Carter Paint and other grateful casino operators. Called to
account for the company's activities in later years, James Crosby
defended the bribes, saying the money helped to "preserve the two-
party system" in the Bahamas.[26]

Davis's shady maneuvers ensured that a second resort owned by
Mary Carter Paint, the Paradise Island Resort, opened on time and in
style. In 1967, the casino and hotel complex opened to great fanfare
with a gala attended by movie stars and jet-set celebrities. Davis escorted
the Hollywood actress Janet Leigh, while James Crosby entertained the
opening's guest of honor, the once and future presidential candidate,
Richard M. Nixon. A photograph from the event shows Crosby in
swim trunks, touring the grounds with Nixon and his friend Charles
"Bebe" Rebozo, both of whom were stiffly attired in suits and ties.[27]
The trio apparently found common ground. Weeks after the opening,
Crosby donated $100,000 (in 33 checks for $3,000 each, plus one
$1,000 payment) to Nixon's 1968 campaign.[28] The Nixon connection
served to underscore that the once-obscure corporation was now playing with the high rollers. In 1968, the company shed its association with
the paint company and christened itself Resorts International, a name
that reflected its growing holdings in the global entertainment market.
In addition to its properties in the Bahamas, which included the Paradise
Island Resort and Villas, the Brittania Hotel (completed in 1969), several restaurants and nightclubs, and undeveloped property, Resorts
owned hotels in the Netherlands, two amusement parks in the United
States, and a substantial stake in Pan American airlines.

Davis loved life on Paradise Island. Initially, he and his family lived
in the Ocean Club, but later they found a house on the island, not far
from the beach. Davis went to the office every morning in casual
clothes, and often would go swimming with his kids in the afternoon.
At night, he spent time in the resort's restaurants and casinos, rubbing
shoulders with whatever high rollers or celebrities were in town.

By 1970, Jack Davis may not have been among the wealthiest members of the Harvard Business School class of 1949, but he was certainly
among its most swashbuckling and controversial. A 49er as casino boss?
Who would have imagined?

Roger Sonnabend would also depart from a path typical for his class-mates during the 1960s. When their father, Sonny, died in 1964, the Sonnabend brothers quickly reached an understanding that preserved family control of the sprawling hotel business. Roger took over as chief executive officer and chairman of the board of directors. Paul served as the company president, and Stephen took a less active role. Following their father's prescription for continued growth, the Sonnabend brothers initiated a buying spree that doubled the number of hotels in the chain within six years. In tribute, they changed the name of the company to Sonesta Hotels International, a combination of the names of both of their parents.

The hotel expansion coincided with a downturn for the industry as a whole. Hotel occupancy rates in the United States dropped from 61 percent in 1964 to 55 percent in 1970, even as the number of operating hotels constricted by more than 6 percent.[29] Overextended and bur-dened with debt in a soft market, Sonesta teetered on the edge of bank-ruptcy by the end of the 1960s.[30]

The hotel chain's difficulties were only part of the upheaval that con-fronted Roger Sonnabend in the late 1960s. The tremendous political and cultural strife that divided the nation during those years profoundly affected him. In 1968, while the country was dealing with the horrors of the Tet offensive in Vietnam, the assassinations of Martin Luther King Jr. and Robert Kennedy, and the upheaval at the Democratic National Convention, Sonesta hotels had their worst year ever. Earnings dropped to $128,000 from $1,836,000 the previous year. Sonesta's losses were compounded by extensive damage to the chain's Washington, D.C., property, the Mayflower Hotel, which was the target of violence during a race riot unleashed by the King assassination.[31] The violence at home and in Southeast Asia moved Roger Sonnabend to reevaluate his life and his place in broader society. "I looked at myself," he told a reporter, "and saw that going along, trying not to rock the boat, would no longer do."[32]

In looking at himself, Sonnabend saw a quintessential member of the American establishment. He had been groomed for success by

Philips Exeter Academy, MIT, and the Harvard Business School. He took the safe path in life, following his father's footsteps in the hotel business. Despite being Jewish, he was a welcome guest at such restricted clubs as Boston's Algonquin. He was a trustee of Radcliffe College and president of the U.S. Squash Racquets Association. He was active in innocuous community groups such as the National Conference of Christians and Jews. He and his family lived in Brookline, a fashionable suburb safely insulated from urban woes. Sonnabend would say later about his early years, "I was a conservative rock-ribbed Republican and a bright, young Jew who wanted to be loved by everyone."

Sonnabend had not been entirely oblivious to social justice issues before 1968. Sonnabend, his father, and others in the family were involved with the American Jewish Committee, which quietly fought discrimination against Jews in Boston and elsewhere. In the early 1960s, the family had run into problems because of its fair treatment of blacks at its hotels. The brothers had opened a hotel in New Orleans in 1960, its restaurant accessible to both blacks and whites—only to find themselves in violation of Louisiana's segregation laws. Louisiana's authorities threatened to prosecute, but decided not to pursue the case. However, the Sonnabends were thrown out of a major hotel association for their defiant behavior. Up north, Roger Sonnabend and his brothers were also breaking new racial ground at the Plaza Hotel in New York, which they had owned for a number of years. They had black employees at the Plaza greet guests and serve in other key roles. This was all very unorthodox for an upscale hotel in the 1960s. Sonnabend recalls that "there was a concern even on the part of my own people that our customers would desert us, they would not want to go to a hotel if they got into an elevator with a black elevator operator." Sonnabend insisted on pushing forward with integrating the hotel staffs. "It was necessary for us, as we began to introduce blacks, to have what I called these 'sensitivity sessions,' for all our executives. And we lost several executives who quit, rather than to have to work with blacks." The struggles at Sonesta reflected the times—an era shaped by Martin Luther King Jr., Malcolm X, the flames of Watts, and Harper Lee's Pulitzer Prize–winning book, *To Kill a Mockingbird*.

By 1968, Sonnabend's early rumbling of a social conscience had turned into a major personal revolution. In that year—the year that King and Bobby Kennedy were assassinated, the year the Tet offensive underscored the futility of the Vietnam War, the year that antiwar demonstrators were beaten by police in Chicago—Roger Sonnabend decided he didn't like what he saw in himself. Complacency at a time of social upheaval was not acceptable. His decision to start rocking the boat on behalf of a more just society would have a tremendous impact on his administration of the Sonesta hotels. His leadership style and personal demeanor changed dramatically. Where he once wore suits and button-down shirts, Sonnabend began to favor a neat beard and modish cloth-ing. Instead of meeting business associates for lunch at exclusive clubs, he began writing confrontational letters urging businesspeople to with-hold patronage from institutions that did not serve blacks, women, or Jews. Sonnabend targeted his old associates at the Algonquin Club in Boston, persuading several business organizations to move their meet-ings elsewhere. And he publicized what he called the "iridescent irony" of being invited to discuss race relations at New York City's Urban League Club, which did not accept blacks or Jews as members.[33] After a lifetime of paying lip service, "trying to live the Wasp life all my years," Sonnabend found it liberating to shake off "the conforming parts of my life that were not really me."[34] Though the changes were personal, Sonnabend's leadership role in the family business gave him an arena in which he could put his convictions into action.

Sonnabend's most ambitious effort on behalf of social justice directly engaged the name and resources of Sonesta International. In 1968, he signed on as a regional chairman of the National Alliance of Businessmen, a federal commission that coordinated its efforts with the War on Poverty's Office of Economic Opportunity. The NAB targeted what Sonnabend called "the paradox of poverty-in-the-midst-of-plenty," the existence of more than 100 million Americans living in poverty during prosperous times.[35] The plan was to provide training and jobs for thousands of hard-core unemployed, the most truly disadvan-taged of the poor population. In a speech to the National Association of Business Economists (future Federal Reserve Chairman Alan Greenspan chaired the session), Sonnabend announced his hotel chain's plan to hire 250 unemployed persons and to provide such basic job skills as remedial education, housing, transportation, legal services, and health care when necessary. He also articulated ambitious goals for improving race rela-tions in other ways, including helping to finance and run a black-owned hotel in Harlem and striving to place minorities in 10 to 15 percent of the corporation's executive positions. Sonnabend urged other business leaders to adopt a similar set of goals. He insisted that good race relations and the War on Poverty were good for business because they strengthened the workforce and increased the purchasing power of the 25 million members of the black community. "Social responsibility—and expanding profitability—are not intrinsically at odds with one another," Sonnabend insisted. "Quite the contrary," he said, "they are two faces of the same coin."[36]

Roger Sonnabend's keen sense of social responsibility showed the ways in which a new generation of corporate leaders sought to promote the quintessential American values of fairness and community through the power of the private sector. While such CEOs were still very much in the minority in the 1960s, the idea of corporate social responsibility would become a major feature of the corporate world in later decades. Jim Burke, Peter McColough, and many other 49ers besides Sonnabend came to see themselves as early leaders in this enlightened movement.

Fellow 49ers viewed Sonnabend's personal transformation during the 1960s with bemusement. "He became kind of a hippie," Marvin Traub said many years later. For other class members, the social upheavals of the 1960s appeared to produce few waves. Even the sexual revolution seemed to have little impact. Fifty years after their graduation, a poll of the class would find that their marriages had remained remarkably intact, with 49ers succeeding in their marriages at higher rates than the rest of the population.

Ultimately, for most 49ers, the decade of the 1960s was anything but a time of social rebellion. It was a time to push bold new business initiatives that confirmed the Harvard Business School's reputation for doing things differently and better. It was a time to move from junior executive to top executive. It was a time to make a name for themselves and, hopefully, a pile of money at the same time. The booming consumer economy of the decade helped class members like Burke and Traub fulfill their wildest dreams. Meanwhile, the dreams of other 49ers were coming true elsewhere in the economy, as new technology and a fast-changing Wall Street opened uncharted business frontiers.

6

Wizards of a New Way

On July 20, 1969, *Apollo 11* set down on the moon as millions of Americans watched on television. The landing was the culmination of a decade-long technological and management enterprise costing tens of billions of dollars and involving thousands of people. Three members of the Harvard Business School class of 1949 followed *Apollo 11*'s triumphant mission with special pride. George Berman's technology company, Unitrode, had manufactured some 3,000 parts used aboard *Apollo 11*. James Chalmers worked on the Apollo program at TRW, a leading aerospace contractor. Eugene Wilkerson helped manage space programs for the Hughes Aircraft Company, another of NASA's leading contractors.

While the American quest to put a man on the moon during the 1960s was largely driven by Cold War rivalry, it also symbolized the technological revolution of the times—a revolution that played an ever growing role in America's economic dynamism during the postwar period. The United States, of course, had always been a country of inventors and pragmatic problem solvers. It was the country of Ben Franklin and Thomas Edison, the country of the steam engine, the Wright brothers, and the Model T. Technological breakthroughs had frequently been instrumental in generating wealth in the United States during the nineteenth century and the first half of the twentieth century. New oil refining and steel production techniques had helped fuel the fortunes of robber barons. The internal-combustion engine helped create vast riches through a booming new auto industry. And across the United States, legions of clever inventors had struck it rich with new gadgets for the factory, office, or common household.

But even by American standards, the 1960s was a time of special innovation—in some ways rivaling the technology revolution of the 1990s. The exigencies of World War II had led to major breakthroughs in science and technology that laid the foundations for more sweeping advances in the 1960s. Numerous fields of innovation unfolded simultaneously during the decade: aeronautics, computer science, composite materials, lasers, nuclear physics, and chemical engineering. New innovations and discoveries in turn led to new products that could be sold or leased, producing wealth for their creators and many others involved in their manufacture and sale. Just as important, technological advancement generated wealth by boosting productivity and allowing processes in the factory or modern office to be done more quickly and efficiently.

The Harvard Business School was not a natural breeding ground for technological innovators. It was a school that trained managers and administrators, not the hands-on types fascinated by science and technology (whose turf was just up the Charles River at MIT). And yet, in the modern industrial era, there was an inextricable link between the drive toward technological innovation and the quest for productivity, efficiency, and new markets. Often, a company couldn't boost its earnings without getting serious about harnessing new technologies. Key 49ers understood this reality better than many of their contemporaries and saw technology as a driver of profits. Other 49ers were drawn to technological innovation as the centerpiece of new business ventures. Still others became enmeshed in the world of high technology through their involvement with U.S. government programs aimed at winning the arms race with the Russians or putting a man on the moon.

During the 1960s, Peter McColough of Xerox would come to exemplify the nexus between technological innovation and corporate megaprofits. Less well known were the success stories of other 49ers who played supporting roles in making the 1960s one of the most technologically dynamic decades in American history. Langdon Hedrick worked as an engineer for different companies at the forefront of the revolution in electronics product design. During the 1960s, he served as the chief engineer for Tektronics. Richard Sykes, another engineer, became involved with early minicomputers and teamed up with his younger brother, John, to start a company that specialized in data storage. They developed a new company, Sykes Datatronics, to manufacture a cassette tape for storing digital data and raised capital for it through a public stock offering. Warren Hayes was a leader in the fast-evolving world of materials research, working with high-temperature metals and composites to create new kinds of materials for industry and consumer products. A number of other 49ers would have particularly interesting careers on the new frontier of technology development. Foremost among them were James Chalmers, Howard Davis, and George Berman.

James Chalmers was unusual in that he came to the Harvard Business School with a technology background. A serious and well-groomed young man with dark hair and a taste for V-necked sweaters, Chalmers grew up in southern California. As a teenager, with America's involvement in World War II growing closer, he and his friends rode their bicycles out to the desert bombing ranges where dive bombers practiced their bombing raids. Chalmers went to military school and then the California Institute of Technology. He served as a navigator on B-24 bombers flying over Germany in the war. After graduating from Harvard, Chalmers gravitated to the fast-moving frontier of aerospace technology. Along with his wife Nancy and their three-year-old daughter Constance, Chalmers moved back to southern California, which in 1950 was on the cusp of an aerospace boom that would transform the sunny region into one of the wealthiest parts of the United States. Chalmers worked first for a company in San Diego, focusing on thrust-enhancing technology for aircraft afterburners. Then he again moved his family, this time north to Los Angeles, where he joined Hughes Aircraft as an engineer. This job soon led to another position, at the Ramo-Wooldridge company, which would soon become Space Technology Laboratories—a missile contractor for the U.S. Air Force.

Chalmers was in the right field at the right time. The 1950s was an era of intense interest in aerospace and missile technology. The United States was developing ballistic missiles during the 1950s, but it seemed that the Russians were developing them faster. The Soviet launch of

Sputnik in 1957 caused widespread panic in the U.S. political establishment and galvanized a huge missile development effort. Amid inflated Cold War claims of a "missile gap," the United States poured vast resources into an intercontinental ballistic missile program. Space Technology Laboratories—later the Aerospace Corporation—was among the leading contractors for the government, and Chalmers found himself at ground zero of a fast-escalating U.S.-Soviet arms race, working on the Atlas, Titan, Thor, and later the Minuteman ballistic missiles programs.

This work was among the most top secret of all Cold War activities. Every morning, Chalmers went to work in a windowless bunker surrounded by armed guards and barbed wire. "It was like working in a bank vault," he remembered. Chalmers's days were long and intense. A tremendous urgency surrounded the ICBM program. "We were in a terrible rush."

The task of developing an ICBM was daunting in its technical requirements: The missiles had to be able to launch on very short notice, carry a nuclear warhead 3,000 miles over the North Pole, and land with great accuracy. The first three ballistic missile programs Chalmers worked on yielded mixed results. The Atlas, Titan, and Thor programs were early-generation ballistic missile programs of limited sophistication—unreliable, inaccurate, and not worth producing on a large scale. However, Chalmers and his colleagues soon moved on to a more promising missile program: the Minuteman. A major engineering success, the Minuteman was a solid-fueled ICBM that became the backbone of America's long-range missile buildup during the 1960s.

The work of Chalmers and his colleagues was followed with avid interest by officials in Washington. Chalmers gave regular, top secret briefings to the Air Force's high command, and a steady stream of Senators and Congressmen came in for briefings. Chalmers traveled regularly to Cape Canaveral, Florida, for missile launches that tested new rockets. A number of the launches failed specatularly, with the missiles exploding in a fireball on takeoff.

Chalmers's job put him not just in the middle of the arms race, but also in an equally competitive space race. That race was well under way by the end of the 1950s. But John F. Kennedy's vow to put an American on the moon by the end of the decade brought the space race to a new level of intensity and triggered a massive crash program by the U.S.

government. Chalmers and his colleagues at Space Technology Laboratories were deeply involved in the effort. Chalmers was sent to Washington for six months to be part of a combined NASA and U.S. Air Force planning effort, an intense experience that "set up the framework for the entire U.S. space program," Chalmers would later say.

James Chalmers was not the only 49er who found himself enmeshed in the military-technological rivalry with the Soviet Union during the 1960s. Two of his classmates, Howard Davis and Lester Crown, were also playing roles in the development of new military technologies that were helping to fuel America's rise as the most technologically dynamic country in the world.

Howard Davis had never been a typical member of the Harvard Business School class of 1949. He was in the air force when he arrived in Cambridge from Omaha with his wife of three years, Mary, and their young daughter Victoria. During World War II, while still in his early 20s, Davis had commanded a bomb group of 28 B-24 bombers and flew 51 missions over German-held territory. The bomb group was based in Italy and would enter enemy territory over the Alps. Davis would always be in the lead airship, the other bombers arrayed out behind him in attack formation. When the bomb group cleared the Alps, German Messerschmitt fighter planes were usually there to greet them, swooping in from all directions with 30-millimeter machine guns blazing. Later, when the bomb group was near their target, the Messerschmitts would fall away and German antiaircraft artillery would open up, filling the sky with flak explosions. The raids were deadly business. Over 200 American flight officers went to Europe as part of Davis's task force. Less than 20 returned alive.

After graduating from Harvard Business School, Davis continued his air force career. He joined a new section of the military known as the Strategic Air Command (SAC), which had control of America's nuclear arsenal. By the late 1950s, Davis had risen to colonel and commanded a wing of 15 B-52s, each armed with six nuclear weapons. Cold War tensions were near their height, and half of the planes in Davis's wing were maintained on a hair-trigger 15-minute alert at all times, fully fueled, armed, and ready to fly into Soviet territory with enough firepower to destroy the country several times over. During the tense days of the Cuban Missile Crisis, Davis's B-52s went to 24-hour air alert, many flying holding patterns within an hour's striking distance of Soviet territory. Davis himself spent long hours at the controls of the lead bomber in his wing, ready for coded orders that would announce the beginning of war.

By the late 1960s, Davis found himself in McNamara's Pentagon as part of the U.S. Air Force's top command, where he was a key thinker and planner. At that time, the air force's great obsession was to build a new U.S. air-to-air fighter jet that could prevail in dogfights over the Russian MiG 21 and its projected successor, the MiG 23. Davis plunged into this work with zeal. One of his first tasks was to convince a skeptical McNamara and his whiz kids that America needed a new fighter at all.

To convince McNamara to see things the air force's way, Davis assembled a team of over 100 computer programmers to conduct a simulation that pitted the F-4—then the leading U.S. fighter—against the characteristics of the new MiG 23. "We duplicated the same thrust, avionics, and design configuration of the Russian MiG 23," Davis recalled. The team then flew over 3,500 sorties of simulated computer combat and finally came up with a fighter design that could beat the MiG 23. Thus was born one of the most successful U.S. weapons programs in air force history: the F-15 fighter jet. Thirty years later, long after Davis had retired from the air force, the F-15 would still be flying.

Lester Crown would have a far less happy experience with the emerging technology of jet fighters during the 1960s. At the beginning of the decade, Crown was one of the most fortunate and wealthy graduates of the Harvard Business School. The younger Crown rose quickly through the ranks of his father's company, the Material Service Corporation, and became involved in its subsidiary, General Dynamics.

General Dynamics had had many problems during the late 1950s, but it mounted an impressive comeback in the early 1960s. By eliminating the commercial aircraft division and cutting costs in other programs, the corporation brought its balance sheets back into the black. Stock prices, which had tumbled to $2 a share in 1960, rallied impressively, tripling in value in 1964–1965 to reach a decade high of $32.[1] The elder Crown continued to play a leading role in the company. Lester Crown, meanwhile, expanded his own portfolio, assuming the title of executive secretary at Material Service (then run by his older brother, Robert) and eventually executive vice president at General Dynamics.

A grand new military contract for the F–111 plane fueled the recovery at General Dynamics and shaped the business future of the Crown family. It was one of the most controversial defense programs in Pentagon history. The contract eventually brought $8.8 billion worth of business to General Dynamics and introduced an era of financial stability at the company that lasted into the 1980s. But the program was plagued with problems and scandals from the start, and the negative publicity surrounding the plane left a lasting mark on General Dynamics' reputation and would be a disaster for the Crown family. Amid the furor surrounding the F–111 contract, CEO Roger Lewis quietly pushed Henry Crown out of General Dynamics in 1966. Lewis had exercised a clause in Crown's contract that allowed the corporation to buy out Crown's 20 percent share of the corporation. In exchange for $126 million, the elder Crown relinquished his stock, his seat on the board of directors, and control of Material Service Corporation. Lester Crown resigned as vice president of General Dynamics and gave up his various posts at Material Service and the Marblehead Lime Company.[2]

Along with his father and brothers, Lester Crown was deeply demoralized by the loss of General Dynamics. Yet they entertained the hope that some day the family could reclaim control of the company.

The arms race with the Soviet Union, along with space race, involved a stupendous allocation of resources. Critics decried U.S. defense programs of the 1960s as responding to inflated assessments of Soviet strength—claims that would later prove largely correct. And the space program as well had many critics who believed that winning a U.S.-Soviet ego contest in space was not worth tens of billions of dollars. However, for all the waste, sustained U.S. government spending on technology did have some spin-off benefits to the U.S. economy during the 1960s and beyond. Defense and space spending subsidized the development of a booming civilian aerospace sector in the United States that used the latest technologies to dominate the global aerospace industry.

The semiconductor industry was another new high-tech sector of the U.S. economy that burgeoned in the 1960s, thanks both to U.S. defense contracts and the contribution of two entrepreneurial graduates of the Harvard Business School class of 1949: George Berman and Malcolm Hecht.

Like James Chalmers, George Berman came to Harvard Business School with a scientific background. He had grown up in the middle-class Boston neighborhood of Roxbury and had gone to college at MIT—like his father before him—graduating in 1945 with a B.S. in electronics. After Harvard, Berman took his first job, which paid $65 a week, and then proceeded to drift around the Boston area for a decade, working in engineering and marketing positions at four different companies. An inventive, curious man with a quick smile and penchant for adventure, Berman found that none of these jobs fired his imagination or commanded his lasting loyalty. Mainly, he did sales work for electronics companies and it bored him silly. "I learned a lot about the care and feeding of customers," he recalled. It was not the kind of life he wanted. "You were not going to put up with colossal corporate crap forever. You were not going to live like that." Berman longed for the thrill of entrepreneurship. "I was always wanting that someday I would manufacture something interesting, something technical, something that people would love and they'd buy it and they'd pay for it."[3]

Berman's opportunity would come at the end of the 1950s. In what he would remember as "a great stroke of luck," he connected with Malcolm Hecht, a fellow 49er who was also fascinated by technology and also hankered for a more dynamic career. Berman and Hecht had never been buddies at Harvard, but they traveled in some of the same Boston-area social circles in the late 1950s. Together, the two men began talking about starting some kind of company. The talk turned more concrete when one of Berman's friends introduced him to an offbeat electronics inventor named Jack Carmen and a group of venture capitalists who were backing Carmen's work to develop new semiconductor devices. Semiconductors were tiny power devices that could manage the flow of electricity in advanced machines like airplanes and missiles. Carmen was a brilliant and creative man, but he was having little success because of his lack of technical expertise. In short order, Berman and Hecht had worked out a deal to start a real company using some of Carmen's basic ideas and paying him and his backers a percentage of profits. They scraped together some start-up money from family and friends, raising around a half million dollars. In 1960, they opened a small company in Waltham, Massachusetts, a suburb of Boston. The company was initially founded to develop and market a single invention in the semiconductor field—a rugged, fused-in glass rectifier.

Berman and Hecht's new company, Unitrode, was not the only firm that made rectifiers. Over two dozen other companies were making rectifiers in 1960, and the market was quickly driving down the price of the devices. Unitrode would thrive because of a critical edge it had in the field: Its rectifiers were virtually indestructible. Before Unitrode came along, most semiconductors were fragile devices. They couldn't "get too cold, too hot," Berman recalled. "You couldn't shock them physically. You couldn't surge. No surge voltages, no surge currents. They had to be handled with kid gloves, electrically." These limitations meant that military and aerospace equipment designed for rough-and-tumble environments could not simultaneously have the most advanced electronics and also be as reliable as they needed to be.

Mac Hecht drew on his background in chemistry to take the lead in using new materials to create more-rugged semiconductors. The development process was filled with technical obstacles, including the building of 30 furnaces and dangerous work with various chemicals heated to extremely high temperatures. The expenses mounted, and Unitrode's start-up money disappeared with alarming rapidity. "We took on something that we should never have taken on," Berman recalled. "It was really scary." Every week there was the fear that something would fail in development, that they would hit a brick wall, and that the money would run out.

Berman had periods of intense anxiety. His hands would shake. He would shout at his daughters. He would worry again and again that he wasn't going to make it. To cut costs, both Berman and Hecht were hands-on managers every step of the way. Berman did the plumbing to bring cooling water to the furnaces. He wired up machines and instruments. He and Hecht kept the books themselves. Neither of them complained. "We wanted to be high-tech entrepreneurs," Berman said. "It was something in us from the time we were kids."

Miraculously, it all worked out. The stressful and expensive development process produced a new kind of very durable rectifier that was well suited to the rigors of the U.S. military and space programs. Unitrode's new device was soon in high demand. Contractors working with the navy on the Polaris missile, a submarine-launched ballistic missile, wanted the Unitrode rectifier. Other defense contractors also wanted it. Berman and Hecht suddenly had considerable business flowing in, and their new technology company took off. In 1963, the company had its first profitable year, with sales in excess of $1 million. The support of a venture capitalist, Peter Brooke, allowed the company to expand dramatically during the 1960s and move to a new location in Watertown, Massachusetts, an early bastion of what would become a booming high-tech corridor on the outskirts of Boston, along Route 128.

Berman and Hecht reveled in their success. It was the kind of entrepreneurial experience that businesspeople dream of. In 1966, that dream came to include significant personal wealth for both men when Unitrode went public, offering shares to the general public on the New York Stock Exchange. "It was hot for IPOs," Berman recalled, and even a small $4 million company like Unitrode could go public and watch it's stock shoot up. "It was wild." With four young daughters, and no shortage of hobbies, Berman had plenty of uses for the money. The first thing he did was buy a big new house in Newton for $70,000, putting half of the money down up front. Mainly, though, the cash generated by the public offering meant more money for expanding Unitrode. In 1967, Unitrode founded a spin-off company, Powercube, and acquired another company called Solid State Products. Through this period, all of Unitrode's products were designed for military or space program use. The Apollo program was a major customer for Unitrode power devices, and Unitrode's public relations department pointed proudly to the fact that *Apollo 11* contained an estimated 3,000 Unitrode parts when it set humans on the moon in July 1969.

Of all the 49ers who had grand visions about the new technologies of the 1960s, no one was better able to parlay his vision into corporate stardom and personal wealth than Peter McColough. During the 1950s, McColough's early years at Haloid had proven unexpectedly promising. The 1960s would see McColough catapult into the ranks of the most successful and admired business leaders in the United States.

In 1959, Haloid unveiled a line of commercial copiers that lived up to the company's most unabashedly optimistic expectations. The Xerox 914 took its name from the size of the largest documents that it could copy, 9 by 14 inches. It was an adaptation of xerography that owed more than a little to a Kodak trademark. The machine used plain paper and an automatic feeding mechanism that allowed operators to make copies by pressing a single button. The copy quality was excellent, and Haloid boasted that it was often impossible to distinguish the copies from the originals.

The 914 copier involved a huge investment by Haloid—so large that the company's fortunes rested largely on the machine's success. "For seven or eight years," McColough recalled, "the company had been spending more on research and development than they'd been earning . . . we were betting the company—buildings, jobs, trays in the cafeteria—on that product. The whole wad was on the table. No 914, no Haloid, period."[4]

The 914's success was far from guaranteed. The Xerox model was no faster than other available copiers, producing the first copy of a document in 30 seconds and additional copies at the rate of 8 seconds per sheet. Copiers using wet processes sometimes produced copies in as little as four seconds, though the operator then had to wait for the copies to dry. At nearly $30,000 per machine, the sale price of the 914 towered over the competition. Thirty-five other models sold for $200 or less, and $429 had until then represented the high end of the copier market.[5] And the Xerox 914 was bigger, weighing in at 650 pounds and too large to fit through an office door at a time when trends in copier technology had reduced most competitors' models to desktop size. Haloid had spent 15 years and more than $90 million to deliver a decidedly ungainly newborn.[6] But Peter McColough and his colleagues thought that the Xerox 914 was beautiful.

Without McColough's marketing strategy, Haloid might have never transformed its ugly duckling into what some regarded as "the most successful product ever marketed in America."[7] Carlson's invention and Haloid's investment made xerographic copying possible, producing a technique that has proven as adaptable and enduring as the internal-combustion engine. McColough's innovative plans moved the Xerox 914 out of the laboratory and into offices all over the world.

The first obstacle that had to be overcome was the 914's price tag, which McColough saw as prohibitive. Other office equipment companies, notably IBM, had enjoyed some success in renting or leasing their big-ticket products. But existing rental plans could not accommodate the tremendous variations in the number of copies that clients needed. McColough's breakthrough was to use a meter much like those used by electric and telephone companies to monitor usage. The $95 base rent for a 914 included the first 2,000 copies, and customers paid for additional copies according to a schedule of rates and charges. Metered pricing kept up-front expenses to a minimum and offered a variety of pricing plans that could be adjusted to the needs of low-volume users and big customers alike.

McColough's marketing team also resolved the difficulties arising from the tremendous size and weight of the 914. Because the sales force could hardly produce the model out of a sample case, it was essential to develop new ways of getting customers and machines in one place. The company decided to offer the 914s on a 15-day trial basis. Xerox technicians helped to deliver and install 914 copiers, a procedure that often required the installation of new electrical lines. Customers who remained unconvinced by the copier's performance could then count on the company to remove the machine at no additional charge. A more dramatic strategy saw demonstrations of Xerox copying at high-traffic locations such as New York's Grand Central Station. Attractive women behind glass walls operated the copiers with the push of a button, and sometimes asked children or gray-suited businessmen to lend a hand. On-site demonstrations brought the 914 mountain to thousands of Mohammeds every day. Television advertising also spread the word, with award-winning ads that showed a tiny tot helping Daddy and then immortalizing her doll in black and white. A more controversial commercial, which featured a real monkey making a Xerox copy, was withdrawn after office workers objected to the comparison.[8]

Even the ever optimistic Haloid executive team was surprised by the response to the 914. Not only did more firms obtain a Xerox copier, but most customers used the machine in far greater volume than anyone had anticipated. While the company projected that each machine would turn out 10,000 copies each month, actual volume exceeded 40,000. The majority of that figure represented copies of copies, an innovation in the spread of information facilitated by the simplicity and excellent quality of Xerox copying.[9] Within large corporations, the purchase of a 914 for one department often engendered bottlenecks and rivalries that could only be resolved by the purchase of additional machines for other departments. Everybody wanted a 914, but only one company owned the rights to use Carlson's invention. That company's balance sheets reflected the unheralded demand. In 1959, the year Haloid introduced the 914, the company's total revenues amounted to $12,897,000.[10] In 1960, earnings stood at $37,074,000. In 1961, the figure increased to $59,533,000.[11] Earnings jumped an additional 70 percent—to $104,472,000—in 1962.[12] "I keep asking myself," exclaimed CEO Wilson, "when are you going to wake up? Things just aren't this good in life."[13]

Peter McColough took his full measure of the good life at Haloid—which changed its name to Xerox Corporation in 1961. Shares of the company's stock were part of the package that convinced McColough to take the pay cut back in 1954, and like other shareholders, he profited handsomely from Xerox's success. Stock prices increased exponentially, swelling shares valued at $9 in 1957 to $372 in 1963 after multiple splits and dividend increases.[14] The son of a civil servant from Halifax rapidly became one of the wealthiest members of the class of 49.

The early 1960s were boom years for McColough's career at Xerox. Propelled by the fantastic success of his 914 marketing plan, he was named assistant general manager in charge of operations in 1963. The title was misleadingly modest. McColough's new responsibilities included sales, finance control, machine and process manufacturing, purchasing, the company's Haloid photo division, business development, and government operations.[15] In 1966, he became the president and heir apparent to Joseph Wilson, whom McColough succeeded two years later as chief executive officer. At 46, he was nearly 10 years younger than the typical CEO of the era. His Xerox Corporation was the marvel of the business world.

One of McColough's greatest challenges as CEO was managing Xerox's astounding growth. In the seven years after the introduction of the 914, Xerox had manufactured and placed 190,000 copiers, and its staff had soared from 900 to over 24,000. The result was a perpetual sense of chaos. "The company was exploding so rapidly," said McColough, "that we didn't have the systems and controls . . . I was concerned that we couldn't pay our bills even or pay the salesmen. Not because we didn't have money, but our records were so lousy. The whole system was falling apart."[16] McColough's response to the crisis was not popular with longtime Haloid veterans: He recruited outside managers from places like IBM, Ford, and General Motors to develop new systems and impose order.

McColough brought distinct management values to his leadership of Xerox. He placed tremendous confidence in the more junior executives that he hired and promoted, perhaps a reflection of his own rise through the corporate ranks. He believed that it was important to allow the company officers a free rein within their area of responsibility. "I don't think I should ever make a lot of decisions," he noted in 1971. "I make the key ones for the company and I am responsible for all the rest. But for me to go around bragging about the 50 decisions I make every week means that I've got a lousy organization."[17] McColough not only allowed his top people to make their own decisions, he also rarely discussed issues with his staff in one-on-one meetings. Xerox's head of marketing, Ray Hay, once commented that he had been in the boss's office only three times during his two years in the job.[18] McColough saw himself as a symbol of the corporation's goals and principles. The "major role of a CEO is to be seen, whether you are tall or short, handsome or ugly," he observed.[19] Making appearances at Xerox facilities across the United States and around the world, he tried to convey his concern for the employees and his pride in their work. He was an early advocate of management by walking around (MBWA).[20]

From his first days as Xerox's CEO, McColough had determined not to lead a monomaniacal corporate life. "When I was made president of the company," he recalled, "I went through about six months of getting congratulations. Instead of feeling elated about it, I was really rather depressed. Up until then I always felt I had the option if I wanted to do something else. I was interested in politics. I had the freedom, if I wanted to, to move into a government job. But then . . . I realized I had taken on an obligation that no matter what I wanted to do, I couldn't leave."[21]

McColough was intent on shaping the job to fit his desires. He rarely worked after hours or on weekends, and he made time for six to eight weeks of vacation every year, saying he needed room in his schedule for "time to think," and he often came back from sailing expeditions and other retreats filled with ideas that set his staff in motion.[22] Public service also ranked high among his priorities as chief. McColough became a U.S. citizen in 1956 and dedicated himself to making his adopted homeland a better place. These activities included corporate projects such as sponsorship for arts and entertainment, minority hiring, and sabbatical leave for employees interested in public service. They also reflected McColough's personal passions as an active member of the Democratic Party. He saw his political activism as more important than other kinds of community service. "I am shocked," he once observed "at intelligent persons who take no voice whatsoever in politics."[23] McColough served on a presidential task force in the Johnson administration and chaired the New York Citizens for Humphrey and Muskie Committee. His political career reached a chaotic climax when he served as a delegate to the 1968 Democratic Convention in Chicago, where he and other delegates witnessed outrageous Yippie demonstrations and police brutality.

Under McColough's leadership, the magnificent Xerox boom of the 1960s continued. Between 1964 and 1974, Xerox enjoyed average annual earnings growth of 24 percent, fueled by 30 percent average annual sales increases. A series of new copier models—the 813 desktop copier, the 2400, which could make 40 copies per minute, the 9200, producing 120 copies per minute, the 4000, which made two-sided copies—kept demand for the latest Xerox products high.

By the time of the Watergate scandal in 1973, the brand name had become synonymous with photocopying to such an extent that Senator Sam J. Ervin Jr. repeatedly used "Xerox" as a verb during his televised hearings.[24]

Harvard Business School had never been billed as a training ground for technological innovators and entrepreneurs. Yet some members of the class of 1949 had their greatest impact on the postwar business world through their roles in developing new technologies. For James Chalmers and Howard Davis, business school training proved key to tackling some of the most complex defense and aerospace technology challenges of the 1960s. Others, like Berman and McColough, represented the real wave of the future: harnessing new technology to corporate profits. This strategy required not just visionary ideas. It required serious investments of company resources, amassed through public offerings in a strong stock market. Research and development had long been a part of corporate strategy. In the 1960s, technology companies like Xerox brought these strategies to new levels of sophistication and poured unprecedented resources into the pursuit of profitable innovation. By the dawn of the 1970s, the United States stood on the brink of a technological revolution that would turn computers and other kinds of rarefied technology into common household items and create a new breed of business titans.

7

Riding the Bull

I f there is one spot on earth that symbolizes the dazzling phenomenon of American wealth, it is the Wall Street financial district. Yet at the dawn of the 1960s, a decade that would witness an astounding explosion of wealth, Wall Street remained a backwater in the U.S. economy. When sophisticated observers of economic life considered the humming engines of American growth, they thought of Detroit, where the auto industry was booming. They thought of Pittsburgh, where the steel industry remained robust. They thought of the sprawling new suburbs that ringed every major city of the United States, the creation of which produced major real estate fortunes. They thought of bustling shipping ports like New York, and they thought of the big department stores. They did not automatically think of Wall Street as one of the great locomotives of economic growth or wealth creation.

For much of the early postwar era, Wall Street was a sleepy place. The hangover from the Great Depression placed a damper on the U.S. stock market well into the postwar period. Bill Ruane and Jack Shad, among the few 49ers who gravitated to Wall Street after they graduated from Harvard, found that "nothing was happening," in Ruane's words. Wall Street would yield excellent returns to investors during the 1950s, but there was none of the excitement of a bull market. The absence of major activity on Wall Street during the 1950s was due to low corporate profits in many sectors and a shortage of extra cash that Americans could put into the stock market. Also, the great stock market crash of 1929 was still a not-too-distant memory to many Americans of the 1950s. In 1952, only 4 percent of Americans owned stocks. A decade later, just over 10 percent did.

Wall Street sprang to life in the 1960s in a big way. That decade would see the strongest bull market since the 1920s, with the Dow Jones Industrial Average breaking 1,000. By the late 1960s, Wall Street would once more become a leading symbol of wealth creation. And in its resurgence, the financial services sector would develop ever more sophisticated mechanisms for aggregating and multiplying wealth. A number of 49ers—George Berman, Tom Murphy, Peter McColough, John Muller, Harry Figgie, and others—would turn to the Street to realize their ambitions of corporate expansion. For fledgling companies like Unitrode, Wall Street was a place to raise large sums of capital that could be used to underwrite business expansion and the creation of yet more wealth. Public stock offerings of companies, of course, were nothing new. Companies had been helping finance themselves this way since the beginning of the stock market. What was new in the 1960s was the manner in which an initial public offering on Wall Street produced tremendous hype—everyone wanted to be in early on the next hot stock—and could yield a rapid and vast infusion of wealth for a company. Unitrode's public offering in 1966, near the height of the bull market, had allowed it to pour major resources into expansion—financing a spin-off company, the acquisition of another company, and new capital investments at Unitrode itself. Xerox was no newcomer to the stock market during the 1960s, but the phenomenal increase in the value of Xerox shares over the decade helped the company finance one of the most lavish research and development efforts ever witnessed within the technology world. Tom Murphy's Capital Cities turned to Wall Street in the 1960s to raise funds for new capital investments and acquisitions, which in turn fueled aggressive empire building.

The strength of the stock market also meant new opportunities for individuals to create wealth. This was most spectacularly true for corporate leaders, like Peter McColough, who accepted part of their compensation in the form of stock. Still a relatively new practice during the 1960s, high levels of stock compensation for company employees took on new meaning in the bull market of the 1960s. The practice meant that an ever growing number of CEOs would become millionaires, even though their heavily taxed salaries alone would have never allowed them to reach that goal.

For the vast majority of Americans, the stock market did not deliver new wealth. Less than 15 percent of American households had money in the stock market throughout the 1960s. However, the decade saw growing investments in the stock market by an increasingly affluent upper middle class. More revolutionary was the explosion in investing by pension funds. The bull market, in fact, came to exist in large part because so many new investors were getting into the stock market. A deluge of new advertising by investment firms lured individuals in, as did tales of friends and neighbors who'd done well. By the end of the 1960s, stock investing was still not the populist activity it would become in the 1990s, nor was it any longer the preserve of the truly rich. And as more Americans—and institutions—put their money in higher-yielding stocks rather than in traditional savings accounts, one more stream of new wealth was added to the growing river of riches circulating through the U.S. economy. For the tiny minority of 49ers who had gone to Wall Street after Harvard, the boom on Wall Street was sweet vindication of a career choice that had initially seemed mystifying to many classmates.

Those 49ers who went to Wall Street would follow different trajectories during the 1960s. In the 1950s, Henry Brandt bounced around a number of investment firms before hooking up with Harvard classmate Bill Ruane. This connection, in turn, led to an association with Warren Buffett, whom he came to consider "the most imaginative and successful investor in the business." Brandt would spend most of the decade helping Buffett establish a thriving investment firm, Warren Buffett Associates. Buffett was not yet a legend on Wall Street in the 1960s, but he was fast on his way to becoming one.

Meanwhile, Brandt's old boss, Bill Ruane, entered the 1960s with the wind at his back. Ruane & Cunniff, the firm Ruane had helped build inside Kidder, Peabody, had been a major success during the late 1950s. Their investing strategy was incredibly basic by the standards of later decades. Ruane and Cunniff observed that the big brokers were making investments only in blue-chip stocks. Perhaps as a reflection of the broader conservatism of the era, few on Wall Street were taking chances on small-company growth stocks. "There were tons of attractive-looking companies out there whose stock was trading for something like 5 times earnings," Ruane would say later, using the lingo of value investing. (A stock trading for only 5 times earnings was considered a major bargain.) Ruane & Cunniff became specialists in small companies and, when they'd done their research, they didn't hesitate to gamble big. These investments in small, growth companies paid off. Between 1955 and 1960, Ruane & Cunniff had a six-year run of making 50 percent gains each year. One transistor company they bought into at 3 times earnings later sold for 80 times earnings.

Ruane's winning streak continued in the 1960s. One of his first big successes in the decade was made possible through 49er classmate, Tom Murphy. In 1961, Capital Cities Broadcasting was clearly moving up in the world, but it was not an obvious stock pick for cautious Wall Street. Cap Cities was still caught up in the struggle to win its first VHF broadcasting license and faced other challenges, too. But Cap Cities also had a lot going for it: a healthy cash flow, monopoly placement within local broadcast markets, and Murphy's leadership, which Ruane trusted completely. "It was a moneymaking machine," Ruane said later of Cap Cities, and the company was using its money wisely, plowing capital into new acquisitions. The company had real potential. Ruane & Cunniff invested heavily. Within a few years, Cap Cities stock would earn Ruane & Cunniff a fortune. Ruane's "discovery" of Cap Cities conformed impeccably to the value-investing model of betting on an undervalued company.

Ruane would score even bigger with another major discovery a few years after his Cap Cities success. In 1964, Ruane was planning a trip to California to check out a supermarket chain he was considering investing in. Supermarket chains, hardware stores, and other unglamorous properties were the bread and butter of value investing—not sexy, but highly profitable over the long haul. Before Ruane left for the West Coast, he ran into a friend who was in show business. His friend said that he should try to hook up with Roy Disney while he was in Hollywood. The friend said that Disney studios had just completed a movie—*Mary Poppins*—that was going to be a huge success. Beyond the prospect of a major hit, Disney had other obvious assets. It had a library of beloved animated films, lots of land in Florida and California, and a studio that produced six or seven good family films each year. Also, there was Walt Disney himself, still engaged in the business and widely seen as a genius.

But Wall Street firms didn't grasp any of this, and Disney stock was not seen as a major investment opportunity. Ruane's friend predicted that this would soon change. Ruane took the tip and called on Roy Disney, Walt's brother, and they talked for a couple hours. He also met with Walt Disney for a fascinating talk. Things were going very well for Disney, including big development plans afoot for the Disney properties in Florida and California. Ruane came away deeply impressed by what he heard.

Back in New York, Ruane bought into the stock, which was selling at only 7 times earnings, in spite of the clear value of the company. *Mary Poppins* turned out to be a hit, as expected. Ruane's investment doubled in value almost right away, going sky-high and remaining one of the hottest stocks on Wall Street for a number of years. Ruane made a killing—although after he sold the Disney stock it continued to climb ever higher.[1] Ruane didn't fret too much. "We sold almost everything too early," he said later. Value investing techniques called for selling at 15 or 20 times earnings. Selling off stocks that later rose higher was an inevitable part of the game.

Even as he became a star on Wall Street during the 1960s, Bill Ruane was different from many investors. The Street of the 1960s was not unlike that of the 1980s and late 1990s. The promise of easy money drew a lot of the wrong kinds of people to investing, and greed brought out the worst in people. Yet Ruane never seemed to lose his moral compass, one that always seemed to point back to his Midwestern roots. In putting the edicts of value investing into action, Ruane talked often with another leading Midwestern disciple of this new religion, his friend Warren Buffett. While Ruane labored in the belly of the beast on Wall Street, Buffett challenged establishment investment techniques from Omaha. In 1956, with $105,000 from friends and family members, he had established Warren Buffett Associates, Ltd. The partnership entrusted its capital to Buffett's hunt for bargains, which proved remarkably successful. By the 1960s, Buffett Associates was enjoying a compounded annual growth rate of almost 30 percent on investments that favored insurance, communications, and other high-cash-flow enterprises.[2] Buffett earned a national reputation as a financial whiz kid when he precipitously sold out of the stock market in the late 1960s. Complaining that high prices had banished bargain properties from the stock market, he liquidated the partnership and consolidated his personal investments in 1969, rewarding his investors with a sizable return. True to Buffett's analysis, the market initiated a prolonged decline.

Buffett encouraged his former investors to seek out Bill Ruane if they still had a taste for playing the stock market. Ruane had served as Buffett's personal stockbroker throughout the 1960s.[3] In 1969, Ruane and Richard Cunniff finally took their shop out of Kidder, Peabody and expanded to handle a mutual fund as well as individual accounts. In July 1970, Ruane established the Sequoia Fund, and many of Buffett's former investors bought shares.

Bill Ruane had made good money on Wall Street in the 1960s. Now, with a major new private fund under his command, even bigger money lay on his horizon.

Ruane's close friend, John Shad, also lived the good life on Wall Street in the 1960s. The 1950s had been a time of intensive striving for the workaholic Shad, and his efforts paid off: a personal fortune made in stocks and a soaring career. In 1963, Shad accepted an offer to set up a new investment banking division at the brokerage firm E.F. Hutton & Company. As vice president for corporate finance, Shad would pioneer Hutton's foray into the biggest and most competitive arena in financial services. Hutton was one of the largest and best-known brokerage houses in the United States in the 1960s, with a nationwide network of branch offices and a strong presence in California, where founder E. F. Hutton had set up shop with a transcontinental wire service in 1904. The firm specialized in retail sales to individual investors. The move into investment banking aimed to strengthen the role of Hutton's New York headquarters vis-à-vis the regional offices and to make a place for Hutton among the great houses of Wall Street.[4] Under Shad, the fledgling division prospered.

Shad's division succeeded because of the hard work, intelligence, and innovative spirit of its chief. Shad quickly established a reputation as one of the sharpest minds at E.F. Hutton—insightful, mathematical, and capable of mastering unlimited detail. His drive to succeed became the stuff of legend. "Many times I would come to see him at 8 A.M. only to find he had been at work all night," recalled a subordinate.[5] During bankers' hours, Shad worked at a furious pace, often holding a telephone receiver to each ear. He loved the deal making, the gamble, and the technical minutiae of each new issue, merger, or acquisition. Shad's example set a frenetic tone for the investment banking department that mirrored the go-go intensity of the field as a whole. Working with vast sums of money on fast-paced deals, Shad's team operated in a kind of permanent emergency mode.

Shad's major contribution to investment banking at Hutton—the successful cultivation of a niche market—reflected a guiding principle of his Harvard Business School education. Hutton's newcomer status in the world of deal making complicated its bid for business among the big corporations. Instead of pursuing the patronage of top-rated companies, Shad worked to identify worthy small corporations and start-ups in need of capital services. Prior to Shad's innovations in banking, most newly established companies had depended on short-term bank loans at floating interest rates to obtain credit. E.F. Hutton under Shad arranged bond-issue financing for companies that the major banks saw as high risk. Because the major bond-rating agencies, Moody's and Standard & Poor's, rated the start-up companies' risk of default as greater than that of established firms, the bonds carried higher interest rates than premium securities. When the firms were successful (and thanks to Shad's careful research, they most often were), the payoff exceeded the margin of top-rated bonds. And Hutton was poised to shepherd its most successful clients through successive rounds of financing, initial public offers of stock, and retail sales through the national brokerage network. "That was the essence of John's strategy," remembered a member of Shad's staff. "[S]ink your teeth into a client and hold on forever."[6]

The issue of high-yield securities, later also known as *junk bonds,* became the cornerstone of investment banking at Hutton. Shad recruited a staff that drew heavily on graduates of the Harvard Business School, including his star protégé, Frederick H. Joseph, who went on to become CEO of Drexel Burnham Lambert, the investment bank that popularized the junk bond in the 1980s. Shad, Joseph, and their team spent weeks evaluating the finances of potential clients. "You check their major customers, suppliers, competitors, and so forth," Shad explained. "You are interested in such critical areas as the integrity and reputation of the officers and directors." Thorough research sometimes uncovered details that "even management doesn't know," Shad said. "A spark-plug executive may be about to quit . . . or a major competitor may be about to introduce a product that will seriously affect the company's earning projections. A key contract may be on the verge of termination."[7] Equipped with all the relevant information about a client, Hutton could proceed with confidence to set a market price for bond-issue securities.

From 1963 to 1969, Shad orchestrated more than 50 corporate financings, mergers, and acquisitions for firms such as Kaufman and Broad Homebuilders, Browning Ferris Industries, and Continental Telephone.[8] What the process lacked in glamour it compensated for in profits. By the end of the 1960s, Shad was a rich man, with every promise of becoming richer still in the years ahead. Just as important, he had the reputation of being one of the smartest men on Wall Street.

For Bill Ruane, John Shad, and other 49ers in the boomtown of New York City in the 1960s, life was about making their mark, along with their fortune. But it was also about friendship, even though the days were long gone of living in the group house on East 11th Street. Through the 1960s, Ruane was close friends with Shad and Joe Amaturo and Tom Murphy. More than anyone, Murphy had emerged in the years since 1949 as something of the social and professional glue among class alums. Jack Davis had landed his job at Mary Carter Paint through his connection to Murphy. Jim Burke's brother worked with Murphy. Ruane made a fortune on Cap Cities because he knew Murphy. Years later, the 49ers would talk with awe about how Murphy supported the friends in his life and was a man who made things happen for people. "Murphy's involved with everyone," Ruane would say.

It was still too early, in the 1960s, for the business press to take notice of the Harvard Business School 49er power network that was taking shape within the business world. Yet by the end of the decade, class members had either taken over, or were poised to take over, some of the most dynamic companies in America. By the end of the 1970s, the class would be a legend and the new trends in business that they had ridden to power would dominate the American economy.

MOVING TO THE TOP

In early June 1974, nearly 300 members of the class of 1949 traveled to Cambridge for their 25th reunion. Most brought their wives and some brought their children, too. They came from as far away as Manila, Calcutta, and Hong Kong. The stars of the class were out in force: Marvin Traub, Peter McColough, Jim Burke, John Shad. But the majority of the class members were far lower profile: men like Walter Scott, head of the J.H. Filbert Company, a firm in Baltimore that made margarine, who called himself a "relatively undistinguished statistic in the class."[1]

Among the 49ers, there were inevitable comments about wider waists and thinning hair, and to many, it was remarkable just how quickly 25 years had passed. World War II, the formative event in the lives of all class members, was becoming a distant memory in American culture, replaced by far more recent traumas like Vietnam and the social turbulence of the 1960s. Many of the children of 49ers were now as old as current students at the Harvard Business School.

But if the America of the 49ers' youth was long gone, the America of 1974 was one that the class was actively shaping from their positions of power and influence—not just in business, but in cultural and non-profit institutions as well. There was a triumphalism in the air at the reunion, and for good reason. Twenty-five years after leaving Harvard, the class of 1949 had marched to the heights of the business world. Nearly a quarter of the class members had already risen to the position of chief executive, and many more held positions in corporate America that carried powers nearly as great. Along the way, the class had assembled fabulous wealth. The wealth, in fact, was one of the great surprises to many of the 49ers, who had never expected to get so rich. A survey of the 376 class members undertaken earlier in the year by *Fortune* magazine yielded stunning numbers: In an America where less than a quarter of middle-aged men made more than $25,000 a year, the median income of a 49er was $53,561 (over $200,000 in 2001 dollars). In an America where a millionaire was still an exotic creature, some 57 class members called themselves millionaires. The combined total personal wealth of the class members answering the survey was nearly a quarter billion dollars, a sum that would be pitiful by later standards of private wealth, even adjusted for inflation, but one that was impressive for the day.

The 49ers had always been a hard-partying crowd, and even in middle age they knew how to put together a weekend of revelry. One of the special elements of the reunion was that it was not simply a nostalgic get-together of former classmates who had long ago fallen out of touch with each other. Instead, the friendships among some 49ers were as intense as they had been 25 years earlier. "My closest friendships are from the class of '49," Jim Burke would say decades after graduation. "A lot of us had interrupted college careers, so these took the place of college friendships."[2] In the mid-1970s, perhaps the tightest friendships from the class were among 10 or so men. In addition to Jim Burke, this clique included Tom Murphy, Peter McColough, Robert Baldwin, Jack Lanahan, Winslow Martin, John Muller Jr., Jack Davis, Frank Mayers, William Hanley Jr., and Robert Landrum.

When they were younger, at Harvard, the men had shared a taste for heavy socializing and adventure. In their early years in business, they made a point of keeping in touch and taking short vacations together. One popular place for such informal reunions during the 1950s and 1960s was the Greenbrier Hotel in West Virginia, then run by Jack Lanahan. Greenbrier is a sprawling 6,000-acre resort that had been popular with Dwight Eisenhower and was the location of a secret relocation center for the U.S. Congress built during Cold War. With Lanahan giving them the run of the hotel, the 49ers would take over the Presidential Suite, which occupied two floors of one wing of the resort and included seven bedrooms, a living room, and a formal dining room. "It was a blast," recalled Jack Muller.

Through the 1970s, the 49ers remained so close that their wives and girlfriends dubbed them "The Group," a teasing reference to Mary

McCarthy's best-selling novel of the time about a group of Vassar graduates.

The men in The Group had taken diverse paths in business: Burke, Murphy, and McColough had aggressively climbed to the top of the corporate world, as had Frank Mayers who was president of Bristol-Myers; John Muller was founder and chairman of General Housewares; Jack Davis was president of Resorts International. But Robert Landrum and Robert Baldwin had moved outside of big business: Baldwin was a Volkswagen dealer in Connecticut; Landrum had left a career in banking to earn a Ph.D. and now led a quiet life as a professor of management at Eastern Kentucky University.

The friendships in The Group endured even as class members were pulled into different worlds and even as they became so busy that their wives needed to schedule time to see them. In the mid-1970s, The Group gathered in Vail one December for a ski vacation with their wives and children. They had so much fun that they decided to make the get-together an annual ritual. Jack Muller volunteered to be the organizer of what became known as Operation Snowflake. A quarter-century later, Operation Snowflake was still going strong. They also maintained various running bets, some going back years. "We gambled on everything in sight," Jack Davis commented.[3] And, of course, there was plenty of career networking among The Group. Peter McColough summed up the reigning ethos among the men in 1974: "We've always been very competitive among ourselves," he said, but "it's nice see to our friends do well."[4]

At the reunion, several days of festivities culminated in a black-tie "Monte Carlo casino" bash at Copley Plaza in Boston. There was no real gambling at the gala, this being Boston in the heart of puritan New England. No matter; the 49ers raptly focused on the roulette wheel and the card games. The high-powered event at Copley drew reporters from the *New York Times, Boston Globe,* and elsewhere. The reporters were there not just hoping for a word with the likes of Jim Burke and Peter McCullough, they also were fascinated with the phenomenon of the class itself.[5]

In that glittering weekend in June 1974, the good fortune of the class was indisputable. Still, the America in which the 49ers lived and ruled was changing in major ways. June 1974 was a strange and difficult time. After more than a year of scandal in Washington, the Nixon presidency was in its final days. The demise of the Nixon White House was a bitter spectacle to many 49ers, who had come of age in a country untouched by political scandals of comparable magnitude. Graham O. Harrison inveighed bitterly to his classmates about the "leaderless, amoral Administration I helped to elect in 1972." A number of 49ers like Jack Davis knew Nixon personally and had raised money for his campaign. Only a minority had sided with George McGovern. One 49er at the reunion who had voted for McGovern was Roger Sonnabend, nearly alone at the festivities in wearing a beard, but seeming to enjoy his status as the most quirky and unconventional class member. "Don't blame me, I voted for McGovern," Sonnabend could quip, quoting a popular bumper sticker of the moment.

Watergate wasn't the only dark cloud hanging over the reunion. In 1974, America was in the middle of the worst recession in 40 years. The slowdown of economic growth was the first significant downturn in the business careers of the 49ers. Oil prices had risen drastically in 1973 as a result of the Yom Kippur War in the Middle East, and the effects on energy-hungry America were profound. Inflation was also skyrocketing, while wage growth was stagnating. Overseas, powerful competitors were rising in the form of America's erstwhile enemies, Germany and Japan. When the first Japanese automobile, the Toyota, had been offered for sale in the United States in 1957, the cars had been something of a novelty and remained so for many years. Not anymore. America's streets were increasingly filled with Japanese and European autos. In World War II, some 90 percent of 49ers had served in the war against the Germans and Japanese. Now, over a quarter century later, many of the 49ers found themselves in a different kind of fight with their former adversaries.

In 1974, the 49ers were on top. But already, the golden age that they had come to take for granted was fast fading into history.

8

New Heights

In 1972, Henry Taft was making $125,000 a year as vice president of the pharmaceutical giant Bristol-Myers. It was a phenomenal amount of money for the time, even for a graduate of the Harvard Business School. Tall and broad-shouldered, a Yale man before entering Harvard, Taft was the spitting image of a big-time corporate leader. At Bristol-Myers, he had considerable authority, and far greater rewards clearly lay in his future.

But it wasn't enough.

Taft was a restless idealist who found the corporate world confining. Around him, in the early 1970s, America was going through a social revolution. For middle-aged Americans like Taft, too old for LSD trips or rock concerts or communes, new questions about the meaning of life were provoked by literature and films that focused on the spiritually empty nature of American life. The novelist John Updike, with his depiction of moral decay and stagnation in suburbia, captured the mood of a generation that had won material success only to find that so much else was missing. Everywhere, people were questioning their values, and Taft found himself asking hard questions about what really made him happy. Years earlier, in 1959, Taft had gone through a similar period of soul-searching after his first marriage had ended in a difficult divorce. Taft had sorted out his life then by sailing across the Pacific and back in a 46-foot ketch. "It really changed my life," he said later.

In 1972, Taft again sought dramatic change. Quitting his job at Bristol-Myers and taking an $85,000 a year pay cut, Taft became president of Outward Bound. The small outdoor education program had something that Bristol-Myers didn't: a philosophy that inspired Taft. It was a philosophy about courage, about exposure to new things, about personal transformation. The organization also jibed with the new environmentalism of the day, a movement that had been gaining steam since the publication in 1962 of Rachel Carlson's seminal book, *Silent Spring*. The first Earth Day had been held in 1970.

To move from Bristol-Myers to Outward Bound meant dropping out of mainstream business life. Taft still had his friends in the fast lane—in 1974 he convinced McColough, Burke, and Murphy to join him for whitewater rafting out west—but Taft was no longer one of them. The times had shifted his values to another orbit.

It was not an easy thing, in the early 1970s, to be a middle-aged member of America's business elite. A powerful regulatory movement, symbolized by consumer-protection advocate Ralph Nader, sought to create new standards of corporate responsibility. Nader's point was a simple one: Corporate greed killed people, and it was a point that he had made in detail in his best-selling book about General Motors' Corvair, *Unsafe At Any Speed*. The values of the corporate world—and of materialism and consumerism—were under siege in American society as they had not been since the 1930s. To focus on making money and to work for the establishment were suspect in equal measure.

This shift in public attitudes was an ironic effect of the explosion of wealth in postwar America. In a time of plenty, many Americans—the young especially—had the luxury to turn to matters beyond material sustenance. The cultural shift to postmaterialism was so powerful that it infected even many who had come of age amid the economic hardship of the Great Depression and world war. Henry Taft was only one of millions of people across generations who were reexamining their values and wondering how they could best make a contribution in the world.

Taft was unusual among 49ers in that his inward gaze at his values led him to a radical shift in lifestyle during the 1970s. Two other examples of this phenomenon were James Craig and Daniel Parker. Craig had spent the 1950s and 1960s helping Roger Sonnabend build his hotel business.

By the late 1960s, however, Craig's interests were turning away from business and toward the political ferment of the times. He attended protests against the Vietnam War, and led a campaign to get rid of the pro-war congressman in his district. He was also open to the cultural experimentation. "The first time I smoked marijuana," Craig recalled, "I thought 'wow, these kids have been hiding great stuff from us.'" In 1971 Craig finally quit his position at Sonesta Hotels. He spent the 1970s devoting tremendous energies to political and social causes, including helping to found the Massachusetts chapter of Common Cause, a national activist organization founded by the liberal leader John Gardner.

Daniel Parker, heir to the Parker Pen fortune, took an even bigger leap out of the business world when he left his successful company in 1973 and accepted an appointment by Richard Nixon to become administrator of the Agency for International Development. There, he would be the point person in the U.S. government for managing foreign aid assistance to scores of country. It was a job that took Parker about as far away from the mundane concerns with products and profits as one could get. Everything was incredibly real. In 1976, for example, Parker flew to Guatemala to assess the damage of an earthquake that killed over 25,000 people. Seeing the wreckage of the shacks and shanties that had come tumbling down on people was something he would never forget. Being in a position to do something about this suffering, rushing U.S. aid to the devastated country, was an experience that Parker would cherish for the rest of his life.

Taft and Craig and Parker were unusual. Even as America went through one of the greatest social upheavals in its history, most of the 49ers continued what they were doing before. Sumner Feldberg, chairman of Zayre, a billion-dollar-a-year discount chain, was among those who questioned his hard-driving life in business but didn't know how to get out. "I'm one of the people who built this business and now I'm a slave to it," he said in 1974. "Every now and then I ask myself: do I have the courage to get off the trolley?" The answer for Feldberg would be no. He stayed on as chairman of Zayre—which ran the clothing store T.J. Maxx—until 1987, and he didn't retire altogether until 1995.

The shift in national values would have its impact by making a number of 49ers more liberal in their politics and social attitudes. In 1949, some 60 percent of class members had identified themselves as Republican. By 1974, that number was down to 48 percent. A poll of 49ers showed that as a group they were very liberal on social issues. The vast majority, for example, supported legal abortion and women's lib. Still, the 49ers remained conservative on economic issues, as might be expected, and very few class members were so affected by the times that they saw the need to leave the business world altogether. Of course, staying in the business world did not mean avoiding the shift in values that was sweeping America, for nearly every sector of American business was affected by the changing American lifestyle.

Nowhere were the challenges and opportunities of the values shift felt more dramatically than in the world of consumer products and services. Despite the economic slowdown, this sector of the U.S. economy thrived as the American middle class continued to expand. The growing ranks of the newly affluent defined the American dream in far more expansive terms than had their parents. Items considered luxuries in the 1950s were now seen as essential. In 1973, a survey found that 88 percent of Americans considered a washing machine to be a necessity, and 57 percent thought the same way about a television.[1] A few decades earlier, of course, the word *necessity* had a very different meaning. It meant food and shelter. In the consumerist America, it meant something very different. And this changing conception of the basics of life provided a gold mine for those with the creativity to mine it. At the forefront of the booming new domestic consumer economy were members of the class of 1949.

On a crisp autumn night in 1972, the vast sales floors of Bloomingdale's store at 59th Street and Lexington Avenue looked nothing like usual. The seventh floor was empty of merchandise and had been turned into a large dance floor; the eighth floor had also been cleared and was filled with 130 dinner tables. Bars were set up on three different floors. Outside, klieg lights shined near the store's entrance. Beginning at 8 P.M., 1,300 people descended on Bloomingdale's to celebrate its 100th anniversary. It was a black-tie crowd, filled with fashion designers, clothing manufacturers, and members of New York society's elite. New York's debonair mayor, John Lindsay, was also there, mentioning to a reporter that he was wearing both a Bloomingdale's tie and underwear. The huge crowd flooded the store, sipping drinks and taking in displays. The event could easily have been thrown at a hotel—it would be two decades before store parties were common in New York—but, as one Bloomingdale's executive explained, "It's cozier to throw a party in your own home."[2] While the party was marking a milestone and celebrating an institution, in retrospect it could be seen as a kickoff for the most successful era of Bloomingdale's—and indeed, the entire history of department store retailing.

The 1970s were the decade that made Marvin Traub famous. Well into his 40s by the dawn of the decade, with combed-back graying hair and heavy horn-rimmed glasses, Traub was nevertheless "with it" and ideally suited to tap into the complex zeitgeist of the era—one that mixed an antiestablishment ethos with chic new sensibilities about fashion and sexuality. While many of his classmates from Harvard, traditional men from the heartland, were confounded by the new counterculture, Traub's brand of cosmopolitanism was easily adapted to the different times.

His flair for showmanship, too, was a gift that translated easily into the new era. In another life, perhaps, Traub might have been in the circus, or maybe an actor, like some of the glitzy friends of his parents who used to visit the Traub apartment on New York's Upper West Side. But Traub had chosen the retail world, and in a time when Americans wanted to be more stimulated and titillated than ever, Marvin Traub knew how to sell. As the 1970s began, Traub's in-store displays were so involved that a new term was coined to describe them: "retailing theater." In one 1971 display, Bloomingdale's created something called "The Cave", a multilevel structure wrapped in white polyurethane. People came to the store simply to gawk at the strange sight. "First of all, they make the store a more exciting place to shop," Traub once said, explaining the heavy investment in in-store displays. "Second, they encourage the development of new products by focusing on a country or theme, and challenging our vendors to come up with new products or suppliers. Third, they obviously reinforce our image of being like no other store in the world."[3]

In another Traub innovation, Bloomingdale's introduced video merchandising, whereby monitors with disco sound tracks were placed around the store to show fashion videos featuring Bloomingdale's clothes. The videos were made in Bloomingdale's in-store television studio and proved to be a huge hit. Even after a video was taken off the store floor, customers would sometimes come back and ask for the clothes that they "saw in the movie."[4] The video monitors were yet one more visual effect that made the atmosphere of Bloomingdale's unique and memorable. Tactics like these, noted one journalist, "transformed the stodgy, family oriented store into a virtual amusement park."[5] Press reports of the time noted that some customers came from as far away as Baltimore just to shop at Bloomingdale's for an afternoon.

Traub could hardly have been happier with the response—from both the public and the press. Make people gawk; persuade them to tell their friends; get them to come back. It was marketing strategy straight out of showbiz. "We try hard to sell the sizzle rather than the steak," said one of Traub's trusted lieutenants, Vice President Joseph Schnee.[6]

For many shoppers, the allure of Bloomingdale's was not just the scenery of the store or the merchandise within. It was also the other customers. Discovering Ralph Lauren in the late 1960s and breaking into the world of upscale men's fashions had been a critical success for Traub. Tapping into this market—and bringing young men to the store in large numbers—facilitated one of the most unique merchandising breakthroughs of the Traub era: Shopping at Bloomingdale's became part of the swinging-singles culture of 1970s New York. The transformation of the department store from a ladies emporium into a meeting place for young people reflected in part the ongoing makeover of the Upper East Side neighborhood around Bloomingdale's. After years as a drab neighborhood, sliced down the middle by the eyesore of the Third Avenue elevated subway, the Upper East Side had begun turning chic in the 1960s. New apartment high-rises were going up around the area, drawing flocks of young people who worked in lucrative jobs in the new office towers that were also going up on the East Side. Upscale restaurants and bars were opening everywhere. The Upper East Side emerged as the home of the Bloomingdale's target audience: young professionals with cash to spare. According to one survey taken in the early 1970s, over 60 percent of Bloomingdale's New York City customers lived or worked near the flagship store. In 1972, as Bloomingdale's celebrated its 100th anniversary, the New York store was among the most famous department stores of its day—or even of all time. It was, in the words of one observer, a "citadel of conspicuous consumption."

The promotion of men's fashions alongside womenswear meant that Bloomingdale's attracted shoppers of both sexes, allowing the store to engage in "young couple merchandising" for housewares and clothing.[7] Advertisements spoke of "The Bloomingdale's Man" as well as

"The Bloomingdale's Woman," providing the punchline for the *New Yorker* cartoon of 1973 that featured "The Bloomingdale's Couple."[8] "Your idea of bringing the two of us closer together always seems to be for me to go with you to Bloomingdale's," noted the male character in the cartoon.[9]

Traub promoted the idea that one could shop around for more than the merchandise at Bloomingdale's, observing avuncularly in 1972 that, "It is a place where the young make dates for the night."[10] Homosexual men, attracted by the men's fashions, also figured prominently in the Bloomingdale's singles scene. As a clearly visible social group for the first time in American society during the 1970s, many gays who moved to New York settled in the bustling new gay scene in the West Village. When they went to shop, the uptown Bloomingdale's—with the clothes of Ralph Lauren, Calvin Klein, and Halston—was a favorite destination. The welcoming atmosphere matched the merchandise offerings as part of Bloomingdale's appeal to gay men. Traub catered to these customers as ardently as any others. Marvin Traub may have come from a generation that was not exactly known for its embrace of alternative sexual lifestyles, but he himself was comfortable with the growing gay world. Ultimately, he was far more the son of his flamboyant parents than the product of the stoic male culture of the World War II era.

The allure that Traub and his colleagues had been striving to create reached a climax in the 1970s, when Bloomingdale's became synonymous with urban glamour. Taking the term "Saturday's Generation" as its catchphrase, the store promoted an image of itself as a "state of mind." Outrageous fun was packaged like a commodity, in store promotions that featured jugglers, fashion shows, parading ducks, and pulsating disco music. "On Saturdays, Bloomingdale's is the biggest party in town," Traub declared.[11] The party brought together the so-called Beautiful People with the fashions that showed their gifts to the best advantage. "I always feel as though I'm surrounded by kindred spirits at Bloomie's," said a customer who rode the train from Baltimore one Saturday in 1972. "It gives me a real high."[12] Drug references, a sign of 1970s chic, seemed to convey the sensation of making the scene at Bloomingdale's, which one observer described as "so heady as to require a tranquilizer."[13] For others, the experience approximated a sexual thrill.

One article of the time summed up the magnetism of the Bloomingdale's scene this way:

> They ooze out of the subway station of the Lexington Avenue Express and into the store's trend lower levels. They march in past the street peddlers who flank the doorways on Third and Lexington Avenues. They ascend and descend the escalators through eight stories of temptation. They come to Blo's to see and be seen. . . . They are the models and the television actresses, the realtor's wives and the agency secretaries (razor thin and stalking the newest hemline), the art directors and the security analysts thronging toward the fat bowties and the Yves Saint Laurent Suits for men, nursemaids pausing with baby strollers and leashed poodles to catch a whiff of Bulgarian rose at a perfume counter.[14]

Traub, who became the chief executive officer of Bloomingdale's in 1976, did not overlook the marketing potential of Bloomingdale's sexy profile. He assiduously promoted the image of Bloomingdale's as a singles destination. Marketing strategies affirmed the principle that sex sells. "We put a man in pajamas along with the model," commented one executive about an ad campaign for a cling-free nightgown, "and what an impact it had on sales."[15] A 1976 lingerie catalog distributed by Bloomingdale's-by-Mail featured provocative photographs by French photographer Guy Bourdin. The catalog, titled *Sighs and Whispers,* included shots of very young women wearing heavy makeup and little else. One showed a woman in underwear standing next to a discarded wedding gown, a man's hand beckoning from the right. Others framed models holding negligees in front of their naked bodies. Gratified by the tremendous publicity and increased sales of lingerie, Traub resolved to continue the sexy motif in catalog photography.[16] A related promotion featured a play on the double entendre of Bloomingdale's nickname, with "Bloomie's" naughtily scrawled across the back of women's underpants. More than 300,000 pairs of the panties sold in the first year, and the line became a perennial favorite.

The edgy, titillating style of Bloomingdale's didn't stop Traub and his store from winning respect from a titan of tradition. In July 1976, Bloomingdale's received one of its most exalted visitors ever: Queen Elizabeth, who made time for a stop at the store in a packed schedule during one of her rare visits to the United States. The store was entirely closed off for the visit, and Bloomingdale's vice president Carl Levine had the honor of guiding the queen and Prince Philip through a 26-minute whirlwind tour of the different displays. Traub, of course, was there too, in a beautiful suit, playing the gracious host and presenting the queen with an authentic Sioux peace pipe as a gift. To make it easier for the queen's motorcade to get to the store, Traub had convinced the city to allow the traffic on Lexington Avenue to flow north instead of south for a short time—no small feat. Traub would later comment of the queen that she "could have used some fashion advice. Her majesty was wearing a sleeveless dress of green dotted swiss with a matching turban, pearl earrings, a triple strand of pearls and her white gloves and handbag. It was attractive, but matronly."[17]

Besides Bloomingdale's, the queen went to Wall Street during her visit to New York. Wall Street and Bloomingdale's. What else, really, was worth seeing?

Bloomingdale's was also a destination for less regal celebrities like Catherine Deneuve and Gloria Vanderbilt. Rumors of such sightings, in turn, fed the store's appeal and brought even larger hordes to Bloomingdale's. Simply shopping at a place like Macy's was nothing compared to the potential of a trip to Bloomingdale's, which included possibly a date and a glimpse of a celebrity.

The success of the Bloomie's underwear line signaled the emergence of Bloomingdale's as a marketable label in its own right. The nickname, while a trifle undignified in the eyes of some observers, was "a triumph of customer identification."[18] The triumph reflected Marvin Traub's careful cultivation of Bloomingdale's as a brand name for chic and his promotion of the Bloomingdale's style in everything from housewares to clothing to novelty items. People from across the fashion and retailing world visited Bloomingdale's to figure out what Traub was up to. "Suddenly every buyer in the country shops Blo's to see what's new," said James Brady, publisher of *Harper's Bazaar.*[19]

Traub's showmanship was richly rewarded during the 1970s. The transformation of Bloomingdale's into a cultural destination and singles scene was reflected in the store's bottom line. Profits soared in the first part of the decade, hitting their peak in the mid-1970s and only partly declining by the end of the decade as the economy began to sour. The flagship store at 59th Street was a moneymaking machine of a kind seldom seen in department store history. With eight floors, the store had a total of 900,000 square feet, about 500,000 square feet of which was selling space. In 1979, the store was amassing annual profits of about $385 per square foot of selling space—outstripping all of its competitors. Through the 1970s, the flagship store had sales of over $100 million per year. This river of money was supplemented by the opening of other Bloomingdale's stores outside of Manhattan—14 stores by the end of the 1970s—and by the creation, in 1978, of major mail catalog business. Now, millions more Americans who had heard of Bloomingdale's could get in on the action. By 1981, the sales volume of Marvin Traub's store would top a half billion dollars a year. During the Christmas season, there were days when the revenue at Bloomingdale's stores was over $4 million in a single day.

Bloomingdale's was not the only store booming during the 1970s. Macy's, Saks Fifth Avenue, and other retail stores saw enormous profits as well. The general surge in retailing came as the huge baby boom generation moved into higher earning phases of their careers and showed an enormous consciousness about fashion. The single most important target audience for Bloomingdale's and similar stores was the fast-growing segment of upper-middle-class Americans, those who earned up to $35,000 a year. Beyond a general increase of wealth in American society, the influx of women into the workplace during the 1970s was another factor that drove up household incomes and created a larger pool of potential Bloomingdale's shoppers.

Ironically, one of the worst aspects of the economy of the 1970s, double-digit inflation, helped increase consumer spending, as people made purchases out of fear that the things they wanted to buy would only grow more expensive the following year, if not the following month. Another piece of bad economic news, the weak dollar abroad, particularly helped retailing in New York City as foreigners flocked to U.S. shores to take advantage of bargain vacation prices. In August 1979, six of New York City's biggest retailers registered a 17.6 percent jump in gains over the previous year—even as most other elements of the New York economy headed into recession.[20] But even in this atmosphere of high growth, Bloomingdale's stood out. "I think Blo's in the last decade has been the most successful store in town," Traub said in 1979.[21] Few people would dispute this claim.

Traub's tremendous success at Bloomingdale's meant not only personal financial rewards—his salary topped $300,000 in 1978—but also a growing profile in New York civic life. Along with his wife Lee, Traub believed that he had a responsibility to give something back to the community. While Lee gravitated toward helping dance and human rights causes, Marvin became interested in strengthening the Metropolitan Museum of Art, in improving Franco-American relations, and in other causes. Traub's personal commitments extended to the policies of the store he ran. He made a point of ensuring that the Bloomingdale's branches outside New York played a role in philanthropy. "I think a department store that clearly participates so much in the growth of a community has a responsibility to help with the philanthropies in that community," he would explain. "And I think using the Bloomingdale's stores to help both publicize and raise money for those causes is absolutely appropriate."[22]

Marvin Traub was not the only 49er who had gone into the retail world and done well. Jack Muller was in the same world, but had taken a very different path to success. After Harvard, Muller had gone to work at Macy's and had spent most of his early career there, becoming manager of drugs and toiletries. Then he had moved on to General Foods, where he spent five years and, in time, found himself not very fulfilled. He had become tired of toiling away in huge companies. Muller wanted more money and more excitement. In 1967, Tom Murphy—ever the career counselor to his friends—told Muller that he should take a leap and get into business on his own. Muller's father, who had barely survived the Depression, was appalled when his son broached this idea. "You've got to be crazy!" Muller remembers his father saying. "You're going to leave a big company to start your own?" Muller forged ahead, undeterred by his father's conservatism. Researching different prospects, Muller was told that he should buy a consumer-products company—a surefire growth industry in the years ahead, as Muller himself well knew.

Taking his research efforts to the display floors of his old employer, Macy's, Muller examined different consumer products. He came across a set of utilitarian products—laundry baskets, ironing boards, and stepladders—that struck him as "dull as hell stuff," but also an area of major opportunity. He located a Minnesota company named J.R. Clarke that made such products, raised $1.6 million from his friends in New York, and bought the company. "I spent six months with no income," Muller remembers.

The venture succeeded. Gathering momentum from his initial success in building J.R. Clarke, renamed General Housewares, Muller took the company public on Wall Street in 1969 with a very lucrative initial public offering. "It was heady wine," he recalls, of the river of cash that flowed in from the IPO. By the mid-1970s, Muller had turned J.R. Clarke into General Housewares, a $56 million per year company. He found the whole experience an amazing adventure. "I was caught up like a girl going to Hollywood," Muller said in 1974. "To have gotten this far has really been exhilarating."[23]

Thirty miles to the south of Marvin Traub's office on 59th Street, at the campuslike headquarters of Johnson & Johnson in New Brunswick, New Jersey, Jim Burke was another 49er trying to understand the thinking of American consumers during the 1970s and capture their allegiance. Burke's office in New Brunswick was uncluttered and elegant. To combat his notorious sloppy side, Burke had long ago dispensed with a desk. He sat instead at a conference table and gave all his papers to his secretaries, asking them to bring him one document at a time. The streamlined feel of the big office made for clear and focused strategizing.

Like Traub, Burke saw himself as an out-of-the-box thinker and a man with an intuitive sense of marketing. Like Traub, too, Burke had particularly strong affection for the class of 1949. Fit and energetic as he hit his 50s, with a receded hairline and a scrunched nose bridge that made him look slightly pugnacious, Burke was a pillar of The Group and valued his friendships with other 49ers above almost all others in his life. In this group of driven men, Burke was perhaps the most driven of all. On a ski vacation in the mid-1970s with McColough and Murphy, Burke was so fixated on the battle to have Tylenol win greater market share that he checked local drugstores to see what kind of shelf space the pain reliever was being given. One day, he dragged Murphy, McColough, and another friend into a drugstore in Denver to literally count the bottles of Tylenol stocked on the shelves. Though titans of the business world, the men were not so recognizable that they would attract notice. Instead, they simply looked odd: a group of middle-aged men in a drugstore counting out bottles of pain reliever.

The episode was pure Burke. Even as Burke's enormous drive allowed him ascend to the plum job at Johnson & Johnson, becoming CEO in 1976 and making over $250,000 a year before bonuses, he remained a hands-on manager. He was the kind of man who wanted to see the data himself, and he was not above poring over spreadsheets and getting into small details. "I make it my business to reach down into the organization periodically to challenge just about anything," Burke explained.[24] For example, Burke would study trends in television programming, observe how health issues were treated, and try to correlate them to Johnson & Johnson's business strategy. A different kind of CEO would simply have tasked this job to marketing or research and listened to a short presentation on the subject or glanced over a brief memo. Not Burke. In the 1950s, as a junior executive at Johnson & Johnson, Burke had developed a reputation for questioning the conventional wisdom. In the 1970s, nothing had changed except for Burke's title. Burke's aggressiveness and curiosity pulled him into all aspects of J&J's operations. "I've never known anyone who is successful who is not curious about everything," Burke once said, underlining his philosophy of life—and management.[25] Burke's hunger for knowledge also drew him to people outside the business world. Fancying himself as something of a Renaissance man, Burke liked to invite various scientists and health thinkers to lunch with the executive committee of Johnson & Johnson.

During all of Burke's years at J&J, perhaps few crusades would more thoroughly harness his personal drive than the battle to establish Tylenol as a leading painkiller during the 1970s. Tylenol, of course, would become famous in 1982 when some of its capsules were found laced with cyanide. But well before the battle to save Tylenol was the battle to establish Tylenol as a leader in the pain-reliever market. This battle was among the most important in J&J's history because of the vast revenues and profits at stake. For Burke, the struggle would be a major turning point.

Tylenol was developed in 1959 by McNeil Laboratories, a J&J subsidiary. McNeil chose to market it as a high-priced drug with high profit margins. But Burke, ever ambitious and always looking for new opportunities, imagined a bigger future for Tylenol. He saw the ever growing amount of consumer spending that was flowing into pain relievers as the American public moved beyond no-frills aspirin bottles and sought to attack their headaches with more sophisticated products. The area was a gold mine—over a half billion dollars by the middle of the 1970s. As with any emerging market, Burke knew that the products that got there first and established consumer allegiance would likely dominate for years to come. Burke urged McNeil Laboratories to turn Tylenol into a contender. He wanted to go for the mass market with lower prices and more-aggressive advertising.

As a subsidiary within J&J's decentralized structure, McNeil had some leeway in deciding how to respond to suggestions from the company's high command. The decision was made to pass on Burke's suggestion. Burke tried an end run, in which he marketed the same product under the name "Truce" through Johnson & Johnson Home Products. "The name Truce was kind of funny," Burke said later, "because there was plenty of warring between our companies when we did it." Truce failed to win the hearts and minds of consumers, but Burke did not surrender.[26]

In 1975, when Bristol-Myers Company introduced Datril, an acetaminophen formula similar to Tylenol at a much lower price, Burke found his chance to again push the mass-market strategy. Burke argued that Tylenol either had to make the leap to mass market or face extinction by Datril. "I didn't feel there was any decision at all," Burke said later. Dick Sellers, Johnson & Johnson's CEO, agreed with Burke.[27]

Reintroducing Tylenol at a competitive price, Burke set out to make it the number one headache reliever on the market. Burke aimed to make Tylenol not just the biggest-selling analgesic brand, but also the biggest-selling Johnson & Johnson product. No expense would be spared in the crusade. Burke had his troops flood doctors' offices and pharmacies with Johnson & Johnson representatives, urging them to recommend Tylenol to their patients and customers. He fought for turf against Bristol-Myers and American Home Products, the makers of the best-selling Anacin. Sweating the details of his marketing strategy, Burke lobbied grocery store managers and drugstore clerks for more shelf space, as he had in Denver with McColough and Murphy.[28] Drawing on his experience in the 1960s with baby products, he unleashed a hugely expensive advertising blitz on television, radio, and print media.[29] Jim Burke wasn't a marketing expert by training. He learned what he knew through his hands-on work with marketers during the 1960s. As he moved up in the company, he continued this style. Ad people who worked with Burke were awed by his intuitive command of the art of selling. "Burke is simply the best marketing man I've ever seen," said Edward N. Ney, a leading ad executive who worked for years with J&J.[30]

Burke's ambitious vision for Tylenol worked exactly as he imagined. By the end of the 1970s, Tylenol sales totaled $350 million annually, a whopping 35 percent of the analgesics market. The hated enemy, Anacin, saw its dominance toppled, and other competition was marginalized. Johnson & Johnson projected a 50 percent market share by 1986.[31]

In another great battle of the 1970s, Burke was the field marshal of a long campaign to introduce J&J disposable diapers and win serious market share in this area. As with Tylenol, Burke first had to fight an internal battle to win support for the idea of moving into the diaper market. Burke prevailed in this struggle, and J&J began pouring tens of millions of dollars into this arena. By 1978, the company had spent nearly $100 million on developing, producing, and marketing its brand of disposable diapers. Again, the investment paid off as the new J&J product began to win a significant share of a lucrative market.

Jim Burke's triumphs during the 1970s made him one of the most respected business leaders in America. But Burke, always relentless in his drive, was typically wary. As he saw it, Johnson & Johnson was playing a risky game in which the company moved ever more deeply into a growth strategy predicted on spending vast amounts of money on advertising in order to win market share for new products and then to protect that market share from competitors. The endless and staggering costs of promotion seriously bit into profits. "The question is whether we are going to be able to achieve margins adequate to generate the capital necessary to continue the kind of growth rates we are capable of achieving," Burke said in 1978. "If we don't, then the company ought to go out and get a new chairman."[32]

Jim Burke could not possibly have known then that diminishing profitability was not the greatest challenge he would face in the next few years. A far more terrible crisis would present itself when a diabolical criminal mind zeroed in on Tylenol.

9

Empire Building

In the early 1970s, Robert Baldwin feared that he was getting soft. Things were becoming too comfortable for Baldwin, who ran a prospering Volkswagen dealership in Connecticut. The business netted him up to $100,000 in a good year, and Baldwin's net worth in his mid-40s was approaching $1 million. Baldwin feared complacency in himself because he had seen it before. After graduating from Harvard Business School, Baldwin had been one of the majority of 49ers who'd taken the safe and easy path, first landing a numbingly boring job in the controller's office at Chrysler and then trading that in for another bureaucratic position in production control at Ford. He endured this kind of life for only a few years before making his big break. He borrowed $100,000 to buy a Ford dealership and, by the late 1950s, had assembled a small group of profitable businesses. But that life, too, had become easy. In 1961, Baldwin sold everything and started again from scratch with the Volkswagen agency in Connecticut.

The first years were challenging, with a mountain of debt hanging over him. But things started getting easier as Volkswagens became among the hottest foreign cars in America. Soon Baldwin paid off all the debts incurred during his start-up. By the early 1970s, he was effortlessly making money hand over fist. And so he feared he was getting soft, losing his nerve. When he looked in the mirror, he saw a middle-aged man with gray hair combed over thinning spots and deep creases in his face. He needed a shot in the arm, but this time, a new business venture didn't seem like the answer.

Baldwin came up with another idea for rejuvenating his spirit and rebuilding his nerve: He took up skydiving.

Robert Baldwin's experience of restlessness was not uncommon among 49ers. Conrad Jones confronted this restlessness in the form of a midlife crisis. At age 52, he was a senior vice president in the premier consulting firm of Booz, Allen & Hamilton in New York City. He had been with the firm for over 20 years, working his way up from a junior position in the Chicago office. His specialty was developing new products, and Jones was considered a leading expert in this field, his advice handsomely paid for by leading companies around the world. Inside Booz, Allen, he was highly respected. He sat on the firm's board and was extremely well compensated. By nearly any measure, Jones was a success in life. Yet he felt that things had reached a dead end. He didn't feel that he was going to rise higher at Booz, Allen, and he worried about sticking around and becoming deadwood. "I came to feel that I was no longer needed," he said later. He sensed that he had reached the end of "life one" and announced to his partners that he was going to take early retirement. After they objected, he agreed to take only a one-year sabbatical.

In 1977, Jones interrupted his 20-year routine of going to the office. Alone with himself and his life, without the distractions of work, Jones made some changes. He decided he wasn't happy in his marriage of 35 years and divorced. He began writing poetry, and by the end of his sabbatical had written a whole volume. His imagination refired, reminded of all the pleasures of life, he determined that he didn't actually want to retire. "I had enjoyed life so much that as I faced the idea of conventionally going over the hill and into autumn, I refused," he said. Jones returned to Booz, Hamilton.[1]

Retirement wasn't even an option in the minds of many 49ers as they hit their 50s. They were an exceptionally driven group. Over the years, they had speculated that the war was responsible for the overachievement ethos among the 49ers. Nearly every single one of these men had had their early lives interrupted by World War II, and for years afterward they had the sensation of coming from behind. It was interesting how this played out as the years went on: Even as they streaked far ahead in the world of business, many 49ers kept racing as if they needed to catch up. Their definition of success, moreover, also tended to be shaped by their generational experience. Yes, they wanted to make money. What business person didn't? But the more powerful drive was to build companies. They were in the game for the joy of creating things, not for superficial rewards like sports cars and beach houses.

The value of building something may have seemed obvious to the 49ers, but it was an idea increasingly moving out of fashion. By the 1970s, the generational divide between the business leaders of the World War II era and the new leaders coming up through the ranks was growing. In 1978, 49ers who paid attention to their alma mater received some stunning news: Nearly a quarter of the Harvard MBA class graduating that June had taken jobs as consultants, some making as much as $40,000 in their first job out of school. The percentage of Harvard MBA graduates going into consulting in 1978 was roughly twice what it had been in 1977—a trend that reflected huge shifts in the business world away from manufacturing and extraction industries.[2]

While many 49ers were perplexed by the trend toward consulting, they were far from out of it as times changed. The tremendous restlessness of leading class members made its mark in one area of business after another in the 1970s as the 49ers did what they knew best: created wealth through expanding businesses.

Of all the 49ers who scaled new heights in the 1970s, perhaps none would be more publicly celebrated than Xerox's Peter McColough. He was seen as a business leader for a new age, harnessing emerging technologies in bold and innovative ways.

In person, McColough was anything but the archetype of the driven corporate leader. His physical presence was uncommanding. He was on the short side, bald with a round and pink face. He was a gregarious, social man, but he spoke with a courtly manner and didn't draw attention to himself. Like his father, a Canadian civil servant, McColough was entirely unpretentious. His lifestyle, too, suggested an altogether different profile than that of one of America's most successful corporate leaders. Even as he drove himself to the top of Xerox and in turn drove

Xerox to the pinnacle of the corporate world, McColough led a life of extraordinary balance. He still took six to eight weeks of vacation each year—enough to travel widely and truly relax.

Part of McColough's downtime strategy was aimed at giving himself time to think freely and creatively. But mainly, McColough simply believed in relaxation as an end in itself. His lifestyle reflected a vow he had made years earlier, while still at Harvard, that he would never work himself too hard. "As a young person, I had some concern that what I didn't want to do in my life was to wake up at some great advanced age having just had a business career, perhaps having made a lot of money, but really just having done that," McColough said in 1979. "Perhaps you've wrecked your health and had no relationship with your family or wife or anyone else, and you've not taken time for recreation. And then maybe you don't have the strength to do some of the things you might like to do."[3] At Harvard, McColough's philosophy of life had translated into minimal studying and maximum partying. At Xerox, it translated into long sailing and skiing trips as well as spending lots of time with his wife and with his three college-age children.

McColough's life philosophy also emphasized valuing public service and making time for it. By the mid-1970s, McColough estimated that he spent maybe 40 to 50 percent of his time on public service. His stardom at Xerox, along with his vast wealth from the company's stock, ensured nearly limitless set of opportunities for such work, and McColough took on a range of roles. He pursued his love of politics, serving as the treasurer of the Democratic National Committee from 1974 through 1976, helping to raise millions for Democratic candidates. He also took a major interest in charity, serving as chairman of the United Way of America for several years. In 1979, he took on the job of chairing President Carter's Commission on Pensions Policy. "I happen to like politics, probably as much as my business," he said in an interview with the *Harvard Business Review*.[4]

McColough's liberal political views were reflected at Xerox, which he made a leader in affirmative action and other forms of corporate responsibility. McColough deeply believed that corporations had an obligation to help solve America's many problems. Like Roger Sonnabend, McColough saw himself as a business leader for a new age of enlightened capitalism. At the annual Xerox shareholder meeting in 1970, an angry woman accused McColough of funding social programs that encouraged student uprisings. McColough's reply took the long view: "This is the worst time in our country's history to show that corporations are only concerned about profits and have no concern for the problems of society. I think that would be suicidal."[5]

As with his long vacations, McColough felt that his public service gave him balance and perspective. "When you are around your own business and you have a lot of problems, you can think that this is the whole world," McColough commented in the late 1970s. "But sometimes I get a little perspective when I drive home at night, and I think, really, if Xerox itself completely disappeared tonight, it would be very bad for stockholders, and employees would lose their jobs, but basically the world is not going to be very different."[6]

Still, even as he put work into perspective, McColough did not rest easily on the company's success. In fact, he shared with other Xerox executives a preoccupation with the long-term viability of the flagship product, xerographic copiers. "The executives knew that Carlson's invention [the Xerox photocopier] had created this enormous market just like that," observed David Kearns, a longtime Xerox official who succeeded McColough as CEO in 1982. "And they feared that— poof—it could disappear just as suddenly."[7] McColough, Kearns, and the others worried that a new invention could conceivably produce copies faster and cheaper than their method, rendering the entire line of Xerox products obsolete. As a result, Xerox laboratories avoided photocopying research. If there was a better method out there for making copies, Xerox did not want to know about it. Instead, the company devoted its resources to diversification, both within the product line and in subsidiary companies. Xerox made a series of acquisitions in educational services, publishing, finance, insurance, and computers that served to hedge its bets against a photocopying revolution. Copier revenues continued to make up more than 90 percent of Xerox's earnings in the 1970s, but McColough was eager to set the corporation on a broader foundation.[8]

The drive to diversify Xerox showcased Peter McColough as a visionary leader, perhaps his greatest strength as a chief executive. Although disaster lay down the road for McColough's Xerox, the vision of the company he articulated in the early 1970s was striking in its simplicity, its logic, and its prescience. The infrastructure of the white-collar workplace in the 1970s, McColough observed, had changed very little during the previous century, even as automation and innovation had transformed many businesses. In a U.S. economy increasingly geared toward services and information, the office remained the backwater of the corporate world, dependent on antiquated machinery like typewriters and adding machines, as well as bulky, unmanageable storage systems. As the providers of the most ubiquitous fully automated piece of office equipment available, the photocopier, Xerox was in a strong position to think big. It had the technical expertise and marketing muscle to change the American office place. Under McColough, Xerox set out to expand the frontiers of possibility by envisioning the office of the future and making the products that would transform it.

Business audiences openly scoffed at McColough's bid for the "nebulous market" in facsimile machines, word processors, laser printers, and "other exotica that is supposed to transform the office much as automation has transformed the factory."[9] When McColough spoke about the office of the future, remembered a financial analyst, "People didn't even understand what he was talking about." There was "no such buzzword" in the business lexicon of the 1970s.[10] Much as it had in the 1950s during the development of the xerographic process, Xerox in the 1970s set out to educate itself about the technology of the future.

If the business community was skeptical, another audience welcomed McColough's endorsement of a new architecture for information as a call to action. Since the early 1960s, a loose confederation of computer scientists, physicists, and engineers had pursued an innovative ideal for research and development. The goal, which first emerged in the U.S. Department of Defense Advanced Research Projects Agency (ARPA), was to create computers that could assist individual users in a variety of information-processing tasks. At a time when computer technology was geared toward macro-users and massive information systems (the first digital computer, ENIAC, completed in 1946, weighed 30 tons and stood two stories high), the idea of a personal computer that served as an electronic partner for individual users was purely radical. When federal funding began to falter, advocates of personal computers moved to academic settings, especially Stanford University in Palo Alto, California, and the University of Utah in Salt Lake City.[11]

McColough was determined to push forward this work with two big, long-term investments. First, Xerox shocked many observers when it laid out nearly $1 billion in 1969 to purchase Scientific Data Systems

(SDS), a mainframe computer company that had been built by Max Palevsky. The move was shocking—and disturbing to Wall Street analysts—because even in its best year, SDS had never made more than $10 million in profits. McColough insisted, however, that the acquisition tremendously increased the corporation's understanding of what he called "the architecture of information."[12]

McColough's second big investment was the establishment in 1970 of a Xerox facility for digital information technology research. The facility was known as the Palo Alto Research Center (PARC), and it created a home for the ARPA dream in corporate America. Embarking on a collaborative venture with inventors and scientists that dwarfed the visionary partnership with Chester Colson in the 1950s, McColough moved Xerox to the cutting edge of information technology. It was the place to be. The year Xerox PARC opened was the year the first floppy disk appeared and, in 1971, Intel Corporation invented the single-chip microprocessor. The future was closer than ever.

The low-slung terraces of the Palo Alto Research Center, which clings to a hillside overlooking the Stanford campus, have been called "the Hanging Gardens of the Information Age."[13] Like a benevolent Los Alamos laboratory, PARC attracted the foremost minds in the field and infused the participants with a bracing sense of purpose. The atmosphere rewarded brilliance and encouraged teamwork, providing academic-style freedoms for its top talents and convening meetings in a "beanbag room" that fostered informality and egalitarianism. Xerox provided the funds—$100 million over the course of the 1970s—but allowed PARC employees to pursue basic research with minimal consideration of marketing deadlines and business priorities.[14]

The results were spectacular. Research at PARC coalesced around the goal of creating a personal computer that "could be owned by everyone and could have the power to handle virtually all of its owner's information-related needs." In 1976, PARC scientists Alan Kay and Adele Goldberg predicted that such technology was not only possible, but that the computer itself would serve as a kind of "dynamic paper" in a case the size of a notebook.[15] Users of Bravo, an early Xerox word processing program, or the graphics software called SuperPaint, could see the text or images that they were creating on the same display as the command icons. The mouse, a pointing device designed by PARC scientist Douglas Englehart, allowed users to input commands or move back and forth between a selection of programs or files at the click of a button. Files in use could be arranged in a series of overlapping windows, which were accessed by using the mouse. Other files could be stored on removable disks.[16] Driven by the vision of the dynamic book, PARC scientists thus pioneered the hardware and operating infrastructure of the computer revolution.

PARC scientists did not develop a notebook computer in the 1970s, but they did succeed in creating the prototype components of the office of the future that McColough had envisioned. By 1973, early versions of the Xerox Alto were in production at PARC and available to a small number of commercial customers. Alto has been called "the most important unannounced computer product of the 1970s."[17] Its bitmapped screen displayed both text and command-driven icons that were activated using the mouse. The machine boasted 64 kilobytes of memory, the equivalent of 64 typed pages in an era when state-of-the-art word processing machines could accommodate only three pages. Other files could be stored on Alto's 2.5-megabyte removable disk drive. Alto's peripheral appliances anticipated some of the most important innovations of the 1980s and 1990s: a high-speed laser printer, an automatic-dial voice-messaging system, a text scanner, and the Ethernet networking system, which allowed computer workstations to share files and communicate electronically.[18] In 1981, Xerox announced that Alto technology had been readied for market in the form of the advanced Star workstation, which possessed 192 kilobytes of memory and 10 megabytes of hard drive storage and used the full range of peripheral office equipment. After 10 years of forward-looking research and development, Xerox was ready to sell the office of the future that McColough had envisioned.

Xerox's Star, unfortunately, arrived too late. By 1981, the innovations that had put the Alto in a class by itself had been widely disseminated among the community of computer scientists and entrepreneurs who had come together in Palo Alto. Ideas developed at PARC found their way into the laboratories of a new generation of information-technology firms, rivals that Xerox had never anticipated. PARC's hardware specialists, including PARC director Lawrence Tesler, Dynabook prophet Alan Kay, and Alto specialist Jeffrey Raskin, took up residence with Steve Jobs and the neighboring Apple Computing Corporation, where they modified Alto designs for the Apple's Lisa and Macintosh

computers. Some of the programmers from PARC began writing soft-
ware for Bill Gates's Seattle-based Microsoft Corporation, which won
the contract to develop IBM's operating system software in 1981.
Others established their own firms, which eventually included Adobe
Systems Incorporated, SynOptics Communications, Inc., and Pixar.
While Xerox succeeded in marketing the laser printer developed at
PARC, the company introduced some of the other discoveries only in
partnerships with other, smaller firms such as Intel Corporation, Digital
Equipment Corporation, and 3Com. So many good ideas made their
way from PARC into the portfolios of competing organizations that
outsiders began to refer to the Xerox facility as "a national resource."[19]

The failure to translate PARC's innovations into Xerox profits was
compounded by other problems facing the company. The acquisition of
Scientific Data Systems had turned out to be an utter fiasco. Despite the
nearly $1 billion price tag and tens of millions of dollars in additional
Xerox investments in SDS, the company steadily lost money. Journalists
mocked it as "McColough's Folly." Max Palevsky, who had sold SDS to
McColough, was rumored to have remarked: "We sold them a dead
horse before it hit the ground."[20] Finally, with nothing to show for its
investment, Xerox disbanded SDS in 1975.[21] At the same time that SDS
was failing, Xerox found itself facing a federal antitrust suit that challenged its monopoly of the photocopying industry. Although the suit
was eventually resolved in Xerox's favor, McColough and other top
executives had their time endlessly siphoned away in long sessions with
company lawyers.

The PARC and SDS calamities reflected the liabilities of
McColough's hands-off management style. While the boss kept his
eye on the future and devoted significant energies to politics and charity, the corporation lost sight of the bigger picture, including its position within the increasingly crowded office products market of the
1970s. Xerox discovered too late that U.S. and Japanese providers of
office copiers—including Canon, Ricoh, IBM, and others—had
eroded its share of the U.S. copier market. The discovery initiated a
scramble to recover the position of its flagship product line that
diverted financial resources and attention away from the long-term
development projects at PARC. The business strategy for Xerox's
information technology also suffered as a result of rivalries between

the Palo Alto–based researchers and the corporate officers at head-quarters in Rochester. The cultural disconnect between the pinstriped professionals who made the business decisions for Xerox and the free-spirited computer crowd created mistrust on both sides. Above all, perhaps, Xerox's fumbling of the future of information technology reflected the classic scenario of corporate Goliaths being felled by entrepreneurial newcomers. While Xerox was working toward the perfect office workstation, Jobs and Gates were catering to the cottage industry of computer hobbyists and Silicon Valley specialists that emerged in the 1970s.

Looking back on the unlikely success of the Xerox Corporation years before the PARC fiasco, McColough noted "that many of the great new industries are not developed by the big companies. Rather they come from unexpected places and from people who don't know any better [than] that they can't succeed."[22] The assessment provided a fitting epi-taph for Xerox's foray into information technology in the 1970s.

Jim Burke once said that if the class of 1949 had taken a vote on who was most likely to succeed, Tom Murphy "would have won hands down."[23] During the early 1970s, another such vote might have been far closer. Murphy was still seen as a class star, but other 49ers were far more in the limelight. Perhaps McColough would have won the vote, or maybe Jim Burke or Marvin Traub. Everyone knew that Murphy had been patiently building a media conglomerate, but many of them didn't fully sense what the long-term trajectory of this effort would be. Com-pared to a superstar like McColough, Murphy was virtually unknown in the 1970s, receiving little attention from the business press. The facts of his career, of course, were extremely impressive: By 1976, at the age of 51, Tom Murphy had built Capital Cities into a $175 million media empire with both print and broadcasting holdings across America and annual profits of $25 million. The company had an impressive track record of increasing its net profits for 21 years straight. Murphy was paid a handsome $260,000 annually, and the value of his stock holdings made him a multimillionaire. Still, outside select circles of business, nobody had ever heard of Tom Murphy. Even in the business world, mention of the name Tom Murphy made people think of Thomas Murphy, the president and chairman of General Motors, not the "other Tom Murphy" of Cap Cities.

The New York headquarters of Capital Cities underscored Murphy's low profile. Located in the elegant Villard building in midtown, the offices were well appointed but inconspicuous, filling a single floor. The staff that managed Cap Cities' far-flung holdings was surprisingly small, with just a few dozen people working in New York. The modest staff reflected Cap Cities' willingness to give wide autonomy to its media businesses. But it also reflected Murphy's business philosophy about keeping operating costs low and not drawing too much attention to yourself.

The low profile was classic Murphy. Friends from Harvard and elsewhere knew Murphy, or "Murph," as the kind of guy who was always at the center of the action but seldom the center of attention. As he became a mover and shaker in the media world, Murphy managed to remain surprisingly down to earth. Bald and somewhat nondescript in his appearance, with a lanky build, thin lips, and a lined face, Murphy didn't stand out in a crowd. He had a relaxed and easygoing manner, his conversation sprinkled with phrases like "you betcha" and "kiddo." Across a room, he'd be ready with a wink and smile. It was easy for those who didn't know Murphy to underestimate him. "I've seen people misread him and think he's just a happy-go-lucky salesman," commented John Grimm III, who came to know Murphy well and saw his iron side not just in the business world but also on the squash court, where the two battled in fierce games several times a week.[24]

Murphy's ascent to new heights during the 1970s was a carefully orchestrated campaign. Since taking over as CEO of Cap Cities in 1966 after the sudden death of Frank Smith from a heart attack, Tom Murphy had mounted one brilliant and risky business gambit after another. He'd put tens of millions of dollars on the line to buy new media properties for Cap Cities. Almost all the ventures succeeded. In 1966, many had doubted that Murphy could ever fill the shoes of Smith. Within a year, it was obvious that Murphy was more than up to the challenge. And by the 1970s, Murphy was seen as something of a business genius in his own right.

Strategizing every move with Murphy was Dan Burke, appointed corporate president for publications in 1969 and the de facto number two at Cap Cities. Burke had originally been at General Foods before starting with Cap Cities in the 1950s. By the 1960s, the relationship between the two men was extraordinarily close. "We finish each other's sentences," Burke would tell friends. Murphy felt a natural affinity for Burke. As Jim Burke's younger brother, Dan Burke was almost family. Murphy trusted him completely in matters of business, and this trust in turn endeared Burke to Murphy.

The tone of their relationship had been set early on when Murphy hired Burke as his replacement at the television station in Albany. "He had no television experience," Murphy would say later. No matter: "I always had a policy that you hire the smartest people you possibly can. You bet on brains, not experience." Burke was flattered by Murphy's estimate of his intellect, but also a bit overwhelmed by the amount of responsibility with which he had been vested: "He left me there in charge, and it was interesting because for at least six weeks, knowing that I had no experience, he never called or checked in." The smart, hard-working Burke excelled at his new job, even more so than Murphy had imagined he might. "It quickly became clear to me that he was the most gifted person at our company." Later, Murphy didn't think twice about elevating Burke to the number two job, and once Burke was in that job, Murphy's natural inclination was to give Burke wide authority and respect. "He very quickly became my equal partner," Murphy said later. "We never disagreed on any major issue."[25]

With Murphy's trusted lieutenant at the helm, print media emerged as the focus of corporate acquisitions at Cap Cities. Still constrained by FCC guidelines, the growing company shifted its focus away from the broadcast industry after trading up to bigger, more lucrative markets with the purchase of Walter Annenberg's Triangle Publications in 1970. For the next 15 years, Murphy and Burke concentrated on print media, nurturing Cap Cities' growing portfolio of magazines and trade dailies, which already accounted for half of the company's revenues.[26] Mass-circulation daily newspapers, however, were the jewels in the crown of the publications industry. In 1970, newspaper circulation was in the middle of long and steep decline—yet newspapers still absorbed almost a quarter of all advertising expenditures, a portion worth nearly $5 billion. Newspaper advertising revenues dwarfed television and radio advertising accounts, which together amounted to slightly more than $3 billion.[27] With plenty of investment capital on hand and his appetite for profits undiminished, Murphy set out to conquer yet another business frontier.

The *Pontiac Press,* later renamed the *Oakland Press,* was Cap Cities' first newspaper acquisition, purchased in 1969. The newspaper served suburban Detroit, including some of the area's wealthiest neighborhoods, with a circulation of 90,000. Acquiring the *Pontiac Press,* Cap Cities got a crash course in the difficulties of the newspaper business. The first three years saw declining subscriptions (as circulation stabilized in the aftermath of a disastrous strike at the *Detroit Free Press*), a consumer boycott prompted by a pro-integration editorial, and a six-day standoff with striking workers from the Newspaper Guild.[28] Undeterred, Murphy and Burke oversaw the acquisition of a second daily, the *Belleville News-Democrat* in the St. Louis area, in 1972.

In newspapers as in the broadcast industries, Cap Cities took care to avoid the appearance of outside tampering. Editorial autonomy remained absolute, establishing a disconnect between corporate and local politics that sometimes jarred Murphy's Republican friends.[29] The New York office left local managers in place and allowed them to make their own operating decisions. "[T]hey showed us how to report the numbers to them, then we never saw anyone for a year," remembered one editor.[30]

Capital Cities entered a bigger market—and encountered more substantial problems—with the purchase of the *Kansas City Star* in 1977. The deal cost Murphy and Burke $125 million. The previous owners had left a troublesome legacy, with excess staff and low salaries for the newspaper's executives, circumstances that seemed ill suited to Cap Cities' practice of permitting autonomy for new acquisitions. Traveling to Kansas City, Murphy ordered a wholesale purge of the deadweight in an assault remembered by employees as "Black Tuesday."[31] In the first 10 years after the takeover, no fewer than five chief editors tried and failed to meet Capital Cities' expectations. Years later, a *Star* employee remarked that there were still plenty of newspaper employees that "hadn't forgotten [Murphy's] steely blue eyes."[32]

Trouble arrived in earnest in 1978 with the purchase of the *Times Leader* in Wilkes-Barre, Pennsylvania, and the onset of a serious strike at the *Oakland Press.* The *Times Leader*'s bargain price reflected problems in its labor relations. After years of working with a highly favorably contract, workers confronted tough negotiations with Capital Cities. When the union elected to strike, the new ownership refused to interrupt publication and a fierce standoff ensued. "It was war from the word go," remembered a union leader.[33] The strike lasted four and a half years, punctuated by extreme measures on both sides. The strikers started publishing a rival paper, the *Citizens' Voice,* which was so successful it survived the strike.[34] Cap Cities, meanwhile, used its massive resources to outmaneuver the opposition, employing a tough labor law firm and importing employees from its other newspapers to keep the presses rolling.[35] By the 1980s, Cap Cities' labor relations were so bad that the AFL-CIO listed the company on its dishonor roll, naming it "the most hard-line anti-union media conglomerate in the nation."[36] Murphy himself did not escape the union's wrath. "If I ever get to hell, I know I'll meet him there," a Newspaper Guild official swore.[37]

The irony of Cap Cities' union-busting policies was that the company was hardly hurting. In the 1970s, corporate revenues increased 390 percent and per-share profits rose 500 percent.[38] While wages were stagnating or falling in real terms for average workers who labored on Cap Cities papers, Murphy and his company were assembling enormous riches. By 1983, Cap Cities would report revenues of $390 million in the publishing division and pretax earnings of $79 million, a profit margin of 20 percent. The earnings fit the pattern of Capital Cities' spectacular overall performance during the company's first three decades, a winning streak that never seemed to end.[39] Under Tom Murphy's careful stewardship—and a tightfistedness that looked like outright greed to unions—the money rolled in with no end in sight.

For those who worked with Murphy or who had known him years earlier at Harvard Business School, it was easy to imagine that the money would keep rolling in forever. Beyond Murphy's track record, one reason to have confidence in him was the supreme confidence that he seemed to have in himself. He was incredibly and unfailingly optimistic about everything. "There are no such things as problems," he liked to say, "only opportunities." His long-term friends, members of The Group like Jim Burke, had seen this quality in him from the earliest days at Harvard. They knew, in fact, that Murphy wouldn't even have been at Harvard if he hadn't been so incorrigibly optimistic that he didn't take no for an answer when he first approached the school about admission.

Decades later, with huge successes under his belt, Murphy's optimism was so uncontainable that his friends sometimes worried that he was not attuned enough to the potential downsides of things. Burke would say, "I used to tell him, 'Murph, the only problem you have is that you don't know when you have one.' " John Muller, another member of The Group, saw Murphy's extreme self-confidence as his one potential weakness: "Because he likes to look at things simply, he can sometimes jump to conclusions."[40]

Beyond print media, Murphy was also winning with his television investments. A key to his success in this area was Capital Cities' close association with the American Broadcasting Company (ABC) in the 1970s, which boosted revenues in the company's broadcast operations. The network scored with the debut of *Monday Night Football* in 1970, a show that virtually created the National Football League.[41] Monday night's lineup also included the *Partridge Family,* the risqué variety show, *Love, American Style,* and the campy *Mod Squad.* By mid-decade, ABC's offerings included the most popular Tuesday night selections of the day, with *Happy Days* and its spinoff hit, *Laverne and Shirley.* On Wednesdays, Americans tuned to ABC for *Welcome Back, Kotter, Eight Is Enough,* and the ratings sensation *Charlie's Angels.* Other time slots featured two hit shows aimed at African Americans (*What's Happening!* and *The Redd Foxx Show*), the *Hardy Boys* and *Nancy Drew* mysteries, and the perennially popular *Love Boat* and *Fantasy Island.* In addition to its regular programming, ABC offered miniseries that set the industry standard, including *Roots,* which premiered in eight episodes in 1977. ABC's daily morning show, *Good Morning, America* hosted by David Hartman, persistently rated number one among A.M. viewers.

Cap Cities' ABC stations had been number one in most of their markets even when the network itself had been running a sorry third in the ratings race.[42] As ABC's fortunes soared in the 1970s, Murphy's affiliates grew ever stronger. KTRK in Houston, for example, held onto $14 million of $21 million in 1978 revenues, a profit margin of more than 65 percent.[43] Murphy was watching his most ambitious dreams come true. "For a long time, most people didn't realize the kind of margins you could enjoy in broadcasting and still run a quality station," he noted with satisfaction. "But they do now."[44] While the 1970s saw developments that would eventually topple the hegemony of network television—the VCR was invented in the 1970s, and a small company called HBO began using satellites in 1975 to broadcast content—the impact of these changes remained years away. For Tom Murphy, times were incredibly good.

Harvard Business School campus at Soldiers Field was built in the 1920s. (*Photo courtesy of Marvin Traub.*)

Professor Georges Frederic Doriot. (*Photo courtesy of Marvin Traub.*)

Extracurricular activities on campus. (*Photo courtesy of Marvin Traub.*)

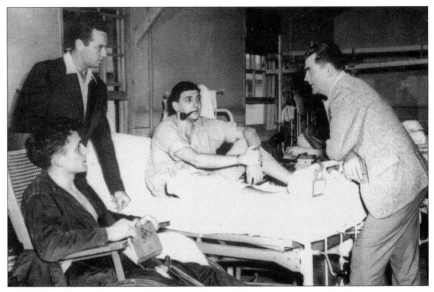

The vast majority of class members served in World War II. Marvin Traub's war experience left him with serious wounds and confined to a military hospital for a year. (*Photo courtesy of Marvin Traub.*)

George Berman and Mac Hecht realized their lifelong dreams of becoming entrepreneurs with their successful technology company, Unitrode. (*Photo courtesy of George Berman.*)

Roger Sonnabend and his family's hotel business took advantage of the explosion of leisure and travel during the postwar era. (©2002 AP Worldwide.)

Bloomingdale's was one of Queen Elizabeth's few stops during her 1976 visit to New York City. Marvin Traub was happy to show her abound. (Photo courtesy of Marvin Traub.)

Jack Davis never intended to go into the casino business. Above, Davis and James Crosby with new slot machines in Atlantic City. (©2002 AP Worldwide.) Below, with wife Caroline and Donald Trump, who bought Resorts International. (*Photo courtesy of Jack Davis.*)

Jack O'Connell (above) left a successful career in advertising to become a filmmaker.
Below, filming his critically acclaimed feature film, *Greenwich Village Story.* (*Photos
courtesy of Jack O'Connell.*)

After a stint in the newspaper business in
Ohio, Clarence Brown followed his father
into politics and became a member Congress. (*©2002 AP Worldwide.*)

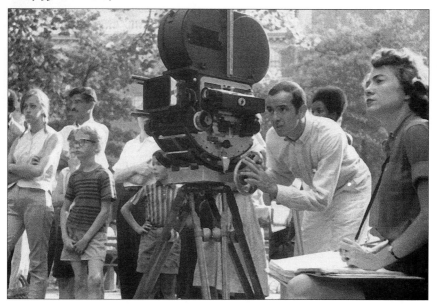

After leading Xerox to the heights of profitability, and then through years of troubled times, Peter McColough turned over leadership of the company to David T. Kearns (left) in 1982. (*©2002 AP Worldwide.*)

SEC chairman John Shad led the prosecution of Wall Street insider trading scandals in the 1980s. Above, testifying to Congress in 1986. (*©2002 AP Worldwide.*)

During college, Joe Amaturo had a job making a $11 a week. By his mid-70s, he was worth millions from buying and selling TV and radio stations. (*Photo courtesy of Joe Amaturo.*)

As a disciple of value investing, Bill Ruane built one of the most successful investment funds on Wall Street. (*Photo courtesy of Alumni Office, Harvard Business School.*)

Tom Murphy's Capital Cities first bought ABC, then sold out to Disney and Michael Eisner (left) in 1995 in a $19 billion merger. (©*2002 AP Worldwide.*)

Jim Burke (right) received high praise for his handling of the Tylenol poisonings. (©*2002 AP Worldwide.*) Below, with Tom Murphy and Marvin Traub, after receiving an award at the Harvard Business School Club in New York. (*Photo courtesy of Marvin Traub.*)

Close friendships between class members lasted for decades. Left, "The Group" at Operation Snowflake in 1995, an annual ski vacation begun in the mid-1970s. Below, an informal get-together at Jim Burke's home on Long Island. From left: Peter McColough, Jim Burke, Jack Davis. From right: Frank Mayers, Bill Hanley, Jack Muller, Tom Murphy. (*Photos courtesy of Jack Muller.*)

Those who became involved with Murphy in business—especially if they were union members—knew that his easygoing personality was ultimately a facade. Murphy was as tough as corporate leaders came. Still, there was an essential truth to Murphy's humility: As with many other 49ers, his great success exceeded his expectations for himself, and he was smart enough to deeply appreciate just how much he had. A classic Murphy story is about the time he traveled to Bermuda on vacation with some of his pals from the class of 49. The group checked into a posh country club estate resort and headed out to the tennis court in their whites. At the baseline of the first-class clay court, about to serve, Murphy paused. He placed his tennis racket and balls on the ground and took in the atmosphere of luxury and privilege with wonder.

"Can this be the young Tom Murphy from Brooklyn?" he asked.

Indeed it was.

Lester Crown had little reason to be awed by his growing wealth and power during the 1970s. It had been something he had come to expect from the time that he was young, and he had been groomed as the heir apparent for Henry Crown's growing business empire for years. Lester Crown would say often as he got older that he felt like the "luckiest guy alive," but his luck was mainly the luck of birth as opposed to meeting the right person at a cocktail party, as Tom Murphy had, or taking a risk on the right obscure company, as Peter McColough had.

Among the elite of supersuccessful 49ers, Crown was something of an outsider. He didn't pal around with friends from his Harvard days and he wasn't a vocal cheerleader for the class's alumni and their accomplishments. Crown also wasn't part of the endless good-natured competition that went on among leading class members. This was probably good for the other 49ers because, even in the 1970s, Lester Crown was on his way to beating fellow class members hands down and becoming the wealthiest of all the 49ers. This fortune would eventually place him among the top 100 richest people in America, and Crown alone would be the 49er who annually ended up on *Forbes'* list of the 400 richest Americans by the 1990s.

In the 1970s, however, Crown's profile remained low. He led a quiet life in Chicago, away from the red-hot media center of New York City. He was involved with his large family of seven children and a slew of charitable activities. In the business world, he was known among insiders as a major player and a comer. But he didn't have the public profile of someone like Traub or McColough. A big reason for this was that, even through the 1970s, Lester Crown remained under the shadow of his powerful father and had little real freedom to become his own man. His situation was the business equivalent to that of Prince Charles of England, who waits endlessly in the wings while his mother, Queen Elizabeth II, lives on and on and on.

The life energy of the formidable Henry Crown—known as the Colonel—was a wonder to behold. Well after most men might have retired and turned the family business over to someone else (a capable son with a Harvard MBA, say), Crown continued to hold on tightly to power as he advanced into old age. In 1970, Crown was 74, but age didn't slow him down one bit and he kept going strong throughout the decade. So Lester operated in the shadows.

The 1970s would be a time of great dramas for the Crown family. The sudden death in 1969 of the oldest son in the family, Robert, cast a tremendous pall over the family for several years. Robert had suffered a heart attack while driving, a tragedy that ended the life of a man whom all had imagined had many good years left. Because of the close-knit nature of the Crown family and the way that business was deeply enmeshed in family life, the shock reverberated through everything. For Lester Crown, losing his older brother was more than a personal event; it also meant that he now stood as the heir apparent—a patriarch in waiting—to everything that the Colonel had built.

Henry and Lester Crown found comfort in a campaign to buy back their influence at General Dynamics, the former jewel of the Crown business empire. Lester and his father firmly believed that the defense company should never have slipped from their grasp in 1966 to begin with. Assisted by Nathan Cummings, a family friend and the chairman of Consolidated Foods (later renamed the Sara Lee Corporation), the effort to recover the company became something of a personal crusade for the Crown men. "It was emotionalism that drove us back," Lester recalled.[45] The Crown family rapidly rebuilt its portfolio to 20 percent of General Dynamics' common stock in 1970 with a total outlay of $60 million. Soon, with control of six seats on the 14-person board of directors, the Crowns reasserted their dominant role in time for the boom years of the 1970s.[46] Material Service Company became folded within General Dynamics as a subsidiary.

With Robert gone, Lester Crown stepped up as his father's chief lieutenant, assuming the responsibilities of president and chief executive officer at Material Service and taking the rank of executive vice president at General Dynamics. Reaping a healthy profit margin of 5 percent on the dollar, Material Service netted $27 million in 1973, but Lester Crown wanted more. Bent on making a name for himself and Material Service within General Dynamics, Lester Crown engaged in a competition with the other divisions of the parent company.

Perhaps it was because of his ambitions—or perhaps it was the loose ethics of the world in which he had been raised—that Lester Crown made one of the great mistakes of his life when he resorted to extralegal tactics to promote Material Service's interests. In 1972, Crown joined with a group of other Chicago-area construction firm executives to lobby for the passage of a new state law to increase the highway weight limits for ready-mix concrete trucks. By raising the weight of individual loads, the construction lobby hoped to increase profit margins on concrete deliveries. They established a $50,000 slush fund to smooth the way with Illinois legislators. As the largest contractor in the area, Lester Crown contributed the most to the fund, giving $8,000 of his own money and, later, a second installment of $15,000. The bill failed, vetoed by Governor Richard Ogilvie, and the sponsoring legislators soon faced allegations of corruption. A federal grand jury subpoenaed records from Material Service, which revealed that Crown had not only contributed to the bribery scheme, but had asked seven company employees to pad their expense reports in order to reimburse his expenditures.[47]

Facing both prison time and fines, Crown adroitly handled the most perilous moment of his career. He cut a deal to receive immunity in return for testimony. In April 1974, a sharply dressed Crown appeared before the federal grand jury and told the truth about his pivotal role in nakedly illegal activities. Later that year, the United States District Court for Northern Illinois named Lester Crown and four other Material Service officers as unindicted co-conspirators in the bribery case.[48] Thanks to Crown's testimony, the indicted conspirators—five state legislators—went to prison. Crown walked free. "The two-bit cigar chompers were found guilty of taking bribes," wrote Chicago columnist Mike Royko, "while Lester and his button-down flunkies went back to the business of getting richer."[49] Longtime observers of the Crown family were less shocked about Lester's behavior than about how the scandal had become public. Obviously, Lester lacked the smooth touch of his father or his dead older brother, and some thought the episode would never have occurred if Robert had still been alive.

The younger Crown found that his illegal activities did little to diminish his standing at General Dynamics. During the proceedings in district court, Lester was elected to the board of directors of Material Service Corporation, thus increasing his clout at General Dynamics. Crown also scored a coup when the Department of Defense granted him a top-secret security clearance in July 1974. This status allowed Crown to be closely involved in the details of General Dynamics' nuclear weapons programs, having access to some of America's most closely guarded military secrets. One problem in all of this, however, was that Crown's application for the security clearance did not disclose his legal improprieties to the Defense Department's examiners. In their proxy statements of 1974, 1975, and 1976, the board of directors failed to disclose Lester Crown's role in the bribery scandal.[50] This oversight had a certain logic from Crown's perspective, since the Pentagon was typically not in the habit of granting security clearances to those who bribed government officials. Crown's illegal omission of information did not attract attention for over 10 years, at which point it triggered an SEC investigation, along with attacks from members of Congress who called for Crown's removal from the board of General Dynamics board.[51]

While Lester Crown's legal troubles would come back to haunt him in the 1980s, they were quickly forgotten in the mid-1970s, after the bribery trial ended in Chicago. The bigger news for the next few years was good news: General Dynamics became a moneymaking machine. Fueled by tremendous contracts in the marine and aerospace divisions as well as by the strength of Material Service's sector, the corporation thrived. In 1973, earnings rose 50 percent, to $40 million, a ratio of $3.84 per share.[52] Every subsequent year showed significant gains.[53] Before running into problems with its submarine construction in 1977 and 1978, General Dynamics generated tremendous wealth.

The Electric Boat submarine, one of the company's most lucrative contracts, had run into problems almost as soon as construction began.

After a series of major problems surrounding construction of new SSN 668s for the navy, General Dynamics found itself saddled in 1978 with a $359 million loss.[54] It was a remarkable turn of fortune.

With the weight of family business growing ever heavier as the 1970s came to an end, it might have seemed logical for Henry Crown to finally give up his tightfisted control. By 1979, Henry Crown was 83 years old. Lester was in his mid-50s, a fairly advanced age to still be taking orders from dad. Yet Henry Crown showed no signs of going anywhere. Every morning, a Cadillac limousine would pull up outside of the old man's 17-room home in Evanston and take him to downtown Chicago. Usually, the big black car would drop him off for a shave at the Conrad Hilton Hotel. From there, Henry Crown would briskly walk a mile and a half to his office in the old Mercantile Exchange Building, arriving at work before eight. Crown would explain to anyone who asked that continuing to work made him feel alive and that he didn't want to "sit in California or Florida and play cards and wait for death."[55]

The elder Crown was proud of his tenacity in the ninth decade of his life, and he bristled at those who automatically assumed that his son Lester was the real decision maker in the company. A *Forbes* reporter who made the mistake of phoning Lester for an interview in 1980 got a curt phone call back from Henry Crown himself: "When I'm retired or gone, he'll be the family spokesman. We can't have everyone saying something different, so I'll do the talking."[56]

The relationship between Lester and his father unfolded behind a thick veil of privacy, so it was difficult for outsiders to gauge the difficulties Lester faced in forever playing second fiddle to the Colonel. What was obvious was that the two men had extremely different backgrounds. Henry Crown had never finished high school and had worked his way up from making cement deliveries by horse and wagon to being an industrial titan. Lester had grown up with every privilege and the best education money could buy before going into the family business. Inevitably, there had to be clashes between the old and the new, between the studied sophistication of a Harvard Business School grad and the instinctual drive of an aging business genius who had grown up in poverty. Whatever conflicts may have existed between the Crowns were carefully kept from public view. To anyone who asked, Crown sang the praises of his father and, clearly, was exceptionally close to the old man.

Lester Crown, it seemed, was happy to wait patiently for his turn to rule.

The 1970s were a rocky time for American business leaders—especially those running large companies. It was a decade of oil shocks and recession and runaway inflation. It was, in fact, the worst decade in American business since the class of 1949 entered the business world. Nearly everything that could go wrong did go wrong.

But what was remarkable about the 49ers was just how many of them prospered during these turbulent years. For every man like McColough or Murphy or Crown who presided over the building of a major, well-known corporation, there were dozens of other 49ers who also hit their stride in the 1970s, scaling up successful businesses and generating enormous wealth. Joe Amaturo was a classic success story of the class: After a number of years in New York doing sales work, Amaturo had struck out on his own in the mid-1950s, investing in a small radio station in Massachusetts. The timing was perfect, as a radio boom was fueled by the wildly popular music of Elvis Presley and Bill Haley and Jerry Lee Lewis and Perry Como. The proliferation of small transistor radios meant that people could tune in nearly anywhere at anytime. From his initial success in radio, Amaturo had built up a media business that was nothing like Murphy's Cap Cities, but very impressive nevertheless. By the end of the 1970s, Amaturo owned over a dozen radio and television stations around the country.

George Berman's Unitrode was another 49er business that took off during the 1970s. In the late 1960s, Unitrode had sales of around $5 million a year. By 1974, sales had climbed to $35 million a year. Disaster struck when Berman's friend, partner, and fellow 49er Mac Hecht died suddenly in the mid-1970s of leukemia—"it was a horror," Berman recalled—but the tragedy didn't stop growth. Berman called on the talents of another classmate, Emmett Wallace, a consultant specializing in organizational development, to help ensure that Unitrode stayed on track. By the end of the decade, the company was approaching $100 million in annual sales.

As impressive as the individual success stories of 49ers were, the truly amazing thing about the class members during the 1970s was their collective success in reaching the top of the business world. Of the 376 class members who responded to the 1974 *Fortune* survey of the class, almost 45 percent were functioning as chief executives or chief executive operating officers. In these positions, the article observed, "Collectively, they exercise command in enterprises that employed approximately 860,000 people and took in some $40 billion in revenues last year."

To describe the great achievements of the 49ers, *Fortune* coined a phrase for them that would stick for years to come: "The class the dollars fell on."[57]

10

Living Dangerously

I f the World War II generation had to choose just a few words to describe themselves as a group, one of them would surely be *courageous*. It's a reasonable claim. The men who stormed Normandy and flew bomber raids over Germany, who fought the island war in the Pacific and hunted German subs in the North Atlantic, were certainly a gutsy bunch. The 49ers themselves were often amazed at the kind of courage they showed during the war, and, unlike the Vietnam veterans, many of them told their war stories for years. Typically, though, the 49ers didn't see their acts of great bravery as anything special. "Courage is universal," observed George Wilkerson, who had fought at Iwo Jima and, later, at Chosin Reservoir. Being courageous was just part of being in a war. "It's really kind of routine."

The postwar period showcased a different kind of courage, as a generation that had come of age during the Great Depression and World War II took major risks to create a new world of business. Among the 49ers, the high-level risk takers were actually a minority: For every Tom Murphy who bet heavily on a questionable venture, for every George Berman who started his own company, there were probably 10 classmates who took the safe and easy path and operated strictly within the system. During the late 1960s and the 1970s, however, a number of 49ers who hadn't taken many risks during their careers got to a point where they finally broke out and tried something new—sometimes because they had no choice. Other 49ers felt secure enough to take bigger risks and push the envelope of their careers.

On a late spring morning in May 1978, Jack Davis rose at 6 A.M. in his home in Atlantic City and went into work earlier than usual. Davis had been living in windy, run-down Atlantic City for less than two years, and it hadn't changed all that much since he arrived: It was still an impoverished city of 30,000 people, filled with crumbling neighborhoods and welfare recipients. "The place was a dump," Davis said. It was not a typical city for a Harvard Business School graduate to choose as home, but then, Jack Davis was not typical.

As the sun rose over the Atlantic Ocean from the east, Davis spent the morning emptying slot machines in Resorts International's newly opened Boardwalk casino hotel. "I love it," Davis told a reporter as he hauled buckets of $1 coins from the slots. The buckets weren't light and took two men to haul them. Each bucket weighed around 80 pounds and contained $1,500. During the first three nights after the casino's opening, the slot machines had grossed over $200,000. Carting this money away was heavy labor. Davis was on bucket duty because New Jersey's stringent rules governing the casino mandated that only a few company employees were allowed to handle the casino's cash. These rules were aimed at keeping organized crime out of Atlantic City. As president of Resorts International, Davis was among those authorized to touch the cash. And so, with a swollen river of money pouring into the Boardwalk casino, Davis pitched in to help empty the slot machines.

Even Davis hadn't fully expected the frenzy of excitement that accompanied the opening days of the first major American casino outside of Las Vegas. After Governor Brendan Byrne of New Jersey cut the orange ribbon in front of the casino on the morning of May 26, thousands of gamblers poured into the Boardwalk. For the next few days, over Memorial Day weekend, lines into the casino would stretch for four blocks, and the place was jammed nearly around the clock. The stampede was so bad that 33,000 square feet of carpeting would need to be replaced afterward. Davis couldn't care less about the carpeting. He walked around the casino dressed impeccably and grinning broadly at the crowd. "You're not going to get this smile off me for a long time," he said.[1] So much money came in that first weekend that Davis and his overwhelmed staff didn't have the manpower to count it. Instead, they stuffed the money in bags and piled them in a locked room.

The opening of the Boardwalk hotel and casino was a major vindication of a high-risk strategy pursued by Resorts International to open up Atlantic City to gambling. For Jack Davis, it was a hell of a ride. But then, that was nothing new.

Jack Davis was a 49er whose career had led him into more risk taking than he was always comfortable with. During the 1960s, it blew the minds of many of Davis's classmates when they learned just how deeply Davis had become enmeshed in the murky Bahamian world of casino gambling—and how naturally he had apparently adapted to that world. Davis himself was surprised by the change in his career plans. "Never. Never," Davis said, when he was once asked whether he had ever planned to use his MBA to go into the casino business. "Nobody talked about the casino business at Harvard." It was a turbulent time getting into this business, but Davis had managed to come through the experience unscathed—both physically and legally. "I never met anybody from the Mob," Davis said later. "And nobody ever came up and said 'We're you're new partners.' " Davis's friends and family supported him and believed that what he did was legitimate. But in an era in which organized crime was still a major presence in American society, especially in the gambling business, others took a different attitude. Many of the people Davis met automatically assumed that somehow his career was unsavory and that he must somehow be in cahoots with the likes of well-known mobster Meyer Lansky. Sometimes, when Davis told people what he did, they would look at him and ask, "How's Meyer?" Davis could and did laugh at this joke—up to a point.

By the 1970s, Davis was looking for fresh excitement. Resorts International entered the new decade completely transformed. In addition to its properties in the Bahamas, which included the Paradise Island Resort and Villas, the Brittania Hotel (completed in 1969), several restaurants and nightclubs, and undeveloped property, Resorts owned hotels in the Netherlands, two amusement parks in the United States, and a substantial stake in Pan American airlines. In the 1970s, Resorts purchased a tennis facility in New York City and a controlling interest in Chalk's International Airlines, which it used to ferry passengers from the United States to its sunny properties in the Bahamas. James Crosby's urge to acquire, however, continued unabated, especially as Resorts faced increasing pressure from the Bahamian government in the mid-1970s. Amid rising taxes, challenges to its gambling licenses, and muted threats of nationalization, the company began to look for a more secure environment for its gambling operations. "We were a victim of the Bahamian government, because they could just squeeze us and squeeze us and squeeze us," Davis recalled.

Resorts had a few problems with the U.S. government as well. Although the drama of the Watergate scandal unfolded mainly in Washington, it also reached Paradise Island as part of an investigation of Nixon's friend Bebe Rebozo. Nixon, of course, had been to Resorts' properties during the 1960s, and he and Crosby were friendly. (Crosby had donated $100,000 to Nixon's 1968 presidential campaign—crucial funds that helped Nixon win the New Hampshire primary.) Allegations were made that Resorts was part of an operation that illegally funneled large amounts of cash into Nixon's campaign via Rebozo's bank account in Key Biscayne. Investigators descended upon Paradise Island, asking hard questions of Crosby, Davis, and other Resorts officials. Nothing ever came of the allegations, but some investigators involved with the episode felt there was wrongdoing involved. "We ran out of time and money," a Watergate investigator told *Barron's*. "We handed it over to the special prosecutor's office. Nothing was solved to my satisfaction."[2] Resorts International had dodged another bullet. And yet, even as the dust from Watergate settled, the Bahamian government kept tightening the screws on the company.

Hard times on the eastern seaboard presented Resorts International with an unexpected opportunity. In industrial New Jersey, where manufacturing centers were hit hard by the oil shock and inflation of the early 1970s, politicians and planners were willing to explore radical solutions to urban blight. A proposal to legalize gambling statewide had failed in a 1974 referendum, but gaming enthusiasts and business interests were convinced that a compromise could be reached. Led by Resorts International, the pro-gambling lobby pushed for a new referendum to legalize gambling only in the formerly booming resort town of Atlantic City, which had lately fallen into disarray. As they had in the Bahamas, Davis and Crosby attempted to minimize resistance to the plan by spreading their money around. "We felt that it could be made to pass," Davis recalled, "that we could help finance the kind of a campaign that would get it passed." Resorts brought in a professional political strategist who had orchestrated referendum victories in California. Resorts also spent more than $200,000 on pro-casino advertising and employed the relatives of key New Jersey legislators as staff attorneys.[3] Meanwhile, the company banked heavily on victory. "We put half our money on the line, and we bought all kinds of real estate," recalled Davis. While Crosby was jittery about the Atlantic City venture, and not keen on moving further into the gambling business, Davis never had any doubts. He worked relentlessly to keep Crosby committed to the venture, pushing Atlantic City as the key to the Resorts' future. In September 1976, Resorts International purchased the Chalfonte-Haddon Hotel, a 1,000-room establishment on Atlantic City's boardwalk, for $2.5 million and additional acreage for $5.6 million. The purchase pushed the stakes even higher. In Las Vegas, veteran casino entrepreneurs like Steve Wynn scoffed at Resorts' investments as a boondoggle in the making.

Victory in the referendum was by no means a given. If the referendum had been voted down by New Jersey voters in November 1976, Resorts International may well have gone under. But Davis and the company survived when New Jersey voters approved the Atlantic City gambling referendum. Indeed, they did much more than survive: Thanks to what Davis would describe to the press as people's "basic urge to gamble," Resorts cashed in big time. Days after the Boardwalk casino opened, Davis had the pleasure of showing Steve Wynn around town to look at real estate. Wynn had hastily flown in from Las Vegas determined to stake a claim in the unlikely new gold rush unfolding on New Jersey's coast.

As the only gambling establishment with its feet on the ground in Atlantic City during the first years of legalized gambling, Resorts International enjoyed a tremendous advantage over its competitors. When the Resorts International casino opened on the site of the old Haddon hotel in 1978 after a $50 million renovation, the management could hardly contain the tremendous demand. Initially, the gaming floor covered 33,000 square feet, with 80 gaming tables and 850 slot machines. But very quickly, Davis realized this wouldn't be enough, so he doubled the size of the gaming floor and put in more of everything—twice as many slot machines, a third as many gaming tables—to absorb the flow of cash coming out of the wallets of visitors to his casino.

With incomes rising and inflation high, the 1970s were years of tremendous popularity for gambling; in 1974, 48 percent of U.S. adults participated in some type of gambling.[4] Resorts International reaped the benefits of hosting the most glamorous type of gambling in the most populated region of the United States, an advantage that was magnified by its temporary monopoly on gambling in Atlantic City. During the first month of operations, receipts exceeded $16 million.[5]

Very quickly, Resorts' casino in Atlantic City was pulling in more money than the largest casinos in Las Vegas. The Boardwalk casino took in a staggering $220 million during its first year of operation—an average of just over $600,000 a day. Like everyone else, Davis was surprised by these numbers. Before the casino had opened, Davis and Resorts had estimated that it would probably take in $60 to $100 million in its first year. When asked to explain the gap between what they projected and what they took in, Davis replied "Nobody's perfect. . . . We always expected it would be a great success. In fact, it turned out to be a huge success."[6]

On Wall Street, there was a stampede for Resorts International stock. Shares soared to $210, splitting three times during the first six months of 1978. While *Barron's* magazine would snipe that Resorts was "Wall Street's own floating crap game,"[7] noting its murky history, the average investor disagreed and the money kept rolling in. Jack Davis, who sold 27,000 of his own shares of Resorts that spring, took home a $3 million profit.[8] This chunk of money came on top of his annual salary of $125,000 a year, plus bonus. Davis boasted mildly that his old friends from business school had taken notice of his latest project, insisting that they used to consider his job "more lightly than they take it now."[9]

Even before the spectacular success of Resorts in Atlantic City, Davis was already beginning to receive significant attention from the media. He found the experience baffling and unfair at times. Once, for example, a reporter asked to interview Davis on Paradise Island and he agreed. But as the date grew closer, his workload became too intense and he couldn't find time to do an extensive interview with her. When she arrived, Davis met with her only briefly. As he usually did during his workdays on Paradise Island, he was wearing a sports shirt. Later, she wrote a book, and Davis was appalled to see how he been portrayed. "She described me as, you know, some guy with a big brown, hairy chest, with gold chains hanging all over me, and I've never had a gold chain in my life." The mainstream press was somewhat more responsible. In a 1979 article, the *Washington Post* said of Davis: "He doesn't gamble, except for occasional forays to Vegas to observe the state of the art.

Most people, his press aide admits, expect Davis to be a swarthy, beefy, tough-talking man with a goon's personality. In fact, he's a button-down, bottom-line exec who jogs on the Boardwalk in the morning."[10]

Resorts International's success in Atlantic City elevated the company to rank among the *Fortune* 500 by the end of 1978. But the position of the company in this exalted and respectable place was far from secure. In fact, Resorts' money machine in Atlantic City rested on an extremely precarious foundation: When it opened its Boardwalk casino in May 1978, the company had only a temporary gambling license. In order to keep doing business in Atlantic City over the long run, Resorts International needed a permanent license, which had to be granted by the New Jersey Casino Control Commission. The application process was a lengthy one requiring public hearings before the commission. Resorts treated the battle with utmost gravity, as they had the referendum campaign in November 1976. Once again, they turned to experts in swaying public opinion, bringing in a high-powered public relations consultant, David Probinsky, who was paid over $1 million before the hearings began and promised a seven-figure bonus if Resorts got the green light.

The campaign got off to a terrible start. In December 1978, New Jersey attorney general John Degnan came out and publicly opposed granting Resorts International a permanent gambling license. Backed by an investigation by the state's newly created Division of Gaming Enforcement, Degan filed 17 objections to the license with the Casino Control Commission. The objections included Resorts International's alleged past ties with organized crime, including racketeer Meyer Lansky, payoffs to Bahamian officials through a slush fund operated by Davis, and mismanagement of its casinos both in the Bahamas and in Atlantic City. The charges were a massive blow. Suddenly, prospects for the permanent gambling license looked bleak indeed—this after an $80 million investment by Resorts in Atlantic City. On Wall Street, news of the charges sent Resorts' gilded stock into a tailspin; it fell to as low as $20 a share. The company's very survival was at stake. Publicly, Davis tried to appear calm: "We're not going to give up without a fight," he said.[11]

Davis's first act of damage control was to suspend one of his closest aides at Resorts, executive Seymour Alter. Alter had been named in the state report as one of the 17 reasons to deny Resorts a permanent gambling license and as a leading example of the sleaze surrounding the company. According to the state, Alter had attempted to bribe a New York judge in 1962 and had also procured prostitutes for Bahamian officials during a trip to Las Vegas. Davis was sympathetic to Alter, who certainly was operating in typical Resorts fashion when he showed the Bahamian officials a good time in Las Vegas. (Alter would also boast about procuring prostitutes for James Crosby.) Still, Davis saw no other option than to clean house and send Alter packing before the hearings began.

With the future of gambling in Atlantic City seemingly at stake, the hearings over the company's license request were closely followed by the press. They were held in the middle of January in a bleak Atlantic City buffeted by cold winds. Resorts officials testified under oath, and the seven-week hearings dredged up all sorts of allegations in the company's past. Harsh questions were directed at James Crosby, who spent days testifying and found the hearings painfully difficult because of a worsening case of emphysema.

Davis didn't testify until the twelfth day of the hearing. Appearing before the commission in a conservative suit, he found himself grilled on long-standing allegations of Resorts' involvement with corruption and organized crime in its Bahamas operations. Davis acknowledged cash payments to Bahamian officials that continued even recently, saying that over $25,000 was doled out in the first half of the 1970s. The payments were made in cash, and Davis himself was often the person who delivered the money. Davis was nonchalant about all this, saying such payments were legal under Bahamian law. "We were not attempting to cover up the fact that we were making payments and giving gifts to Bahamians," Davis told the commission. "Top Bahamian officials knew this was going on, right to the very top."[12] Like Crosby, Davis would spend days on the witness stand being peppered with questions. At night, the Resorts' executives would gather in a war room to plot strategy with their lawyers. "It was a very heavy time," Davis recalled.

After the hearings ended, Davis and the top executives of Resorts International waited anxiously for the decision to come down. Finally, on February 27, the commission granted the license, saying the state had not proved its case that Resorts was unfit to run a casino. The commission's decision was unanimous. "Now it's back to business," a jubilant Davis told the press.[13]

To keep the Casino Control Commission happy during Resorts' tenuous first two years, the company engaged in constant efforts to appear to be the most upstanding business Atlantic City had ever seen.

Davis made various promises about improving the poverty-stricken city, offering to build middle-income housing units and a new sports complex. Davis even said that the company would spend $1 million to build a new church to replace one that was in the casino development zone. Meanwhile, Resorts was constantly working to keep its hotels up to the high standards that the Casino Control Commission expected. It was hard work. During one grueling hearing with the Casino Control Commission lasting over 13 hours, Davis found himself being loudly berated by the commission's chairman, Joseph P. Lordi, for the company's failure to make promised improvements at its Boardwalk casino hotel. "I'm not sure that the Resorts International is ready to maintain that hotel as a first-class hotel," Lordi said. "We're not going to allow paint and patch jobs in any situation."[14]

Davis was unruffled by his hazing by Lordi and the Casino Control Commission. It was nothing compared to the two cliff-hangers he'd been through in the past three years, the referendum and the licensing hearing. Davis was getting used to the rough-and-tumble. What did bother him, however, was the frenzy of construction going on in Atlantic City as other companies moved to break Resorts' monopoly on east coast gambling and build their own casinos in "Vegas East." As the construction steamed ahead, Davis was smart enough to know that his company's venture in Atlantic City faced its greatest test yet.

Jack O'Connell was another risk taker in the class of 1949 who sometimes feared during the 1970s that his dreams were too grandiose.

At Harvard, O'Connell had been a compulsive joke teller and among the most creative members of the class. He regularly wrote comedy for the *Harbus News,* the biweekly student publication of the business school. "He'd write stories that would make you piss in your pants," recalls Joe Amaturo, who also worked on the *Harbus News.* O'Connell was also the 49er who had run around campus with a camera filming *Tomorrow's Leaders Today.* The movie was filled with funny little snippets, including Harry Figgie cheating on the golf course. While the film was mainly a joke, O'Connell had serious fantasies during his Harvard years about becoming a filmmaker.

These fantasies remained largely buried for a decade as O'Connell pursued an advertising career in New York. The closest he got to film-making was producing hundreds of television commercials. The work wasn't very satisfying, but he was a star in the ad world. By the late 1950s, O'Connell was making a huge salary, and he lived the good life in Manhattan, with a large apartment on Madison Avenue on the tony Upper East Side. As he went through his high-paced career, O'Connell inched closer to his true ambitions with the help of psychoanalysis. He also saved money religiously, sending checks every month to his good friend Bill Ruane, who invested the money in stocks. Finally, in 1959, O'Connell left behind the fat paychecks and pushed his way into the film world. Through friends in advertising, O'Connell landed a job being an assistant to the Italian director Michelangelo Antonioni for his new film, *L'Avventura*. Before leaving for Italy, O'Connell put himself through a crash course in Italian and managed to pick up the basics of the language. When O'Connell arrived in Rome, Antonioni was there to greet him at the airport and they drove south from the city, to a party in a seaside town. On the way, Antonioni informed O'Connell that funding for the new film was not yet in place and shooting would not start for a month. Fortunately, one of the guests at the party that day was the famous filmmaker, Federico Fellini, then in the middle of shooting his classic, *La Dolce Vita*. Fellini offered to have O'Connell come and work on that film while waiting for Antonioni's funding to come through. O'Connell jumped at the offer.

The jobs in Italy were just a stepping-stone to O'Connell's true ambition of making his own films—writing, directing, and producing. In 1960, O'Connell formed a film company called the Astron Film Corporation and set out to raise money for his first feature, *Greenwich Village Story*. With the help of his close friend Harry Weyher, a Harvard-trained lawyer, O'Connell proposed to set up a limited partnership to finance the movie, an arrangement never used before in the film industry. The IRS approved the innovative plan, which provided a tax shelter for investors in the film, and O'Connell set to work finding backers. He turned to his Harvard classmates to help fund the film, budgeted at $75,000. The money came in from friends like Ruane, Frank Mayers, Joe Amaturo, and many others, and production began. After shooting started, the film's costs rose higher than expected, ultimately to $135,000, forcing O'Connell to dip deeply into the personal nest egg that he built with Ruane's help during his advertising career.

Greenwich Village Story, shot in black and white, dealt with a theme that O'Connell could relate to intimately: art versus selling out. The film was about a group of young people in Greenwich Village living the lifestyle of beatniks. It focused on a young Beat writer struggling to publish his first novel and his ballet-dancing girlfriend, who has just learned that she is pregnant. Another character in the film is a stiff advertising executive who secretly longs for the creative life yet doesn't have the courage to give up the security of his mainstream career. The film ends darkly with a botched illegal abortion that claims the life of the ballet dancer.

Greenwich Village Story was a critical triumph that received enthusiastic reviews in the *Daily News* and an invitation to the Venice Film Festival, one of only two U.S. films that year to receive this coveted honor. Columbia Pictures arranged a private screening of the film with its executives in New York. Afterward, it offered O'Connell a distribution deal. O'Connell hesitated. Columbia had the reputation of being highly dishonest in its accounting practices. The studio offered no advance money, and also made it clear that they would be keeping the books. O'Connell knew that numerous filmmakers had been ripped off this way, so he turned down the deal.

Greenwich Village Story played at theaters across the country, but netted only low returns. Not only were O'Connell's investor friends out a huge amount of money, but O'Connell himself took a massive financial hit that left him flattened. O'Connell found himself without enough money to live on, and took a temporary job that paid less than half of what he was making in advertising. O'Connell managed to make several other independent films in the 1960s, including a film called *Christa,* later renamed *Swedish Flygirls.* While that film played in thousands of theaters, and should have netted O'Connell several million dollars, he was swindled by the distributor and saw few profits.

The emerging counterculture remained a keen interest of O'Connell during the 1960s. In 1966, on a visit to Los Angeles, he met some young people in a park smoking marijuana and dressed in colorful clothes who called themselves "hippies." O'Connell sensed that something big was happening in the culture, and heard that there were even more hippies up in San Francisco. Through a contact made through his Harvard classmate Frank Mayers, O'Connell got backing from RKO in New York to go to San Francisco to make a television movie about the hippies.

O'Connell arrived in San Francisco with a seven-person film crew in June 1967. In the coming months, he shot a film he called *Revolution*—later renamed *Hippie Revolution*—a feature-length documentary that focused on the famous Summer of Love in Haight Ashbury. The film featured interviews with hippies and others in the Haight. Through creative camera work, O'Connell tried to re-create the experience of LSD trips, and captured the idealistic thinking of beautiful hippie girls with names like Today Malone. Years later, a reviewer would call *Revolution* "a crude but heartfelt time capsule, released in the summer of '68, just before the Haight-Ashbury scene turned into one big, unwashed bummer. And even if director Jack O'Connell may not have made a great movie, he was at the right time, at the right place, and (most important) with the right tripped-out attitude." Jack O'Connell had wandered far indeed from the world of mainstream business.

United Artists agreed to distribute *Revolution,* which opened to strong reviews in a movie theater on 12th Street in Greenwich Village. Night after night, the theater was packed, and United Artists had plans to distribute the film to theaters nationwide. O'Connell had a major hit on his hands. Then, unexpectedly, the union projectionists at the theater announced that they would no longer run the film. The reason was that, in making *Revolution,* O'Connell had used a film crew from a fledging new union that was trying to challenge the industry hegemony of The International Alliance of Theatrical Stage Employees (IATSE), the main union that controlled all aspects of film production. Unwilling to challenge IATSE's power, United Artists abandoned O'Connell. *Revolution* went from being a hit to being a flop.

While most of the 49ers would watch the countercultural movements of the late 1960s and early 1970s from afar, cocooned within the buttoned-down world of business, O'Connell engaged with the times and would later be seen as one of its leading cinematic chroniclers. O'Connell also proved to be a pioneer with his invention of a limited partnership to finance *Greenwich Village Story,* an approach to financing films that helped transform the movie industry. Still, even his best-grossing films produced little in the way of earnings. O'Connell's investors rarely received any returns—that is, beyond losses that they could charge against their taxes. "I'm not the most successful film producer in history," O'Connell commented in the late 1970s during a less hopeful moment. One of his weaknesses, he decided, was that he overreached his actual talents—by writing, directing, and producing. "I blame myself for indulging myself too much," he said. "The hard facts out there are well taught at HBS, but not to somebody who thinks he might be some sort of artist."[15]

By 1979, O'Connell's fortunes had dipped so low that he was thinking of going back into marketing. He was toying with the idea of starting a company to distribute independent films, which he saw as a profitable niche. The problem with his idea was that it required some venture capital to get off the ground, and by this time O'Connell had exhausted the goodwill of even his most loyal financial backers. Beset by bills, O'Connell barely managed to hold onto his one-bedroom rented apartment on West 22nd Street and began looking for work in advertising.

A dejected return to Madison Avenue never came to pass. Instead, tragedy struck O'Connell when he was mugged and assaulted in Washington Square Park. The attack took place in broad daylight. One moment O'Connell was taking notes on a film idea he was working on; the next thing he knew he was on the ground, barely conscious, with two police officers hovering above him. The assault was a savage one, resulting in a massive head injury that almost killed him. At the hospital, the doctors delivered a grim prognosis to O'Connell's brother Bob, who had rushed up from Washington, D.C.: that he might never recover his mental faculties again. After being released from the hospital, O'Connell could recognize people but couldn't understand them or communicate. A friend volunteered to nurse him full time. In his small Chelsea apartment, with its perfect view of the skyscrapers on Manhattan's southern tip, O'Connell began a difficult rehabilitation process with no clear outcome.

Harry Figgie was another of the class's great risk takers. In the 1970s, his zest for charging into the unknown would make him one of the more successful businessmen in America—albeit one that generated mixed emotions among his classmates. Figgie was a conglomerate builder in the old style, with a hard-driving style and a loud voice. Raised in Ohio, he was the son of a self-made father who had started out poor and become vice president of Rockwell International. Figgie sought to carry on the family's upward movement by fulfilling much grander ambitions. After earning an engineering degree in Cleveland, he flirted with a career as a major league pitcher before deciding to go to Harvard Business School. Over six feet tall and weighing in at 200 pounds, Figgie was hard to miss around campus. After graduation, he was unusual among 49ers in that he went into consulting. His drive led him to become one of the youngest partners in the history of the consulting firm of Booz, Allen.

Consulting didn't satisfy Figgie. Like so many others of his generation, he wanted to build something and to generate wealth in the traditional way. In 1963, Figgie made his big break: In a period of just 19 days, Figgie scraped together $1.3 million in venture capital—enough money to buy an unglamorous company that had come up for sale called Automatic Sprinkler. The company had $22 million in sales, but was on the verge of bankruptcy.

Nobody could quite understand why Figgie chose Automatic Sprinkler as the company to launch his grand career. Even the outgoing board chairman of Automatic Sprinkler told Figgie: "You're the dumbest man alive." Figgie's reply was defiant: "No, the second. You sold."

Figgie threw himself into Automatic Sprinkler as if it were a holy crusade. In very short order, he had turned the company around. During the first full year under Figgie's leadership, the company showed a profit, and by 1966 it was so profitable that Figgie was able to take it public under the name of A-T-O, International. On the day that A-T-O appeared on the Big Board, Figgie showed up outside the stock exchange riding a hook and ladder and wearing a fire hat—a publicity-generating stunt of the sort seldom seen on the Street. A more sophisticated PR effort was spearheaded by Hill & Knowlton. A-T-O publicity man William G. Borchert brazenly predicted that the company would have $1 billion in sales by 1970. In the overheated stock market of the late 1960s, these claims convinced plenty of investors to buy in, and A-T-O's stock rocketed skyward, reaching a stunning high of $74 in 1968. The cash from the public offering made A-T-O flush enough to serve as a platform for Figgie's empire-building ambitions.

And what ambitions they were. In just five years, Figgie bought 72 companies of all kinds. Mainly, he focused on industry, buying firms that made things like cement mixers and road graders and mining tractors. Figgie fit well the profile of the swaggering empire builder. He was tall and athletic, with a square chiseled face and plastic-framed glasses that looked as if they could withstand a boxing match.

Figgie's old-style conglomerate building attracted its share of skeptics on Wall Street who didn't see a method to Figgie's buying madness. It seemed the guy was just buying companies for the sake of buying them and wanted to get big for the sake of being big—a business philosophy better suited, it seemed, to the turn of the century. Figgie scoffed at these critics. "Hypocrites!" he said. "If you're an old company that sees the need of going into different product lines, they call you diversified and say you're smart. If you're a new company that's based on different product lines, they call you a conglomerate, as if it were a dirty word. The hell with 'em."[16] For a time, the healthy profits of A-T-O kept Wall Street in line and its stock did phenomenally well. Figgie was called a "supersynergist" by the business press for combining disparate business elements into a successful empire. Figgie was also seen as a turnaround guy, a man who bought struggling companies and turned them into moneymaking machines. Much was made of his degrees in engineering, law, and management. Figgie was not just a doer, but a thinking man's businessman with a superior skill set and a soaring vision. By 1969, A-T-O had sales of $340 million.

Then came a series of problems that almost killed the company, including an investigation by the SEC that A-T-O had lied about its assets when it went public and revelations that it had been technically bankrupt twice but hadn't shared this news publicly. In another damning revelation, it was learned that Figgie had secretly sold some 80,000 shares of his own A-T-O stock when it was at its height. Some of these shares were unloaded just before bad news about A-T-O was made public. Other key company backers also unloaded shares with insider knowledge of the company's twists and turns. "Despite appearances the SEC never went after Figgie and his friends for their insider trading," *Forbes* would note. "Figgie had an excellent legal counsel and carefully kept within the letter—if not necessarily the spirit—of law."[17] Figgie's reputation on Wall Street took a major beating: Not only was he seen as a conglomerate builder, but an unscrupulous one at that. It was a trying time for him. "There isn't enough money in the U.S. for me to take the kind of punishment I've taken in the last year," Figgie reported to the Harvard Business School Bulletin in 1969. "But I'm not money motivated. I just believe in what we are trying to do."[18]

A-T-O's stock went into a terrifying plunge. By 1970, the price of a share of A-T-O stock had fallen by $68, to $6 a share. And it would continue falling over the next couple of years, bottoming out at $4 to $5 a share in the mid-1970s. Inside the company, there was constant turmoil caused by Figgie's tyrannical style and poor management. "When I came there A-T-O had problems everywhere," said James H. Goss, who worked for three years as Figgie's number two man before being pushed out in 1971. "Figgie was—and is—just a management consultant. He is interested only in acquisitions. He is simply not interested in operations."[19] Figgie was often not in the office and instead was out on the road wheeling and dealing. Goss would sometimes go days without being able to reach him. After Goss was forced out, a new president came, John Tanis, who continued Goss's work of trying to bring order to chaos. Tanis considered himself something of a friend of Figgie's, but found working for him unbearable. In 1971, Tanis's wife died, but Figgie was entirely unsympathetic. Tanis resigned in 1972, only to find that A-T-O immediately canceled a compensation package that had promised him certain benefits upon his departure from the firm. Tanis ended up suing A-T-O for $200,000. Tanis's story was typical: In the early 1970s, A-T-O had a 74 percent turnover rate among its top corporate executives.[20] Even as Figgie earned the distrust of his own managers, he earned the fierce detestation of organized labor. A die-hard conservative Republican, Figgie hated unions and often dealt with them irrationally and abusively, triggering major strikes like the one that paralyzed operations at A-T-O's bottling machinery company in 1977.

Figgie's behavior ensured that he spent the 1970s attracting criticism and being derided as a charlatan. In 1978, as Figgie's stock finally began to climb back upward, moving toward $15 a share, *Forbes* ran a searing profile of Figgie entitled "Will the Fish Bite Again At the Same Old Bait?" The article opened by snidely mentioning that Figgie was overweight at six feet tall and 230 pounds, and it was all downhill from there. Figgie's long list of past sins was recounted in detail, and A-T-O's weak corporate foundations were dissected. The article ended on a cautionary note: "Investors, and their advisors, would do well to look skeptically on claims that A-T-O has turned around."[21]

During the 1970s, with the business press gunning for him, Figgie tried to lay low. Beyond an unsuccessful bid to buy the Boston Red Sox team in 1978, Figgie didn't attempt to buy any new companies during much of the 1970s, and he organized A-T-O into a number of divisions that made the company seem more logical and less chaotic. Quietly and without fanfare, Figgie built A-T-O into a major player in the business world during the 1970s. "We are in danger of becoming a good company," Figgie said in 1978. "Gosh, if I could build a $20-million company to $630 million, imagine what I could do from this plateau. It would be like shooting fish in a barrel."[22]

Indeed, A-T-O did keep growing. Those naysayers who wrote Figgie off during the early part of the decade and then forgot about him in the late part of the decade would find themselves in for quite a surprise when Figgie's company made the *Fortune* 500 list in 1982, with sales approaching a $1 billion.

Figgie was not just a bygone archetype in his ham-fisted approach to empire building. He was also a classic podium-pounding businessman-philosopher of the old school—one who felt an intense obligation to warn anyone who would listen about the threats facing America's future. In the late 1970s, Figgie saw these threats as proliferating. In his profile for the 30th reunion, Figgie unleashed a tirade about American decline:

> The danger of inflation continues and grows without an attack on the fundamental source. The dependence we have on Saudi Arabia could bring us financial disaster within five years. . . . The Russians surpass us now in weapons excellence at ALL levels. We are becoming a second rate country because of our poor political leadership and much of the ownership of our industry will pass to the hands of foreigners within the next decade because of the weakness of our currency.[23]

Around A-T-O's office, Harry Figgie had a reputation as being a tough boss and a shouter. These same characteristics shaped his public persona. Figgie wasn't alone among 49ers in believing that the country had major problems as the 1970s wound down, but he complained more loudly, more publicly, and more caustically than nearly any other class member. To be sure, Figgie was especially affected by America's declining economic preeminence because of his heavy investment in traditional U.S. industries that were getting walloped by foreign competition.

But there was something else going on in the complaints of Figgie and others of the World War II generation about the American decline: It was simply hard to accept the reality that the golden age of American business was finally coming to an end.

11

Taming the Bear

I n the spirit of the competition among them, the 49ers loved to tease and incite each other. Robert Baldwin, a core member of The Group, was particularly good at baiting his classmates. One day in the early 1970s, while having lunch at the "21" club with Tom Murphy, Baldwin and Jim Burke had some fun with Murphy. Baldwin complimented Murphy on how well he had done with Cap Cities. Murphy had the reputation in the class as having accumulated more wealth than anyone else—an estimated $3 million fortune. It was really very impressive, Baldwin said. Then Burke, on cue, entered the conversation. He said he had recently seen Peter McColough and found out some interesting news: McColough's huge portfolio of Xerox stock was doing extremely well. In fact, McColough estimated that he was now worth over $12 million—four times Murphy's own fortune.

Wasn't that interesting news, Baldwin and Burke commented. It looked like Tom Murphy was not the richest 49er after all. Boy, that Peter McColough sure was impressive.

Among the 49ers, trumping Tom Murphy was no small accomplishment. That McColough could snatch away a little of Murphy's sheen was due to his enormous good fortune with the stock market. But McColough, of course, wasn't the only 49er to benefit enormously from the stock market. Among the many other gifts and opportunities handed to the class of 1949, the long-term growth of the stock market rated high in importance, even though during the 1970s the stock market was not noted for its stellar performance. It gyrated wildly, going from the worst bear market in memory to a bull market and then slumping again. Still, the market doled out huge wealth to the 49ers, gravy on top of the salaries they earned for their hard work. Beyond McColough and Murphy, the ranks of stock market winners in the class was considerable over the decade: George Berman became a millionaire as Unitrode's stock soared; Harry Figgie financed his conglomerate building with money generated by a stock market offering for A-T-O, International; John Muller received a huge payday when General Housewares went public in 1969; and Lester Crown got even richer when General Dynamics' stock became hot.

For 49ers trying to figure out how to harness the stock market to their ambitions, there was never any shortage of advice from old classmates—especially Bill Ruane and John Shad.

In his physical appearance, Bill Ruane looked the part of the investor. Over the years, he had managed to hold onto all of his hair, which he kept combed back and parted neatly to the side. Youthful and alert in his 40s, Ruane's suits were expensively made and his shirts were always impeccably pressed. He was so well put together that, at first glance, a potential investor might think Bill Ruane perhaps was just a little too slick. This impression, however, could not survive even the briefest conversation with Ruane.

In his personality and philosophy, Ruane was exactly the opposite of the stereotypical stock investor. He was contemplative and soft-spoken. He didn't engage in hype. He didn't pay much attention to the hot stock of the day. Amazingly, Bill Ruane didn't even bother to watch the ticker tape most of the time. His ideal day was spent like that of a scholar, hidden away someplace, quietly studying financial data about prospective investments. He sometimes described his profession in questionnaires as "Bill Ruane, research analyst." In another manifestation of Ruane's laid-back style, he was a Wall Streeter who actually tried to maintain a normal schedule, telling his classmates from Harvard in the 1970s that a major goal in his life "is to achieve a proper balance between enjoyment of family and enjoyment of my work." In a further contrast to the culture of Wall Street, which had turned brasher and greedier in the 1960s, Ruane didn't have a burning sense of entitlement. "Basically I feel like a lucky man," Ruane said in 1979, a comment that friends knew reflected his entire outlook on life.[1]

Take away the expensive suit and Bill Ruane might be mistaken for a small-town hardware store owner from the Midwest, or maybe a serious manager at a medium-size business. Indeed, the comparison to a small businessman is one that Ruane would probably have welcomed, even as his success grew in the 1970s. In his mind, a traditional business approach was the precise thing that distinguished him and his firm from typical Wall Street investors, whom he tended to deride as gamblers. "Most fortunes," Ruane said in 1973, "have been made by people who went into business, not by speculators. . . . How many speculators do you know that have become rich?"[2]

Bill Ruane's value investing was the antithesis of speculation. In his fortieth-floor office at the tip of Manhattan, not far from the giant construction site where the Twin Towers of World Trade Center were going up, Ruane and his colleagues used a commonsense logic that was surprisingly foreign to modern Wall Street. "What we do basically is go into a good business, hopefully at what we think is a bargain price—and live with it until we think it is no longer a bargain." It was that simple.[3]

Ruane's stable, almost stoic approach to investing was ideally suited to a decade of tremendous turbulence on Wall Street. It was a decade that crushed speculators left and right and took the glamour away from stock market investing. While the 1960s had drawn legions of fortune hunters to the gold rush on Wall Street, the investors who hung in with the business during the 1970s needed plenty of resilience and an appetite for surprises. Bill Ruane didn't mind the rough ride one bit.

The year Ruane founded the Sequoia Fund, 1970, was the worst year on Wall Street that anyone could remember. As one analyst said about 1970, "Everything that could go wrong for the market went wrong."[4] The war in Vietnam was creating serious economic strains, especially in combination with the expansion of federal spending programs under Presidents Johnson and Nixon. Inflation, which had been practically irrelevant for the previous two decades, spiked in response to acute deficits in the federal budget and the balance of payments. The political crises of the early 1970s, including the invasion of Cambodia, the Kent State and Jackson State University killings, and the Watergate scandal, exacerbated the economic malaise. Wary investors pulled money out of the stock market just as Ruane & Cunniff were buying in. By the end of 1970, the Dow stood at 631, a figure that represented a 50 percent decline in real value since 1966.[5]

The next four years offered little relief, as the oil shock of 1973 compounded existing problems. In 1973 and 1974, the stock market experienced the worst disaster since 1930, with the Dow Jones Industrial Average dipping below 600.[6] Seats on the New York Stock Exchange, for which Ruane & Cunniff paid nearly half a million dollars in 1969, were selling for as little as $65,000.[7] Bill Ruane's first years as an independent investment adviser coincided with the worst Wall Street blight since the Great Depression. Asked about his strategy during the early years, Ruane said, "We hid under the desk and wondered if the storm would ever clear."[8]

In fact, the decline in stock prices created exactly the kind of conditions that value investors favored. When a *Forbes* reporter asked Warren Buffett how he felt about the current market in late 1974, Buffett described himself as "an oversexed man in a harem."[9] While Ruane might have found himself short of money to invest, bargains were in plentiful supply. Ruane spent the early 1970s acquiring a series of beauties for Sequoia's portfolio. Buying low and selling high, Ruane led the industry in posting gains. For the three years ending in 1977, the Sequoia Fund was the best-performing mutual fund in the field, with returns of 133.1 percent.[10]

Ruane's success did not go unnoticed by the business media. He was profiled by *Forbes* in 1973, in an article tinged with skepticism, and again in 1977, in a more glowing article entitled "The Tortoise and the Hare." Bill Ruane, as Wall Street learned, was the tortoise that unexpectedly was beating the pants off his competitors.[11]

Trained to be skeptical of market swings, Ruane kept his success in perspective. "We're not as smart as the current results might indicate," he told his investors in 1977, "nor were we as dumb as we felt back in 1973 and 1974 when the stock market dropped the prices of our companies to levels that appeared to predict the end of society as we know it."[12] Sequoia succeeded because Ruane and his partner followed strict guidelines in selecting properties. Steadfast to his principles, Ruane chose not to invest at those times that he didn't see stocks worth buying. In 1977, when his reputation as a stock market maestro reached an early peak, the Sequoia Fund held 20 percent of its assets in cash. "Our attitude is still that stocks are basically cheap," explained Rick Cunniff. "We just haven't been able to find as much stuff as we would like to put our dollars in."[13]

The mid- to late 1970s witnessed major changes in the operation of U.S. equities markets that created significant long-term gains. The most important of these grew out of the 1974 Employee Retirement Income Security Act (ERISA), which redefined the duties of the trustees of corporate pension funds. In the past, most pension fund managers had invested conservatively in bonds and government securities, often disregarding the growth potential of their funds. Under ERISA, managers were encouraged to consider a broader portfolio that included corporate equities and other high-yield investments. The change channeled billions of dollars in corporate pension funds into the market, and encouraged other large institutional investors (such as state governments) to do likewise. Over time, the flow of pension and endowment funds into the stock market significantly expanded market capitalization.[14] A second provision of ERISA created tax deferments for individual retirement accounts (IRAs), a measure that ultimately encouraged the growth of mutual funds.

Mutual funds remained a cottage financial industry as late as 1970. Investors' trusts had been popular in the 1920s, but the exposure of mismanagement and corruption among fund administrators by the 1929 crash had seriously damaged the credibility of the trusts. A series of new regulations and the use of the term *mutual fund* (which evoked the stability of mutual savings banks and insurance companies) restored a measure of consumer confidence.[15] Mutual funds of the 1960s and early 1970s continued to serve a small number of investors, mostly through investment in stocks and occasionally a mixture of stocks and bonds. The diversification of mutual fund portfolios and the broadening of their investment base was yet to come.

In the short term, however, the boosts to the stock market were insufficient to offset the continuing economic malaise of the 1970s and early 1980s. Beset by a second oil crisis and demoralized by the decline of manufacturing and heavy industry, the U.S. economy suffered the twin indignities of dramatic inflation and high unemployment. Interest rates, climbing since the mid-1960s, soared to terrifying heights.[16] With the prime rate at the all-time high of 15.27 percent in 1980, droves of investors (including Ruane) switched to bank deposits and other interest-bearing securities. Market doldrums resumed in earnest. By the end of the decade, the percentage of Americans with money in the stock market had actually fallen.

Bill Ruane's success with the Sequoia Fund gave him the freedom that every stock investor dreamed of. He was his own man with his own fund during the 1970s, beholden to nobody except his partners, whom he dealt with as equals.

John Shad would have a very different experience on Wall Street during the 1970s. It would be one of frustration and setbacks. Shad embodied the fierce work ethic that made Wall Street famous, but his professional persona fit awkwardly into the model of the rakish tycoon that made the Street notorious. The culture of the Wall Street workplace, in Shad's day and always, celebrated the rugged individualist, the sly huckster, the sleek sophisticate. More narrow in its homogeneity than the terms *all white* and *all male* can convey, the coterie of Wall Street bankers operated within a relentlessly rigid social tradition. A handful of types that ranged from the icy Wasp insider to the tough Irish fighter to the smart, abrasive Jew dominated the range of acceptable gestures and styles. In this charged masculine environment, Shad cut a less-than-dashing figure. "As brilliant as he was, he could be equally comical," said a former vice president at Hutton. "He's kind of ugly, and he wears these terrible suits that always seem two sizes too big."[17] Neither wit nor eccentricity compensated for his homely appearance and ample girth. Shad's nonconformity offset some of the advantages of his professional achievements. His career at Hutton arrived at an early and insurmountable plateau.

Shad won election to E.F. Hutton's board of directors and was named executive vice president, but remained outside of the firm's inner circle. Shad's standing at Hutton suffered a dramatic setback in 1970, when CEO Sylvan Coleman reached mandatory retirement age. Coleman's preferred successor was Keith Wellin, the president of Hutton. But a movement to displace Wellin quickly cropped up. Leading the revolt was Robert Fomon, a 45-year-old senior vice president in charge of Hutton's West Coast corporate finance department. Fomon had his own ambitions for the top job, but he pursued them through the vehicle of John Shad, pushing Shad to make a bid for the CEO slot.

Shad's prospects were shaky from the start. Many at Hutton secretly mocked Shad's potential for leadership. He was seen as a technician lacking vision, a man adept at analyzing the mechanics of deals and mastering the minutiae of financial details. He was known for arriving at meetings tremendously prepared, with reams of data that his staff had laboriously developed to answer every possible question—and yet managing to leave people unimpressed because of his personality. When it came to the core of the business that Hutton did, nobody could doubt John Shad's competence. In some quarters of Wall Street, John Shad was highly respected as a brilliant analyst who had not only made millions for himself by the time he was his mid-40s, but had also helped make Hutton such a profitable firm. More than anyone, Shad was responsible for establishing Hutton as a leader in the investment banking world during the 1960s. Nobody denied Shad credit for that. At the same time, many others around Wall Street and at Hutton believed that he lacked the long-range thinking, management prowess, and overall gravitas of a company leader. "While no one doubted that Shad was a superb banker, they feared that he was more of an individualist than a team player," wrote Mark Stevens, in his history of E.F. Hutton, *Sudden Death*. "Absorbed in his work, committed to his own buying and selling and deal making, he had neither the time nor the inclination to step away from his personal pursuits to lead the firm."[18]

Shad would be the first to acknowledge that he was no big fan of administration and management. He had always been indifferent to those aspects of his work at Hutton. Yet he saw himself as smarter, tougher, and more hardworking than most of the prima donnas on Wall Street. At Hutton, Shad was known as a legendary workaholic who virtually lived at the office. "Many times I would come see him at 8 A.M. only to find that he had been at work all night," recalled colleague Paul Bagley. "Others who got holed up in the office now and then on emergency projects said they'd find Shad there, too, wandering around at three or four o'clock in the morning. The man had an unlimited capacity for work."[19]

Shad's self-identity was rooted in a long-standing personal narrative that had always emphasized extraordinary discipline and determination:

his leaving home at the age of 17 and working as a riveter on the grave-yard shift at night and then going to college during the day; his nights spent studying during the 1950s when he got a law degree while holding down a full-time job and making a fortune; his killer hours during the 1960s as he moved up the ranks of Hutton and expanded his personal fortune. Always, since as long as he could remember, Shad had been running forward, pushing himself relentlessly. "I've grown up on stress," Shad once said about himself. "My whole life has been stress." Shad's detractors may have seen this narrative as the reason he was such a dour and uncharismatic figure. The guy had beaten the life out of himself. But Shad saw his past as evidence of exceptional fortitude and intelligence. He was simply a better man than most.

Shad didn't relish the open battle required to try to seize the top job at Hutton. Once in that battle during the winter of 1970, however, Shad brought his formidable energies to bear. It was among the most important battles yet of Shad's career. He enlisted two lawyers to help him and began an effort to woo votes from the partners of Hutton. After intense political lobbying, Shad and his rival Keith Wellin both emerged with just over a third of the partners supporting them—with the rest uncommitted. Robert Fomon was the key to victory, holding the loyalties of a number of partners. One of Shad's lawyers asked Fomon to call in his promised support, and Fomon said that the votes would be there to put Shad over the top at the annual meeting of partners on February 11, 1970. But shortly afterward, disaster struck: Wellin struck a deal with Fomon that made Wellin vice chairman and Fomon president in exchange for the votes that Fomon had promised to Shad.

It was a stunning double cross that played out dramatically in a meeting among Hutton's directors held in the Hutton conference room in New York. One by one, the directors voiced their support for the deal that would put Fomon in charge of day-to-day operations at the firm. Still, Shad refused to back down. As all the directors looked on, Shad launched into an impassioned plea for the top job. He said he had the experience, the intelligence, and the stature to head the firm. Then Shad turned to Fomon, who had initially backed him for the top job and asked: "Who do you think should be president?" Fomon was rattled by the question. "Everyone in the room has just said that I should be president, John," Fomon remembers saying. "Do you want me to tell them that they are wrong? That you should be?"[20]

Shad said nothing. His bid for power was crushed and Fomon was put in charge of E.F. Hutton.[21] "Shad was betrayed—no question about it," said one Hutton participant in the election. "By the time John figured out what had gone on behind the scenes, he was staggered."[22]

Despite the betrayal, Shad stayed on as Fomon's subordinate at the head of Hutton's banking operations. He would endure hard times during his second decade at Hutton. CEO Fomon proved to be a character straight out of the Wall Street pantheon and just short of dysfunctional. A strutting masculinist, he boasted about his sexual escapades and told reporters that he thought women should be seen and not heard. A newspaper article showed him holding a branding iron in the shape of the letter F, gesturing with his thumb and finger and saying of a dispute with a fearsome rival, "Merrill Lynch scares me about that much."[23]

Fomon targeted Shad for humiliation with a passion born of the awkward circumstances of his succession. A favorite forum for Fomon's abuse was the executive dining room, where Fomon was wont to unleash loud harangues at Shad. The situation was so bad that Shad began avoiding the dining room altogether. At those times that he did show up, Fomon's behavior could be unbelievable. Shouting across the executive dining room, Fomon publicly denounced Shad's clients as small fry and delivered personal insults. Fomon sometimes left his seat to harangue him as Shad hung his head over his plate. "This is a first class house," he demanded. "Is this the best you can do?"[24]

The CEO's behavior encouraged more junior officers to join in mocking Shad. One wickedly funny story had Shad taking notes on matchbooks during a sales rep's standard stump speech (Shad was a heavy smoker). At the next stop on their tour, Shad asked to do the speech himself and then pulled the matchbooks one by one out of his pocket and read from them aloud to give his speech.[25]

Pushed to the margins, Shad grew irascible and condescending. Shad had always been a difficult person to work for, and this only got worse under Fomon's reign. Working killer hours himself, Shad expected his subordinates to do the same. He also was guilty of many of Fomon's worst sins. "Some managers use diplomacy, but Shad used fear and humiliation," said Paul Bagley. "When subordinates presented ideas that he rejected for one reason or another, he'd tear into them in front of others, dissecting their argument, humiliating them. Tact? The man never heard of the word."[26]

One of the ironies of Shad's falling star at Hutton was that the firm's investment banking business actually did very well in the early 1970s under Shad's leadership, with the firm's investment banking fees tripling between 1970 and 1972. In 1972, Shad was named Investment Banker of the Year by *Finance* magazine. Still, the high command at Hutton wanted Shad out of the firm—no easy matter given Shad's sizable stock holdings and his allies with key partners. Increasingly, however, Shad himself looked for honorable exit strategies. Wall Street was bereft of major opportunities during the early 1970s, but public service beckoned Shad. A lifelong conservative Republican, Shad drew on his contacts in Washington to try to get positions in the Nixon or Ford administration. At one point, he narrowly missed out on the opportunity to head the Overseas Development Corporation in 1970.[27] Meanwhile, E.F. Hutton declined around him even as a national advertising campaign proclaimed, "When E.F. Hutton talks, people listen."[28] Perhaps demoralized by the erosion of their boss's power, prominent members of Shad's staff, including Frederick Joseph, migrated to Drexel Burnham Lambert, where they found in Michael Milken a more outspoken advocate of the high-yield bond. Worse, Hutton's sprawling retail sector initiated a hidden pattern of criminal behavior that may have been sanctioned in the upper echelons of management.

Still, Shad soldiered on, steadied by the increasingly large portion of corporate earnings derived from the investment banking sector.[29] A 1981 *Business Week* article described E.F. Hutton as "one of the best-managed firms on the Street," an estimate that the next five years would prove disastrously wrong.[30]

A DIFFERENT TIME

On a summer day in 1986, John Shad made one of the more difficult phone calls during his time as chairman of the Securities and Exchange Commission. The call was to Fred Joseph, chief executive of Drexel Burnham Lambert, the company that employed a little-known merger and acquisitions specialist named Dennis Levine. Levine was about to be arrested by the SEC for insider trading. The investigation had been going on for months; the evidence against Levine was airtight. Finally the SEC had decided to move.

"I'm sorry it's your guy," Shad told Joseph. Many years earlier, at E.F. Hutton, Shad had hired Fred Joseph. He considered him a friend and something of a protégé.

"Don't apologize," Joseph said. "This is your job."

Catching criminals on Wall Street had always been a central function of the SEC, and John Shad knew this well when he was appointed its chairman by President Ronald Reagan in 1981. But neither Shad nor anyone else could have imagined that the 1980s would witness the biggest criminal cases in the annals of the financial services sector.

The arrest of Dennis Levine was just the beginning of a massive insider trading investigation that John Shad would shepherd for months on end. It was nerve-racking work that took aim at some of the most powerful figures on Wall Street, along with leading investment firms. Shad, a notorious workaholic and a heavy smoker, was used to intense stress. But this was something else altogether. The investigation would result in charges against such titans of finance as Ivan Boesky and Michael Milken. When it was finally over, the insider trading scandals of the 1980s would stand as a symbol of one of the more turbulent and corrupt decades in the history of American business.

The 1980s saw wealth creation in America on a scale unseen since the 1960s. It was the kind of boom era that transformed 24-year-old stockbrokers into millionaires. The hit television shows *Dynasty* and *Dallas* brought the fantasy of fabulous wealth into millions of living rooms every week. It was the time of Donald Trump and Leona Helmsley and Carl Icahn, a time when even religious figures like Jim Bakker were in the thrall of greed. *Forbes'* introduction in 1982 of its wildly popular list of the richest 400 Americans helped solidify a new pecking order of wealth that, in the 1980s, seemed to be the only hierarchy that mattered.

The decade would be good to the 49ers, some of whom rose to the height of their success, others who retired with plenty of money in a surging stock market. But the business world of the 1980s would not belong to the 49ers in the way the 1970s had. A different generation was moving into power during the decade and, with them, a different set of values. The 49ers had come of age in an industrial America where getting rich meant making something of value. The 49ers' generation of business leaders had built on this idea and helped create a broader American economy that milked the potential of technology and created new consumer markets where none had existed before. There was an idealism in the early careers of the 49ers—a sense that the winners in business would always be those who worked the hardest, who were most dedicated to quality, and who had the right mix of American know-how and plain gumption. The same values that won World War II were the values that drove the 49ers in creating the new economy of the 1960s and 1970s. "After the war, we all believed that good can prevail," Jim Burke would say in 1986.[1] "We went to school with a set of values forged by the war, and life has reaffirmed those values."

And yet, even as many 49ers had abundant evidence—and wealth—to underscore their triumph in the 1980s, the ways of their generation were clearly in retreat. The 1980s saw the rise of a very different kind of business world and a different set of leaders. To these leaders, business was less about making quality products or delivering quality service and more about making as much money as possible—and then flaunting it. It was an attitude embodied by Sherman McCoy, the thirtysomething protagonist of Tom Wolfe's *Bonfire of the Vanities,* who fancied himself a "master of the universe" and felt supremely entitled to his multimillion-dollar bonuses and 14-room Park Avenue apartment. New York socialite Brooke Astor, who lived on Park Avenue in real life, would say about the 1980s and its impact: "Everyone became obsessed with money and went higgledy-piggledy scampering after their fortunes. People with money used to often care about the people who had no money. Not always, but often. Now, it is rare to find people with money who care at all about people with no money."[2]

The values of the 49ers—sacrifice, humility, loyalty, belief in government as an agent of national advancement, and dedication to "giving something back"—were increasingly being pushed aside in the business world of the 1980s. *Newsweek* magazine dubbed 1984 "The Year of the Yuppie." Winning, and winning big, was the goal in the new game. Greed, of course, had always been part of the postwar business world, but shared social norms had kept it in check. As the drive for riches infused the fabric of American business culture in the 1980s, these norms would be swept away. It was the young people, the would-be Sherman McCoys, who were the worst. "These kids are smart," said 49er Ned Dewey about the new young business elite, including the Harvard MBAs. "But in my business I'd as soon take a python to bed with me as hire one. He'd suck my brains, memorize my Rolodex, and use my telephone to find some other guy who'd pay him twice as much money."[3] Things in the business world were just not the way they used to be.

Evidence that the 49ers' day was passing came forth, ironically, in the growing media attention to the class. On a spring night in 1986, Marvin Traub hosted a small party to celebrate the publication of a book about the class entitled *The Big Time* by Lawrence Shames. Some 15 members of the class showed up, including leading luminaries like Jim Burke, Jack Shad, Bill Ruane, and Jack Davis. They were greeted by nearly twice as many journalists and publicity people. The *New York Times* ran a story about the event, as did other publications. The valedictory theme of these stories was different than those articles that had run during the 1970s, most famously the 1974 *Fortune* article, "The Class the Dollars Fell On." The articles in the 1970s depicted a group of business leaders at the height of their power. Writings about the class in the 1980s acknowledged their tremendous continuing power—"They are the generation that runs the nation," said the *Times*—but the articles also had a sheen of nostalgia, with wistful references to the GI Bill and to values forged by the Great Depression and World War II.

The 49ers themselves, in their comments to the press, reinforced the impression that they were from a bygone era. "All day long we deal in millions, billions," Bill Eiseman, a top bank executive, told Shames. "But to this day, when I look down and see a fifty-dollar bill in my wallet, I feel this instant of boyish excitement, I almost want to fold it up and put it into my shoe. I remember when having that much cash at once qualified you as a wealthy man."[4] Perhaps the most significant indicator that the era of the 49ers was passing was the fact that more than 60 members of the class were no longer alive to greet the publication of Shames's book.

Still, even as the day of the 49ers was passing, many of them were at the pinnacle of their success.

12

Wise Men

J im Burke's first five years as Johnson & Johnson's chief executive, beginning in 1976, were years of enormous corporate prosperity. From the polished conference table of his uncluttered office in New Brunswick, not a stray paper or file folder in sight, Burke presided over a growing empire. Finally, his moment had arrived. After years of working his way up through the ranks and tolerating all the narrow thinkers and cautious corporate bureaucrats, Burke now had the control he needed to make things happen. Johnson & Johnson was turned into a marketing powerhouse, a company known for aggressively pushing products and a willingness to take risks. This hunger in business was the Jim Burke way.

Burke's personality was something else entirely. Even as he reigned at the top of the corporate world, there was still something of the nice country boy in Burke. He connected warmly with people and was unintimidating. "Burke is very intuitive, a very sensitive guy, who has that ability that some women but not many men have to listen to a conversation at a dinner table, say, and to understand the vibrations underneath," Peter McColough told *Forbes* when the magazine did a major profile of Johnson & Johnson in 1981.[1] It was these kind of human qualities rather than showmanship that seemed to account for Burke's tremendous success. He was a marketing genius, but there was nothing especially flashy about Burke. With plastic bifocals and white hair thinning on top, his face sagging a bit as he hit his late 50s, his conversation calm and quiet, his baby-blue eyes twinkling, Burke hardly conveyed killer instincts or a steely determination. He kept in shape through skiing and other sports, but he didn't look particularly fit or convey the sleek athleticism of some of the younger CEOs coming up through the ranks of corporate America. Jim Burke, in fact, looked a bit on the dowdy side. And yet, in his business, where market dominance could slip away before one knew it, where profits could vanish in a single quarter, where stock could plummet on news of weak earnings and wipe out millions of dollars in shareholder wealth, Burke was relentless in his drive. He viewed the world as a continuous battle for the upper hand. Burke liked to be a winner.

And win he did as Johnson & Johnson's CEO. Thanks in large part to Burke's drive, Johnson & Johnson had established itself as the preeminent health care brand. Amid the general economic downturn of the 1970s and early 1980s, the company's earnings were very high, rising 16.7 percent in 1981 with projections for even more dramatic growth the following year. Tylenol played an important role in this prosperity. Burke's mobilization of vast resources to advertise the drug had paid off spectacularly by the early 1980s, with the pain reliever capturing an amazing 35 percent of America's $1 billion analgesic market. In 1981, Tylenol contributed some 7 percent of Johnson & Johnson's worldwide sales, but a hefty 15 to 20 percent of its profits. It had even surpassed Crest toothpaste as the world's top health and beauty product.

Burke could not have been prouder. Tylenol had been his baby, a personal crusade in the mid-1970s. Now he was being vindicated. All told, at the beginning of 1982, Johnson & Johnson had over $5 billion in annual sales and owned nearly 150 companies. In just two years, the company's stock had risen from the low 20s to $46 a share.

Burke's own personal wealth increased along with the company's fortunes. He didn't have the kind of fortune of Peter McColough or Tom Murphy, but like many of his classmates from Harvard, Burke had done infinitely better in life than he had ever imagined. He was thankful for the life he led and the opportunities he had. He enjoyed going into work every day to the unassuming redbrick headquarters of Johnson & Johnson.

In September 1982, over Labor Weekend, the executive committee of Johnson & Johnson held its annual strategic planning review. The exercise was meant as an opportunity to step back from the fray of daily operations and look into the future. Given the company's health, the mood at the retreat was upbeat. But Burke played the role of the skeptic and the worrier during the discussion. Things were so good for Johnson & Johnson on that warm late-summer weekend that Burke kept wondering aloud about what might go wrong. "We had been marveling at how lucky we were to be in our industry, to have some very profitable brands doing so well," he remembered, "and I said, offhand, what if something happens to one of them, like Tylenol?"

Burke took some teasing at the meeting for playing the role of naysayer. Anyone who had known him for years, of course, was not very surprised that Burke—with all his drive and his penchant for a fight or a crusade—would be a bit at a loss about what to do with himself when life was so good. "Nothing is impregnable, but it was such an extraordinary business, there didn't seem to be any downside," Burke recalled of the meeting over Labor Day. "Nobody could come up with anything."[2]

The bolt out of the blue hit several weeks later.

On the morning of September 30, a pleasant, sunny day, Burke was having a meeting with the company president, David Clare. It was a quiet, regularly scheduled meeting in which they were catching up on a variety of nonpressing matters. Clare had just come back from a stress test as part of the company's health program and he was talking about how he was in good shape with low stress. Then Arthur Quilty, one of the top executives, burst in. He breathlessly reported that terrible news had just come from Chicago: The Cook County Medical Examiner's Office was reporting that three people had died as a result of taking Tylenol capsules laced with cyanide. More bad news would soon be on the way, with another four people in Chicago dying in the same terrible manner.

Much later, the FBI would say that the killer was thought to be a middle-aged man, probably white, certainly intelligent, and most likely withdrawn and antisocial. The motive? Nobody could ever figure that out. And why Tylenol, as opposed to thousands of other products? These questions would never be answered. The mentality of the killer would baffle leading criminal psychologists for years to come.

After the news from Arthur Quilty on that fateful morning, Burke quickly swung into action. His first move was to appoint one of his trusted executives to be the leading point man on the crisis. He chose David Collins, the 48-year-old chairman of McNeil Consumer Product, the Johnson & Johnson subsidiary in Pennsylvania that made Tylenol.

Although Collins would be the point man at McNeil, Burke himself personally led the crisis response in the weeks ahead, delegating the rest of his responsibilities at Johnson & Johnson to other executives.

The first days of the crisis were chaotic. "You couldn't find anything more traumatic," Burke recalled.[3] Hundreds of calls flooded the switchboards at the New Brunswick headquarters—panicked consumers, pharmacies and doctors, poison centers, and terrifying false alarms—posing questions that Johnson & Johnson could not answer. Scattered around America were some 31 million bottles of Tylenol. It was impossible to say how many were contaminated. "It looked like the plague," Collins would say later. "We had no idea where it would end. And the only information we had was that we didn't know what was going on."[4] A staggering amount of information needed to be rapidly sorted out—about where the cyanide-laced Tylenol tablets had been purchased, when they had been produced, when they had been shipped and stocked. Within the first day, Collins's staff had at least figured out one clear fact: It was highly unlikely that the poisoning of the capsules had taken place at the McNeil plant in Pennsylvania.

As the crisis unfolded, Burke saw his first responsibility as preventing more deaths. His instinct was to push for a nationwide recall of Tylenol capsules. The recall of 31 million bottles of Tylenol would not only be a major undertaking logistically, but with a retail value of $100 million, it would mean a huge financial loss for Johnson & Johnson. Even so, Burke was ready to do it. What other choice was there? Several days after the poisonings, Burke traveled to Washington and met with the Federal Bureau of Investigation and the Food and Drug Administration. The Feds, surprisingly, were against a recall. "The FBI didn't want us to do it," Burke recalled later, "because it would say to whomever did this, 'Hey I'm winning, I can bring a major corporation to its knees.' And the FDA argued it might cause more public anxiety than it would relieve."[5]

A day after the meeting, strychnine-laced capsules appeared in California in what appeared to be a copycat crime. In the wake of this incident, the federal agencies approved the recall, and bottles of Tylenol swiftly vacated the shelves that Burke had worked so hard to secure years earlier. The poisoning and the recall were huge news. Suddenly, the word *Tylenol* became associated with instant and untimely death. Macabre jokes about Tylenol proliferated. Tylenol didn't just relieve headaches, it cured them permanently. The outlook for Johnson & Johnson's premier brand was grim.

Having addressed the immediate danger to human life, Burke quickly turned to the danger to Tylenol's survival and Johnson & Johnson's corporate health. "We were still in a state of shock," Burke said later of the weeks after the poisoning. "It's like going through a death in the family."[6] Burke wrote notes of condolence to all the families of the poison victims while sorting through advice about what to do next. An atmosphere of crisis pervaded the headquarters of Johnson & Johnson, with meetings around the clock that included top executives and marketing specialists.

Ultimately, Burke rejected all proposals for permanently ending the Tylenol product line and reintroducing it under a different name. Instead, he resolved to fight to keep the Tylenol brand alive. "Even in our worst-case scenario, where we get back only half the base we had before," he reasoned, "it would still be the market leader."[7]

Burke's first step on the road to recovery was to undertake polling of consumer attitudes toward Tylenol. The results were sobering. Nearly 100 percent of Americans knew about the Tylenol poisoning, and even though most people didn't blame the maker of the drug for this episode, a majority said they were not likely to buy Tylenol ever again. Certainly there was no shortage of other choices for consumers. American Home Products, Burke's bitter enemy from the 1970s, had shifts working around the clock to produce Anacin, the pain reliever that Tylenol had only recently vanquished. Recapturing Tylenol's former glory and market share seemed to be a hopeless endeavor. As tens of millions of recalled Tylenol capsules were burned in incinerators, many, if not most, consumer analysts believed that the brand name was dead forever.

Burke's strategy for rebuilding confidence in the product was three-fold. First, McNeil reintroduced Tylenol in a tamperproof bottle that soon became the standard packaging design for all over-the-counter medications and many foods, cosmetics, and vitamins. Second, Johnson & Johnson sponsored a major advertising campaign that featured a coupon for new tamperproof bottles of Tylenol at a discounted price. Finally, at the end of October, one month after the crisis began, Burke held a pep rally for over 2,000 Johnson & Johnson salespeople. "We're coming back," he declared.[8] Then he gave them marching orders to go out and persuade doctors and pharmacists to begin recommending

Tylenol again to their patients and customers. For Jim Burke, the job of selling Tylenol against adverse odds was a familiar routine.

On November 11, Burke held a videoconference broadcast in 30 cities. "In every sense of the term this has been a national tragedy, and everyone in America shares a part of that grief that it imposes," he said. "It has introduced us to a new form of terrorism and brought the potential for new fears and concerns close to our homes. It has alerted the consumer to new dangers and touched off a revolution in consumer packaging that eventually will reach all areas of the marketplace. I will begin by stating that as a company we have made the unequivocal commitment to rebuild this business under the Tylenol name. We are coming back." Four days later, Burke appeared on the *Donahue* show. He explained how the tamperproof packages worked and played up the coupon offer. His demeanor was calm and reassuring, that of a man who could be trusted with the lives of American consumers. Burke also made an appearance on *60 Minutes* to promote his message. Like many others, Burke believed the Tylenol killer would eventually be found. He hoped that the $100,000 cash reward offered by Johnson & Johnson for the killer would help ensure that justice was done. Yet a year after the poisoning, law enforcement officials remained stumped. "With Tylenol there was never a message or a clue to the reason," said one Illinois law enforcement official. "Not only can't we say who, but we can't say why."[9]

On January 3, 1983, three months after the poisonings, the first new advertisements for Tylenol ran on television. It was the beginning of a major new marketing assault that would continue relentlessly through the year. The comeback effort succeeded. In defiance of many predictions, Tylenol reclaimed 80 percent of its former market share within a year of the poisonings. Johnson & Johnson swallowed $50 million in losses and a $56.8 million increase in advertising costs but kept moving forward.[10] "It's a miracle, pure and simple," Joseph Riccardo of the Bear, Stearns investment banking firm told *Time* magazine on the anniversary of the poisonings. "The consensus among shrewd advertising executives on Madison Avenue was that the brand name would never recover."[11] Kudos came not just from ad execs, but from Jim Burke's alma mater, Harvard Business School. "It's been about as effective a rescue job as I've seen in marketing," said Stephen Greyser, a professor of marketing at the school.[12]

Burke was not above giving himself and Johnson & Johnson some pats on the back, especially for undertaking the recall. "It showed that the credo works," Burke said, invoking the company's hallowed—if often ridiculed—ethical code. "The Tylenol recall isn't going to pay our bills for the next year or two, but in the long run it will be worth it in values."[13] As the one-year anniversary of the poisonings came and went, Burke acknowledged the shadow that the terrible episode had cast. "It isn't that easy to put behind us," Burke said in an interview. "It still permeates the company. But no one's obsessed with it anymore."[14] A few moments in the next year or two would bring Burke back to the terrible days of the Tylenol poisonings. In 1983, five people died from medical complications surrounding the use of the arthritis drug Zomax, and Johnson & Johnson recalled it. Later that same year, three people died when a Johnson & Johnson kidney dialysis machine malfunctioned in November 1983. Also, misreads from a Johnson & Johnson CT scanner in New York prompted an FDA investigation that same year. In December 1983, after this year of problems, a Wall Street analyst described the company as "snake-bitten."[15] But there was nothing in all these episodes that remotely compared with the trauma of the Tylenol incident. Slowly, life returned to normal and Johnson & Johnson continued to move forward as a vibrant and flourishing company. Burke focused his restless energy on other challenges.

For Burke, the Tylenol poisonings actually had positive consequences. Before 1982, Burke had never been on television during his 30 years in the business world. Now he was well known. The incident tremendously raised his profile and established for him a national reputation as a miracle worker, capable of overcoming the worst odds. Burke received many invitations to speak, and he often used these occasions to stress the importance of corporate ethics and talk up Johnson & Johnson's credo. Burke even paid for a study that showed that 15 companies with written codes of ethics outperformed the Dow Jones Industrial Average by 600 percent over a 30-year period.[16]

Certainly, Johnson & Johnson seemed to offer evidence of something being done right. As the boom of the 1980s kicked in, Johnson & Johnson's fortunes soared, its stock hitting all time highs. Tylenol completely recaptured its lost market share, and company executives again dreamed of seizing half of the vast pain-reliever market for the drug.

During Burke's better days, the seven poisoning deaths in Chicago could almost be forgotten. Other times, he would have bad dreams of that terrible time, or not be able to sleep at all, especially on the anniversaries of the poisonings. With the killer still at large, it always seemed possible that he or she might choose to strike again. "It hung like the sword of Damocles," Burke said. David Collins, chairman of McNeil, also felt the weight of dread. "When the phone rang at night," he said, "you were always sure that either one of your kids had been hurt in a car wreck or that there'd been another Tylenol murder."[17]

One of Burke's bad dreams occurred on a cold Saturday night in early February 1986. He dreamed that the poisoning was happening again and that people were dying. He awoke relieved that it was just a nightmare.

Only it wasn't.

The day before Burke had his nightmare, on February 7, a 23-year-old woman named Diane Elsroth was visiting her boyfriend in Yonkers, New York. Late in the evening, she complained she wasn't feeling well. Her boyfriend opened a new bottle of Tylenol, breaking the safety seal and giving Elsroth two Tylenol capsules. She then went to bed. The next day, when her boyfriend tried to wake her, she was dead. The county medical examiner undertook an autopsy, along with blood tests.

The bad news arrived at headquarters on the afternoon of February 10, in a call to Johnson & Johnson's president David Clare from Joe Chiesa, president of McNeil Consumer Products. Chiesa had been informed about the death of Diane Elsroth and the results of the autopsy. Potassium cyanide had been in the Tylenol capsules taken by Elsroth.

Clare hurried across the eleventh-floor executive suites to Burke's office. "We've got a real problem," he said. Remembering the terrible dream, Burke knew instinctively what the problem was.

Burke and other top executives held their breath, terrified that news of more poisonings would follow. They prayed the Elsroth case was an isolated incident. In the meantime, they took dramatic action. The company posted a reward of $100,000, canceled all Tylenol advertising, and moved to hunt down all Tylenol capsules that were part of the same lot as those taken by Elsroth.

On the night of February 10, after long hours of crisis management with Burke, David Clare went home with a headache. From the medicine cabinet in his bathroom, Clare took out a half-empty bottle of Tylenol and shook out two capsules. Then he paused, scrutinizing them closely before popping them into his mouth. A long road lay ahead for the company.[18]

Five days after the news of Elsroth's death, Burke received a call from FDA commissioner Frank Young, who asked, "Are you sitting down?" Young reported that a second contaminated bottle of Tylenol had been found in Westchester. "Frank, that is the worst news you could give us," Burke responded.[19] The FBI reported that there was no evidence of tampering with the Tylenol packages, raising the possibility that the poisonings took place within the manufacturing center.[20]

Burke insisted again on trying to save the Tylenol brand. The only hope for Tylenol, he argued, was to abandon the capsule format, which allowed would-be murderers to hide the poison where it would not be detected.

Executives at McNeil objected to Burke's proposal, pointing out that capsules constituted 30 percent of total sales. But Burke was adamant with his counterparts at the subsidiary. He began to push them relentlessly. "Give us a plan. Have you got a new package? Have you got a new capsule?" He argued that there would never be a tamperproof package and that the company could not survive a third incident. "Not only do we risk Tylenol," without an alternative, "we risk Johnson & Johnson."[21] Burke's will prevailed and the Caplets form of Tylenol was rapidly developed.

With the new strategy in place, Burke took to the airwaves. "We fought our way back from the Chicago tragedy," Burke said at a news conference where he announced the discontinuation of all capsule drugs. "We will do it again this time. . . . What we've done is say, 'You're not going to defeat us.' "[22] Burke again appeared on *Donahue* and other shows. He carried an oversized model of a Tylenol Caplet, a coated pill that would replace the capsule in all Tylenol products. The switch would cost $100 to $150 million, not calculating sales lost to those who continued to prefer capsules.[23] In his public statements, Burke expressed sympathy for the family of Diane Elsroth, saying that his company's tremendous losses did not compare with the loss of the Elsroth family. Elsroth's aunt had a stinging reply: "Bring back my niece. Can they do that?" Elsroth's mother, meanwhile, called Burke's decision to end capsule use "three years too late."[24]

Burke's determination and reassuring presence triumphed over the odds. In a marketing coup, Burke made Johnson & Johnson look farsighted and responsible with its new Caplet. "They're getting people to question capsules rather than Tylenol," a competitor complained.[25] Tylenol Caplets began to look like the safest analgesic product on the market.

Burke's successful efforts on behalf of Tylenol and public health made him a hero. "Jim Burke of Johnson & Johnson, you have our deepest admiration," said President Ronald Reagan that fateful February. Reagan praised Burke for embodying "the highest ideals of corporate responsibility and grace under pressure."[26] In fact, most of the commentary about Burke's role in the episode was filled with praise. In 1987, Johnson & Johnson was found to be among the 10 most admired companies in America. But at least some observers didn't think that Burke or Johnson & Johnson had done anything particularly amazing. Leading PR expert Herbert Schmertz, for example, would later say that the Tylenol poisonings were not examples of a true corporate crisis. "J&J did nothing wrong and the press knew this," he said. "The company was a victim rather than a party to creating the crisis. J&J was very open, cooperative and available but it's easy to be open when no one is going after you."[27] Burke himself was not particularly impressed with Johnson & Johnson's response. "All we did was what we thought any responsible company would have done in our position—and people reacted as if this were some radical new departure for American business. My God, what did people expect we'd do?"[28]

Among those who expected more of Burke and Johnson & Johnson was the family of Diane Elsroth, who slapped the company with a $94 million lawsuit. The suit accused Johnson & Johnson and McNeil of reckless disregard for the public, citing "defects in the design, manufacture, assembly, packaging, marketing, advertising, testing, inspection, distribution, warning and sale" of Extra-Strength Tylenol.[29]

Tylenol analgesics recovered in full, producing $500 million in sales by 1989. Buoyed by Burke's confidence, the Tylenol brand expanded to include a line of products for the common cold and a successful sleep aid, Tylenol P.M. Johnson & Johnson continued its program of diversification and globalization, becoming one of the most successful corporations of the 1990s. Jim Burke resigned as CEO in 1989 and was named to the Business Hall of Fame in 1990.

No other 49ers would match Jim Burke's stature or visibility during the 1980s. If the circumstances of Burke's rise to prominence hadn't been so horrific, there would have been plenty of envy among his superambitious classmates. As it was, Burke was tremendously admired, and other 49ers saw him as typifying the kinds of values that their generation believed in and sought to live by.

Another 49er who shot to prominence in the 1980s also attracted widespread admiration from class members, although no one was surprised at his success.

The 1980s would be the decade that Tom Murphy hit the big time.

In many ways, of course, Murphy had been a heavyweight in the business world since the early 1960s. Among those in the media business, Murphy was seen as a star for his success in building Capital Cities into a moneymaking machine. But beyond these circles, Murphy was not very well known. At events with other corporate movers and shakers, the tall, bald, and nondescript Murphy did not naturally draw a large amount of attention. His photo had been in the mainstream business press only a few times during the 1970s, and his name didn't immediately ring a bell. People who met Murphy without knowing the amazing Cap Cities story were not instantly impressed. He didn't radiate intensity or talk of grand visions or drop names. It's not that he was boring or colorless. Far from it. Lanky and easygoing, Murphy had plenty of natural, folksy charm. It was just that he was down-to-earth and unassuming in a way that superpowerful people usually were not. He was shy, even. Murphy and his wife Suzanne lived in Rye, Westchester County, and he didn't throw his multimillion dollar fortune around socially in the city. Also, the fact that he didn't drink or smoke and was religious set him apart from New York's glitterati. Tom Murphy flew under the radar and actively avoided the spotlight. Once, an acquaintance of his, business columnist James Brady, ran into Murphy on Park Avenue. Brady asked when the hell Murphy was going to sit down and do a real interview with him, and Murphy replied, "You know me, Jim, I hate publicity."[30]

As the 1980s began, Murphy was satisfied with his success and not overtly hankering to be seen as a bigger fish. According to the media rumor mill, one or more of the three networks had tried to lure Murphy away from Cap Cities with offers of big, high-profile jobs. Murphy wasn't interested. Still, while he didn't seek fame, the drive to relent-lessly grow Cap Cities was in Murphy's blood. After two decades of endless buyouts and takeovers of media properties, Murphy didn't know any other life. He was eternally restless and easily bored with the day-to-day details of business. The quiet wood-paneled calm of Cap Cities' elegant offices on East 51st Street, behind St. Patrick's Cathedral, might have looked like the headquarters of a company content to coast on past successes, but in fact Murphy was always shopping. "He looks at everything," a colleague reported.[31] With Cap Cities' annual pretax revenues soaring to $663 million in 1982, Murphy needed to search for new ways to reinvest. In 1976, *Forbes* magazine had commented on "Tom Murphy's pleasant cash flow problem." The comment was facetious, but by the early 1980s, the challenge of putting this river of money to work, and to keep buying new properties, was growing.

Beyond having plenty of cash to be able to buy and buy big, Murphy also had a major advantage when it came to shopping for companies: Cap Cities was trusted and respected. In fact, it had one of the best reputations in corporate America, with earnings increasing for nearly 30 straight years, television holdings that consistently outperformed the competition, and a reputation for keeping costs low. Murphy's low-key style may not have been winning him lots of ink in the business press, but it impressed company analysts. In a corporate world filled with flash and bloat, people took note of the fact that Cap Cities practiced what it preached. It had no corporate jet, no public relations staff, no legal department, and fewer than three dozen employees in its New York headquarters. In another reassuring sign, the top management of Cap Cities was also remarkably stable, with hefty bonuses for performance and little turnover.

Wall Street could not get enough of Cap Cities. Its infatuation with the company, begun in 1961 thanks in part to Bill Ruane, intensified into a love affair as time went on. At first, the "conventional wisdom on Wall Street was that Capital Cities would be just a nice little company," Murphy's Harvard classmate John Muller observed. "But Murphy surprised them."[32] Boy, did he. In March 1983, Cap Cities stock climbed to nearly $150 a share, with 80 percent held by large institutional investors who knew value when they saw it. (With Murphy's own considerable stockholdings in Cap Cities, his net worth climbed to more than $20 million—this on top of a salary and a bonus compensation in

1983 reported to be $6.1 million.) One of Murphy's greatest admirers in the investing world was Warren Buffett, the Omaha-based investor who had been introduced to Murphy by Bill Ruane in the late 1960s. A friendship between the two men had flowered over time, and Buffet never flagged in his enthusiasm for Cap Cities' leader. "Murph is the best manager of any publicly owned company that I know of," Buffett once said. High praise indeed from a man who had made a vast fortune analyzing companies.[33] Like so many others, Buffett saw Murphy's even-keeled personality as key to his success. "He has none of those complexities of character that screw other people up and make for irrational behavior," Buffett would say.[34]

For many media companies interested in selling, Cap Cities was an ideal suitor. (Although unions saw things differently; Cap Cities was universally despised by organized labor.) And it was not just because Wall Street was squarely behind the company. It was also Murphy's style. While Dan Burke ran day-to-day operations at Cap Cities, Murphy was the man who did the flirting with potential acquisitions. It was a role he excelled at. His uncomplicated, straight-shooting manner was reassuring to smaller companies that didn't want to be eaten by some New York shark. People also took note of the cool confidence with which Murphy and Burke ran their shop, giving their media holdings plenty of autonomy. "You don't have to call the powerhouse in New York for answers," said one TV syndicator.[35] Years earlier, when he had first turned over the Albany television station to Dan Burke, Murphy had given him a tremendously long leash. As Cap Cities grew, he practiced this philosophy on a larger scale. "There's no magic to it," Murphy would say. "We hire the best people we can find and let them do their jobs."[36]

The main limiting factor on Murphy's acquisitive tendencies was finding media properties worth buying. "What you have to do is be patient," he had explained to a reporter in the 1970s, "and that's not necessarily easy for a fellow like me." The right opportunities would come around, he thought. "I think I get paid not just to make deals but to make good deals."[37] In Cap Cities' 1983 annual report, Murphy basically apologized for not finding enough properties to acquire.

Cable television looked to Murphy like a good deal in the 1980s. By the early 1980s, more than 20 million U.S. households subscribed to cable services, and Capital Cities Communications began to get in on the action with some initial purchases.[38] In fact, cable seemed like the

only way to keep the company growing once it had reached the maximum number of broadcast stations permissible by the FCC and had
acquired the big-market franchises and added 10 daily newspapers to its
list. In the early 1980s, it appeared as though Capital Cities had finally
reached its limit in the advertising-supported industries.

An FCC ruling late in 1984 opened a new door to Capital Cities'
expansion. Yielding to the conservative passion for deregulation at the
apex of the Reagan era, the commission agreed to expand the number of broadcast franchises permitted for individual owners. In the
wake of this ruling, Tom Murphy intended to more than double the
number of television and radio stations under his purview and also to
expand further. By the mid-1980s, Capital Cities had holdings in television stations, radio, cable, magazines, and newspapers—in short,
the company had a foothold in every advertising-supported media
market except one: television networks. The networks were not the
most lucrative wing of the entertainment industry. In fact, the television networks performed erratically and took home a much smaller
proportion of advertising revenues than their affiliates and related
industries. "The network business is not a great business, it's true,"
Murphy admitted.[39] But Cap Cities' bottom-line management had
succeeded more than once in its efforts to squeeze profits from a lackluster acquisition. Besides, the television networks were themselves
diverse multimedia conglomerates whose assets included television
and radio stations in the top U.S. markets. A single acquisition, a
megadeal, could transform Murphy's company overnight into the
biggest show in town.

The most likely candidate for acquisition by Murphy was ABC,
which had fallen behind since its glory days in the 1970s. By the early
1980s, the network was struggling with declining earnings and sluggish
ratings. Its longtime chairman, the legendary but aging Leonard Goldenson, knew that he had to find a successor capable of holding together
the network he had built from scratch in the face of pressure from cable
broadcasting, videocassette recorders, and hostile takeovers. ABC
seemed ripe for a friendly buyout, but Capital Cities presented itself as
an unlikely suitor. The television network was roughly three times larger
than Murphy's media conglomerate, with $3.7 billion in annual rev-
enues, compared to Cap Cities' $939 million. ABC's television affiliates
had a lock on the largest broadcast audiences in the country in New

York, Chicago, Detroit, Los Angeles, and San Francisco. And ABC's cable stations, led by the sports channel ESPN, were industry leaders, reaching millions of homes in dozens of different countries. If Capital Cities were to succeed in buying ABC, observed a Cap Cities employee, it would be like the minnow that came to swallow the whale.[40]

Murphy understood well that buying ABC would not be like buying anything else. For one thing, the network lived under a constant glare of publicity and media scrutiny. In a nation obsessed with television, the successes and failures of ABC's main programs were dissected endlessly. Its news anchors and leading reporters were major celebrities—Peter Jennings, Ted Koppel, Sam Donaldson—and its decisions about how to cover news often generated storms of controversy. In this kind of fishbowl, the personalities of ABC's top management figures did not escape scrutiny, either.

Early in the process of approaching ABC, Murphy had a candid talk with Dan Burke, Cap Cities' president and Murphy's friend and trusted lieutenant. Murphy talked about how buying ABC would put both men in the spotlight as never before. They would become public figures and could expect their share of the kind of rough treatment that public figures received. Gone would be the anonymity that they took for granted at Cap Cities. Was Burke ready for this? Burke said he was, although like Murphy he led a quiet, low-profile life that included a home in Rye. Neither Burke nor Murphy aspired to live in a fishbowl, nor was either man afraid of the big time.

Murphy approached the prospect of buying ABC gingerly. Never before in American history had a television network been bought. There were complex regulatory issues involved, as well as myriad financial considerations for both parties.

It was in December of 1984 that Murphy first broached the idea to the aged Goldenson with his trademark combination of charm and directness. "Please don't throw me out the window of this building, but I have a suggestion to make," Murphy said to Goldenson. "What about merging our two companies?"

Goldenson's response was one of cautious interest: "Maybe it makes good sense, but I'd have to think about it."[41]

Murphy argued that the merger would work, especially if the FCC made expected changes in its rules to allow for more-concentrated ownership of television stations. In January, the FCC did make the new changes and Murphy went back to Goldenson. "Do you want to pursue the thing I talked to you about?" he asked.

Again, Goldenson was interested. "Yes, but give me a little more time to think about it." Goldenson did think about it, and serious negotiations got under way in February. One of Murphy's first phone calls was to Buffett, whom he wanted at his side for the negotiations. "You're not going to believe this, pal!" Murphy said. When Murphy let Buffett in on the secret that he might be able to buy ABC, Buffett came quickly to the question of how it might affect Murphy's life. "The first thing you've got to do is figure out whether you really want to do it. Forget about the mathematics. What you're considering means a basic lifestyle change. You and your wives will have to decide that."[42]

Murphy and Burke definitely wanted to do it.

Goldenson's willingness to entertain Murphy's offer was testament to the sterling reputation both of Cap Cities and of Murphy. Cap Cities expertise in managing a media empire was well known, and Goldenson was intrigued by the possibility of streamlining ABC's operation through Cap Cities–style cost cutting. Murphy himself, moreover, seemed like the kind of strong leader that could take Goldenson's place at the network. Goldenson's logic made perfect sense. "If ABC is going to pick any company," observed a financial analyst, "there isn't any that's better managed, better known, or more well thought of than Capital Cities."[43]

Work on the huge and intricate deal unfolded in tremendous secrecy through the first half of March. A leak of the news could have destabilizing effects on the talks and would open the way for insider trading. Only four people at ABC knew the talks were under way, and most top executives at ABC would hear the news only one day before the public announcement. On the Cap Cities side, Murphy worked only with Burke, Warren Buffett, and takeover lawyer Martin Lipton.

The negotiations did not always go smoothly. The price tag for ABC became a major sticking point, almost killing the talks. And even after the price was agreed upon, various details were still being negotiated up until 30 minutes before the ABC board voted on the deal. "He was a tough trader, just impossible," Goldenson later said, only half joking, about Murphy. "And I, like a weak little lamb, [was] ready to be taken to the slaughter."[44]

The final deal called for Capital Cities to acquire ABC for cash and options valued at $3.5 billion—the biggest non-oil-industry merger in

American business history. To raise the cash, Murphy did not even stop at the bank. Instead, he called on his friend Warren Buffett, who was just beginning to make his reputation as an investing titan in the mid-1980s. Buffett agreed to contribute $517.5 million to the deal, purchasing 19 percent of the outstanding shares of the combined companies. Buffett described his role in the deal as that of the "500-pound gorilla"—a presence so formidable that the remaining financing would fall into place, a stockholder so insurmountable that he virtually ensured the newly created "Cap Cities/ABC" would not succumb to a hostile takeover.[45]

On March 18, 1985, the deal was publicly announced. Quickly, the merger received the full endorsement of Wall Street investors. Stocks in both corporations jumped sharply after the announcement in March 1985, and Capital Cities shares gained 22 percent in a single week.[46]

With the ABC deal, the business media finally discovered Tom Murphy. Profiles of him appeared in *Business Week* and the *New York Times*. The articles described Murphy as a reserved, no-nonsense power broker who was so low key he didn't even have a press agent. He was "the consummate deal man" and an "empire builder without usual ego."[47] After a quarter century of great accomplishment but little limelight, Murphy got more press in one week than he'd gotten over a lifetime.

Thomas Murphy of Brooklyn had arrived. He was a player.

Two days after the deal was announced, the *Times* wrote that Murphy had joined "an exclusive club of network super-executives." But friends who knew Murphy well suspected that he would remain his usual modest and private self. Quiet evenings in Rye with Suzanne would not be pushed aside by too many black-tie affairs. "It has nothing to do with rubbing elbows with the greats," said Hugh Beath, who had known Murphy for nearly 20 years. "He is not interested in that kind of life. I think he bought ABC because he thought he could make it better. He likes challenges."[48]

If Wall Street and the business press took pleasure in sanctioning the deal and christening Murphy as a new star, ABC employees greeted news of the merger with concern. Veteran reporter Sam Donaldson said he felt as though "someone had died."[49] Insiders feared that the network programming would suffer from an ensuing culture clash between the irreverent, sometimes racy ABC content providers and the straitlaced, churchgoing executive team at Capital Cities.[50] And from the world of organized labor came a cascade of voices that pointed out that Murphy and Cap Cities had a terrible reputation. "No one is worse than them," said the president of the Newspaper Guild.[51] In 1983, the AFL-CIO had placed Cap Cities on its dishonor roll for being the "most hard-line anti-union media conglomerate in the nation."[52]

Murphy and Burke had nothing to say in their defense on the labor issue. But they did point to the company's history of promoting autonomy for new acquisitions. "[Y]ou're not going to find me reading scripts or wearing a beret," said Murphy.[53] True to form, Cap Cities stuck with ABC's programming chiefs and interfered minimally in programming decisions. Even Donaldson had to admit that Cap Cities was not a threat, saying, "Their record has been good and there's no reason they should change it now."[54]

While the worst fears of ABC loyalists would never come to pass in terms of content on the network, costs and spending were entirely different matters. One business columnist put the situation this way: "All I know is if I were a senior ABC executive in the Los Angeles office with a small cocaine habit and a large expense account, a couple of girlfriends and a marginal efficiency rating, I would this very afternoon exercise my stock options and get out. . . . Murphy and Burke don't mess around."[55]

Changes were coming indeed. Within a month of the deal, ABC accelerated cutbacks in anticipation of the Cap Cities takeover. "Network executives rediscover the taxicab," said *Newsweek* in a story called "Taking the Knife to ABC."[56]

More than half a year elapsed between the time when the merger was publicly announced and the time when the money actually changed hands to complete the sale, during which Murphy and Burke occasionally had nerve-racking second thoughts about whether they were making a terrible mistake in taking over a huge and ailing network. One such doubt occurred when they were at ABC's offices in late March and noticed that several expensive paintings were missing, including a Jackson Pollock and a Willem de Kooning. "My God, they're selling artwork off the walls," Burke whispered to Murphy. As Burke said later, "We thought, 'Wow, this is sort of frightening.' "[57]

Murphy and Burke held steady, and ABC was officially theirs on January 3, 1986.

In Murphy's ideal takeover of a company, the high command of Cap Cities remained hands-off owners. But this wasn't possible with

ABC, which was troubled by losses. Inevitably, Murphy wielded a heavy hand in trying to pare down ABC and control costs. Soon, the six private dining rooms at headquarters, the penthouse suite at the Plaza Hotel, and the spread of snacks laid out for guests of *Good Morning, America* were eliminated.[58] Soon, David Hartman, the beloved host of *Good Morning, America,* was gone, when Murphy and Burke decided not to renew his $2 million contract. Murphy and Burke also forced ABC to cut 1,500 employees, 10 percent of the total, from its payroll. Meanwhile, Murphy practiced what he preached. On his first visit to the Los Angeles headquarters, he was greeted at the airport by a long white limousine. The next time he returned to Los Angeles, when he was firmly in command of the network, he took a cab from the airport. "The business of business is a lot of little decisions every day, mixed up with a few big decisions," Murphy said. "If the boss is chiseling, everyone else will feel they have a right to chisel."[59]

The cuts were controversial in themselves, especially those targeted at the news division, and this turbulence was heightened by various missteps. In one high-profile error, among those who left ABC during this time was ABC president Frederick Pierce, whom Murphy wanted to keep but who resigned when he was stripped of important responsibilities. Murphy was assigned the blame for the blunder. Another embarrassment occurred when there was an outcry over a plan at ABC to use drug-sniffing dogs in the offices of an ABC affiliate. Again, Murphy took heat for the fallout. The word around the media business was that Tom Murphy was in over his head. In 1987, the *New York Times Magazine* ran an article on ABC and Murphy titled "Not Ready for Prime Time?" It portrayed Murphy as struggling to meet the challenge of life in the big time, saying that "the network business is proving more painful than Tom Murphy ever expected. Every move is scrutinized by the press and the public."[60]

Murphy had enough self-confidence to handle the lukewarm press. But the real problem with ABC was declining earnings in spite of Murphy's austerity program. In the first year that Cap Cities was in control, ABC's profits continued falling and ratings remained lackluster, leading analysts to wonder what had happened to Tom Murphy's magic formula for turning businesses around. In 1981, *Forbes* magazine opined, "At Tom Murphy's Capital Cities, whatever can go right, usually does." Suddenly this pattern, what the magazine dubbed "Murphy's Law," didn't look so hard and fast, and by 1987 *Forbes* ran an article titled "An Exception to Murphy's Law?"[61]

Murphy's attitude about his struggles at ABC was typically forthright. "I'd like to be doing better with the network," Murphy said in 1988, after three years of fighting for a decent profit showing. "I'd also like to have a full head of hair and I'd like to be 38."[62] Ultimately, Murphy said, the work of turning around ABC was a long-term undertaking. "It will take some time. We will make some mistakes. But we will fix the network. It didn't break in one year and it will take three or four years to fix it."[63]

With the attempted turnaround of ABC becoming the fight of his career, Murphy opted for more hands-on management than ever before. By 1988, he was even spending time reading and watching pilots for television shows—something he'd promised he would never do.

Tom Murphy was going to fix ABC if it took him the rest of his lifetime.

13

Shady Business

arly in 1987, as his tenure was winding down at the SEC, John Shad decided it was time to give something back to the business school that had helped launch his career four decades earlier. Shad's gift to Harvard was an extraordinary $20 million pledge to create an ethics program at the business school. In addition, Shad promised to help raise an additional $10 million. The announcement of Shad's gift attracted considerable media interest, especially because of Shad's prominent role in uncovering one of the biggest business scandals in Wall Street history. It was unusual, to say the least, for a public official to put up his own money to combat the problem he'd been fighting in government. But Shad had always been an unusual guy, one who took his passions very seriously. And what disturbed him so much about the insider trading scandals was that many of the people involved should have known better. In explaining the gift, Shad said, "I've been concerned over the rash of insider trading cases that have recently been brought against leading graduates of business and law schools, the cream of the crop, many of whom are now convicted felons serving time in penitentiaries." Shad well knew that Harvard Business School had an impact that went far beyond those who graduated from the school itself: Its case studies and research materials were disseminated far and wide. Thus to make ethics a centerpiece of the business school would have wider implications. "Ethics and integrity are their own rewards," Shad said. "They also make good business sense." Shad hoped his millions would help drive home these basic points to future American business leaders.

A number of observers sneered at Shad's gift: "Ethics for the greed-heads," said the *New Republic*. "Can schools and corporations inculcate ethical behavior, or are they merely paying lip service to a widespread business problem?" asked *U.S. News & World Report*. In the atmosphere of the late 1980s, this skepticism was understandable. The 1980s saw America's business class badly tarnish itself with its ethical lapses and naked greed. The scandals were not just on Wall Street, but elsewhere, as takeover mania swept the corporate world and corners were cut along the way. Mostly, the abuses of the decade were perpetrated by a younger, hungrier business class. The 49ers and others of the World War II generation had a distinctly different set of values in that they tended to be grateful for their successes as opposed to impatient that the wealth wasn't coming faster. Marvin Traub once commented that he himself looked at any decision with the thought, "How would I feel if it was on the front page of the *New York Times*? And it makes it very easy to decide. . . . I think those values run right through our class."

But the 49ers would not be entirely immune from the excesses of the era. John Shad would get to know the darker side of American business more closely than he would ever have imagined. And, in one high-profile scandal of the decade, the 49ers would watch as one of their own—Lester Crown—struggled to save his reputation.

Lester Crown turned 60 in 1985. Longevity and good health ran in the Crown family, and the passing years had been kind to Crown. He had a full head of dark hair that he kept neatly combed back, and though his jowls were fleshier than they once were, he was tall and trim. A tennis court behind Crown's two-story brick Georgian house in the Chicago suburb of Wilmette helped him keep fit, as did an indoor pool and a basement filled with health equipment. In the winter, Crown often sported a tan picked up on the ski slopes outside of Aspen, where he and his wife Renee owned a townhouse. To meet Lester Crown at the age of 60 was to encounter a man very much in his prime, a man who felt that life had smiled on him.

Still, it was not so easy to be Lester Crown, and his sixtieth year would be among the most trying of his entire life. Ever since he'd been a young man, fresh out of Harvard, Crown had lived in two worlds. First, there was the world of his father, his family, and business "the Chicago way." In 1985, the dark side of that world dogged Lester Crown as never before, as he came under fire for sins committed in early years. At the same time, Lester was no clone of his father. He was part of the ethically cleaner, more modern world of business the Harvard way. Compared to his father, who told colorful stories and seemed a throwback to an earlier, corrupt era in Chicago, Lester was seen by many as a plain-vanilla, conventional, and earnest professional.

Working for his father made Lester's balancing act a daily reality. By the early 1980s, Lester had spent three decades as the dutiful Jewish son in Henry Crown's business empire and would-be dynasty. Crown rarely talked publicly or privately about his father, but when he did, it was with reverence. He would describe his father as "absolutely brilliant" and "the most humble person I have ever known."[1] Dynastic thinking came naturally to Lester. Even as he worked for his father, Lester was cultivating his own seven children to take over different aspects of the family's business and carry on the dynasty. His children took readily to the work. "The Crowns love business," said one Chicago real estate developer. Not only did all of Lester Crown's children have a concrete stake in the family business, but so, too, did various uncles, cousins, nieces, and nephews. The complexity of the family's business holdings was so great that it was difficult for even Crown to figure out who owned what or how much he was worth.

Crown often worried that the situation was a recipe for family squabbling. "One of these days we're going to get hit in the back of the head because we did this," he commented in 1986.[2] Fortunately, unlike the dysfunctional business families that dominated television during the 1980s in shows like *Dynasty,* the Crown clan was known around town for steadiness and loyalty. They were also known for not flaunting their wealth and for their interest in giving something back to the community. Although Crown was chauffeured into work every day, he felt compelled to explain that it was a luxury he accepted only in order to get work done during his morning commute.

As the 1980s began, Henry Crown endured as the indisputable patriarch of the far-flung Crown family even as he entered his 90s, with

Lester still operating in his father's shadow. The Crown offices on the twelfth floor of the Mercantile Exchange Building in Chicago seemed to say it all. Henry's Crown's office was spacious and regal, with a huge mahogany desk. Lester's office down the hall was small and spare, with a few sports mementos, some model planes, and photos of his family. It was the workplace of an underling, not a corporate titan. However, as the decade unfolded and Henry Crown's health began to wane, the old man's big office would increasingly be empty and the transfer of power to his son would rapidly accelerate.

Lester Crown was finally becoming his own man.

General Dynamics was the focal point of Crown's triumphs as well as his travails. In the early 1980s, the company generated cash as never before. The new Reagan administration embarked on a $2 trillion defense-spending binge, and the Pentagon showered General Dynamics with work. Stock prices for the company surged, profits skyrocketed, and the Crown family got richer and richer. Henry and Lester Crown put this money to work. Father and son invested their profits in a mushrooming financial empire that included a million shares of stock in Hilton Hotels, 45 percent of the Aspen Skiing Company, which owned three of four mountains in the fast-growing resort, 10 percent of the New York Yankees, 27 percent of the Chicago Bulls, and more than $500 million in stock and wholly owned operating companies.[3]

The Crowns kept a tight rein on their empire, paying special attention to the crown jewel of General Dynamics. Lester's autonomy and influence within General Dynamics increased in his role as an executive vice president and a member of the board, but the elder Crown continued to call the shots into the early 1980s as the éminence grise behind the scenes. To the outside world, the Crowns pretended that the corporate leadership of General Dynamics had wide autonomy, and its CEO, David Lewis, was depicted as his own man, who, with his top executive, P. Takis Veliotis, ran the company with minimal interference from the Crown family. Although Lester Crown was an executive vice president in the company, the official story was that he didn't try to exercise major authority. "I have no line responsibility," Lester would say.[4]

The reality was something different. With their huge, controlling interest in General Dynamics, Lester and Henry Crown were not about to be hands-off managers of the company. Every month, at executive committee sessions before full board meetings, Henry and Lester Crown would give Lewis his marching orders. All major decisions had to be cleared by the Crowns, including the hiring of top executives like Veliotis.

The reason that the Crown men tried to play down their central role at General Dynamics was simple: The 1980s would see major scandals at the company.

In 1980, the Securities and Exchange Commission opened an investigation into charges of insider trading at General Dynamics and concluded that the company improperly arranged to buy back 157,500 of its shares before it announced the payment of a large cash dividend in 1978.[5] The SEC also looked into inconsistencies in the company's proxy statements from 1978 to 1982, which failed to disclose problems at its Groton shipyards.[6] Meanwhile, a dispute with the navy over submarine contracts was threatening to become explosive. "If the shipbuilding issues were ever fully investigated," Admiral Rickover declared in 1984, "it would be a scandal bigger than Teapot Dome."[7]

P. Takis Veliotis symbolized decay within the General Dynamics organization. Veliotis was the aristocratic scion of a Greek shipbuilding dynasty. He had enjoyed remarkable success in turning around operations at General Dynamics' troubled commercial shipyard in Quincy, Massachusetts, and was soon promoted to run the famous shipyard at Groton that built nuclear submarines. Lester Crown strongly supported the promotion. It would be a major mistake.

The trouble with Veliotis began in 1982. A grand jury in New York asked Veliotis to testify in a case concerning possible payoffs made by the Frigitemp Corporation in exchange for General Dynamics subcontracts. Soon enough, the proceedings implicated Veliotis in an elaborate kickback scheme in which he allegedly accepted $2.7 million in illegal payments from Frigitemp.[8] Facing indictment, Veliotis fled to his native Greece where he lived as a pampered fugitive from justice through the mid-1980s.

Lester Crown was stung by the events. "I didn't have any idea Veliotis was the louse that he was," Crown would say later. "I, like David [Lewis], was absolutely fooled by him."[9] Veliotis's exit proved to be only the beginning of the fallout from the scandal. Veliotis took documents, audiotapes, and a burning resentment toward General Dynamics with him into exile. The shipbuilder refused to take the fall for business practices that he insisted were commonplace at the parent company. In

1984, the U.S. Justice Department offered him immunity in exchange for evidence and testimony of wrongdoing by General Dynamics. Veliotis responded with what some saw as proof of hundreds and millions of dollars in fraudulent claims against the government. In all of Lester Crown's career, never had he faced a scandal of this magnitude.

The Veliotis inquiry initiated a multifront assault against the defense industry giant. In addition to the Justice Department inquiry, General Dynamics faced hearings in Senator William Proxmire's Joint Economic Committee, an SEC investigation, and Defense Department proceedings. The most damaging revelations came out of the House of Representatives, where John D. Dingell's Committee on Energy and Commerce subpoenaed hundreds of documents that confirmed some of the worst of the charges. High-ranking navy officials appeared on the company payroll, including Admiral Rickover himself, who accepted nearly $70,000 in gifts from General Dynamics prior to the disputes of the 1970s and 1980s.[10] Veliotis testified that the company used bribes to sell military equipment to governments in Egypt and South Korea.[11] Other revelations were simply embarrassing. In an incident that came to symbolize the corruption of the defense industry, a receipt showed that General Dynamics had billed the government $9,609 for a wrench. In another instance, Crown was among a group of General Dynamics executives who went on a luxurious retreat to the Caribbean with their wives—and charged the $100,000 excursion to the Pentagon and U.S. taxpayers.[12]

The Crown family took a major beating during the scandal. The investigations coincided with the long-anticipated transfer of power from Henry to Lester Crown, as the Colonel's health deteriorated in his early 90s. By the beginning of 1985, Henry Crown was ill, as was his wife, and Henry stopped coming to his spacious office in the Mercantile Exchange Building. Lester would tell reporters that his father no longer had a "directional presence" but that "we keep him up to date and use him for advice."[13] Finally, the torch was being passed.

Lester's new and central position of influence in the family empire required him to answer for many of the charges against General Dynamics. Crown took to this task awkwardly, not willing to admit just how corrupt the company had become. "We didn't do anything wrong," he said at one point in 1985, "but it wasn't right either. . . . I have to say there was some foolishness and stupidity on our part not to look ahead and say 'What could this look like on the front pages?' "

Crown himself also became a direct target of investigators. Interestingly, the attack on Crown was not over any of the myriad illegalities at General Dynamics, but rather focused on his top-secret security clearance. The trouble began in 1984, when congressional investigators probing General Dynamics learned of Lester Crown's involvement in the 1972 bribery scandal. Congressional officials began asking hard questions: How could a man like Crown, who had admitted to bribing state government officials in Illinois, ever get a top-secret security clearance? And why should Crown be allowed to keep his security clearance and be actively involved in running General Dynamics, whose work involved some of the most sensitive nuclear weapons secrets of the U.S. military?

On February 7, 1985, Representative John Dingell fired off a harsh letter to Defense Secretary Casper Weinberger. "Bribery is a major felony involving serious moral turpitude," Dingell wrote. "The election to, and the retention on, the board of directors of an individual who admittedly was actively involved in the commission of a major crime is a statement on the integrity of the management of our nation's largest defense contractor."[14] Three weeks later, a chastised Weinberger replied, saying that General Dynamics hadn't properly disclosed all information about Crown's past. Had the Pentagon had all the information, Crown might not have been granted his security clearance. Weinberger promised a full reevaluation of Crown's clearance, including a hearing before a Defense Department examiner.

And so began what the *New York Times* would call "the ordeal of Lester Crown."

Crown's battle to retain his security clearance involved enormous stakes. Losing the security clearance would make it very difficult for Crown to continue serving on the General Dynamics board, which discussed national security secrets as a matter of course. It would also be devastating to his reputation. In 1985, as a respected leading businessman, the very last thing that Lester Crown wanted to be reminded of was a scandal from his past. The whole episode was deeply embarrassing, and Crown would privately compare the publicity to being "boiled in oil."[15]

Keeping the security clearance was an uphill battle. In Representative John Dingell, Crown had a formidable adversary. Dingell had considerable clout in the Democrat-controlled Congress, and the Pentagon was anxious to keep the powerful Congressman happy. In April

1985, Dingell's committee presided over a fierce interrogation of General Dynamics and Defense Department officials. "You have got a crook on your board of directors," Representative John Bryant of Texas berated David Lewis. "He is a crook. He bribed people. He falsified documents."[16] Crown's critics focused not just on the 1972 bribery episode, but also on alleged false testimony give by Crown in a 1975 antitrust action after Crown and a group of investors attempted to purchase the Chicago Bulls. Dingell and his colleagues placed enormous pressure on the Defense Department to revoke Crown's security clearance.[17] The Crown camp fired back. One of Crown's spokesman blasted John Bryant for his comments in Congress, saying they were "a horrible lie."[18]

Despite the fiery public rhetoric, along with news stories in major papers, the drama of the security clearance battle played out mainly behind closed doors. Ready to spend any amount of money to prevail, Crown retained two of the most powerful lawyers in Washington: Lloyd Cutler, former counsel to President Carter, and Leonard Garment, former counsel to President Nixon. In March 1986, after a year of wrangling, a Defense Department examiner named Burt Smith conducted three days of hearings on Crown's fitness to retain his security clearance. The hearings took place in an office tower in Arlington, Virginia. To defend his integrity, Crown and his lawyers lined up an all-star cast of political heavyweights to give testimony to the examiner. Those vouching for Crown included Henry Kissinger, Robert McNamara, and David Packard. Following the hearings, the examiner deliberated for over three months. Finally, on July 30, Smith delivered his verdict: Crown's security clearance was upheld. The examiner's statement said that it would be "unjustified to assess the Applicant's overall trustworthiness solely through a microscopic examination of two isolated incidents that occurred over ten years ago."[19] The decision was a tremendous victory for Crown, although one that was short-lived. Three weeks later, the Pentagon filed an appeal of the decision, and the controversy dragged on through the end of 1986.

Lester Crown was defiant. "I'm angry over the time and effort this has cost me, my family, and my friends," he complained.[20] Old friends could never recall seeing Crown more furious and unsettled. Crown's defenders were emphatic that the man should just be left alone. Even the federal prosecutor in the 1972 case, James Thompson—now Illinois governor—commented that the scandal "appears to have been an isolated aberration in what has otherwise been an exemplary life."[21] Crown himself was forced to largely remain silent for legal reasons, but on occasion he could not resist speaking out. He not only defended himself, but General Dynamics as a whole. "We didn't do anything wrong," said Crown. "[T]here isn't a cultural, ethical change required in this company.[22]

Ample evidence painted a different picture of General Dynamics. Four of its current and former executives, including NASA director James M. Beggs, were convicted of fraud in 1986, and the Convair division had to surrender its security clearance temporarily due to charges of mishandling classified documents. The Department of Defense withheld payments to the Electric Boat division for several months in 1985 and suspended the company from submitting bids in a handful of contract competitions.[23] General Dynamics made arrangements to pay back the $244 million in overcharges uncovered by the investigations.[24]

Still, all was not lost. In February 1986, the company negotiated a comprehensive immunity deal that shielded it from prosecution on matters related to any past military contracts.[25] And even amid the uproar of the scandals, General Dynamics quietly picked up $6.7 billion in new government business in 1985 alone, an 85 percent increase over the previous year.[26] General Dynamics prevailed over charges of corruption because it was too big and too vital to the national defense not to.

In March 1987, Lester Crown himself finally prevailed when a three-person Pentagon appeals board upheld the 1986 decision to allow Crown to retain his security clearance. Two years after beginning, Lester Crown's ordeal had come to an end.

During the same years that Lester Crown was defending himself from a government investigation, John Shad was working on the other side of the fence. As chairman of the Securities and Exchange Commission, he prosecuted criminals who operated in the most exclusive reaches of the business world.

The SEC job was something of a dream come true for John Shad. He had long toyed with a career in public service. During the early

1970s, he had been considered by the Nixon administration to run the Overseas Development Corporation, and his name had floated around in regard to other possible jobs in the Nixon/Ford years. Government service looked good to Shad because he was miserable at E.F. Hutton, and, as a multimillionaire, there was no pressing need for him to endure the abuse of Hutton's president, Robert Fomon. Also, Shad truly believed in his obligation to give something back to the world. He would often say that the goals of his life were "learning, earning, and serving." His intense workaholism had certainly ensured that the earning part of his life was a smashing success. Shad had worked himself into the ground making his fortune—gaining weight, often going without sleep, and assaulting his lungs with a chain-smoking habit. He had also terrorized untold numbers of subordinates with his driving, type A personality. By the late 1970s, Shad's face showed the wear and tear of his career. He had a sallow, unhealthy look, with dark circles below his eyes and deep creases around his mouth. The weight he had gained showed in his neck and cheeks, and his teeth bore the nicotine stains from a four-pack-a-day habit. One of Shad's few hobbies outside of work said everything about the man: He was a skydiver. In the late 1970s, Shad didn't want to stop working—the thought had never even occurred to him—but he did want to channel his manic intensity into something with higher meaning.

Shad's opportunity to serve finally came in 1980. With Hutton fast declining under Fomon's reign, Shad was more anxious than ever to find an exit. Fortune smiled on Shad in the amiable guise of Ronald Reagan. Shad, whose zeal for deregulation and concerns about the moral legacy of the 1960s had increased with time, was a longtime supporter of the California conservative. In early 1980, he was the first major figure on Wall Street to endorse Reagan during the presidential primary.[27] Shad also served as head of Reagan's campaign finance committee for New York State. His efforts helped raise millions for Reagan.

After Reagan's victory over Carter, when the time came for Shad's reward, his appointment as chairman of the SEC was a logical fit, and it reflected Shad's career credentials. Shad was elated. Government service for Ronald Reagan wasn't just any old job; it was an ideological crusade to push the conservative agenda.

Shad was an unusual pick for the job of SEC chairman. In the almost 50 years since the term of the first SEC chairman, Joseph P. Kennedy, only one of the chief enforcers of the nation's securities laws had been selected from the ranks of Wall Street insiders.[28] Shad's appointment signaled the Reagan administration's business-friendly outlook. Some critics excoriated the appointment, suggesting that it was akin to letting the fox guard the chicken coop. This impression was reinforced by Shad's early announcement that he favored easing regulatory requirements wherever possible.[29] The former banker described the "adversarial attitude" between the securities industry and the SEC as "a thing of the past."[30] Shad also announced his intention to scale back operations at the SEC in a cost-cutting exercise aimed at spending less than the annual budget authorized by Congress. Lower spending by the SEC, of course, meant less enforcement. The cutbacks conformed to the Reaganite ideal of smaller government and less regulation. Government, Reagan liked to say, was the problem, not the solution.

"The other day I was asked if I knew what a 'damn shame' is," Shad observed in a joke that career SEC staff probably found less than amusing. "I learned that a damn shame is a busload of government officials going off a cliff—with five empty seats."[31]

A Wall Street observer captured the popular reaction to the Shad agenda: "John will have to work overtime to avoid the appearance of favoritism toward the [securities] industry."[32] In his early days in office, Shad hit the ground running. He brought to the SEC the same round-the-clock work habits and nervous energy that had made him his fortune on Wall Street. Shad's agenda was ambitious as he took on the huge burden of work to undo the edifice of government regulation. In what the *Wall Street Journal* called "the most sweeping deregulation in the agency's 50 years," Shad oversaw the dismantling of stock registration rules, corporate disclosure requirements, and brokerage-house regulations.[33] SEC staffers staggered under the load. Shad's budgetary cuts at the agency meant layoffs even as the boss's new projects increased the workload on SEC lawyers and analysts. "You see people walking around glassy-eyed and tired," a former commissioner observed of the Shad regimen.[34] Shad responded to complaints by noting, "when school lunches are being cut, it's hard to say the SEC should get more people."

The Shad effort to downsize the SEC was greeted with horror by Democrats in Congress and within liberal business circles. Even other Republicans were aghast at the apparent abdication of the SEC's role in enforcement. "Wall Street is a cesspool of hanky-panky and the biggest gambling casino in the country," complained a Republican former commissioner in 1982. "The SEC has got to let the industry know that there's a cop on the beat."[35] In early 1983, Shad was blasted by his colleagues at the SEC when four of them publicly disputed Shad's contention that his budget cuts weren't hurting the SEC's enforcement powers. Shad was also widely criticized for his poor political instincts, and his large personal stockholdings on Wall Street ensured that he was dogged by conflict-of-interest charges.

Mistrust of Shad's caretaker agenda escalated as a boomtown atmosphere descended on Wall Street in the mid-1980s. In 1982, the Dow Jones Industrial Average stood at a lowly 770, a figure that represented a 75 percent depreciation (in real value) since the market high in 1966. By 1987, the Dow had exceeded 2,000 and was rapidly climbing toward 3,000 points, an increase of more than 250 percent.[36]

The 1980s bull market responded to strategies for manipulating stock prices through Wall Street maneuvers, especially mergers and acquisitions coordinated by the most powerful investment banks. New financial services and products—the leveraged buyout (LBO) and the junk bond—ballooned U.S. capital markets. Huge new bond issues flooded corporations and Wall Street offices with money. The complexity and pace of the new financial market created conditions ripe for criminal exploitation.

Yet even as opportunities for crime on Wall Street grew, the enforcement powers of the SEC shrank under Shad's antigovernment reign. "The SEC is horribly overmatched by the bad guys in the marketplace," Royce Griffin, a leading regulatory expert, said in 1985. That same year a report by the American Bar Association stated that the SEC's enforcement staff may be too small "for the commission to effectively discharge its statutory responsibilities." A front-page *Wall Street Journal* article called the SEC inundated, with many claims of criminal activity going uninvestigated by overworked and demoralized staff.[37] Shad's cutbacks, many believed, had effectively disarmed the agency.

The new corporate raiding mentality on Wall Street only made things worse. As a pioneer in high-yield bond financing in the 1960s and 1970s, John Shad had helped to perfect the debt structure that facilitated the most dynamic and dangerous innovation of corporate finance in the 1980s—the leveraged buyout. During the early 1970s, Shad had occasionally intersected with another pioneer in the junk bond field,

Michael Milken, a humorless workaholic who had set up Drexel Burn-ham Lambert's high-yield bond division in 1971. When Shad left E.F. Hutton for the SEC in 1981, junk bonds made up about 12 percent of the $45 billion corporate debt in the United States. The majority pro-vided growth and operational capital for corporations through nonin-vestment-grade issues; early junk bond success stories included MCI Communications and Turner Broadcasting. By 1986, junk bonds made up nearly 25 percent of a total corporate debt that had increased by a factor of 10 in the past half decade to $225 billion.[38] The use of junk bonds to finance hostile takeovers accounted for the difference.

Hostile takeovers had been a Wall Street taboo before the 1980s, but this changed as Salomon Brothers and other respected banks demon-strated the premium prices and fees such transactions could deliver for shareholders, executives, and financial service providers. In the absence of legal or institutional margin restrictions on acquisitions, junk bonds offered ready and unlimited capital to would-be purchasers. In 1984, Drexel executed the first successful hostile takeover leveraged with high-yield securities, the purchase of National Can Corporation by Nelson Pelz for $465 million, less than 10 percent of the total in equity.[39] The ensuing bonanza saw 25,000 corporate mergers completed from 1985 to 1987, 21 of which featured capitalization in excess of $1 billion.[40]

The mergers and acquisitions (M&A) craze pumped up stock prices, substituting a debt-financed retail value for such traditional indexes of corporate worth as the price-to-earnings ratio. The potential for quick riches also helped usher in a wider era of greed on Wall Street. Self-styled corporate raiders became symbols of this new time of excess. In a Wall Street atmosphere where everyone wanted to be one of the big winners, the impulse to find shortcuts was inevitable. As the M&A boom unfolded, John Shad found himself in a curious position. After several years of battling to downsize government and roll back regula-tion, he suddenly began to worry about the unfettered free market that he himself had helped to create. The risks of the new era came to pre-occupy Shad no less than his liberal critics. Leveraged buyouts had fun-damentally altered the financial landscape of the 1980s, overwhelming existing securities laws and inviting a new range of abuses. Early in his tenure, Shad had said publicly that he wasn't worried about mergers and that they tended to be a good thing for efficiency reasons. Now Shad worried that the increased debt would place an unhealthy burden on corporations, draining revenues from research and development and unbalancing financial portfolios. "The more leveraged buyouts today, the more bankruptcies tomorrow," he warned in 1984.[41] Buyouts also created fertile opportunities for financial professionals with inside information about pending mergers who were willing to break the law to cash in on inflated stock prices. Shad had predicted a showdown over insider trading at the outset of his tenure at the SEC, promising in 1981, "We're going to come down with hobnail boots to give some shocking examples to inhibit this activity."[42] At his first public speech after taking office, Shad had inveighed harshly against the greed of inside traders. But if Shad's tough talk sent one message, the downsizing of the SEC sent another. Insider trading accelerated as the LBO boom gained momentum. By 1985, strong surges in stock prices—a sure sign of insider trading—preceded three-quarters of all takeover bids.[43] Determined to crack down, Shad endorsed legislation to triple the cash penalties for insider trading, achieved breakthrough concessions from Swiss banks to facilitate investigations, and increased the number of cases under review.

Shad tried to place his campaign against insider training within his ideological framework of small government. Rather than a kind of new regulation, Shad argued that prosecuting insider trading cases would enforce commonsense laws that had governed the securities industry for decades. The campaign responded to popular concerns about the proliferation of buyouts without claiming to interfere in the market dynamics of mergers and acquisitions, easing Shad's tense relationship with congressional critics who were demanding a more activist role for the SEC.[44] New technology permitted electronic surveillance of trading patterns in thousands of stocks, providing an early alert of suspicious behavior and statistical information that could be used in insider trading prosecutions. People convicted of insider trading were subject to fines in addition to criminal penalties, fines that contributed to the SEC's operating accounts. As penalties mounted to a total of 110 percent of the taxpayer-supported budget, Shad would delight in calling his SEC a government "profit center."[45] Still, even as Shad played the tough enforcer, he was pessimistic about his effectiveness, saying in 1982 that "insider trading had proliferated to the extent that no law enforcement agency can ever expect to fully reach . . . a lot of people have gotten away with a lot of insider trades."[46]

Insider trading was not the only crime going down on Wall Street. In the mid-1980s, scandal engulfed Shad's former firm, E.F. Hutton. A three-year Justice Department investigation culminated in May 1985, when E.F. Hutton pleaded guilty to 2,000 counts of mail and wire fraud in connection with a nationwide check-kiting scheme. The SEC also brought charges against Hutton for defrauding its mutual fund customers. The case shined a spotlight on Shad's old nemesis, Robert Fomon. However, whatever pleasures Shad may have taken in going over Fomon were denied him when he recused himself from participating in the investigation. In the end, the Hutton case led to more pain than satisfaction for Shad. Controversy over what some saw as easy settlement terms—Hutton paid a $2 million fine and avoided criminal penalties—focused attention on the Reagan administration's lax regulatory attitude and Shad's recent and prominent association with the brokerage house.[47] Shad's vigorous pursuit of miscreant financiers during the mid-1980s reflected in part an effort to disassociate his own career from Wall Street wild men like Fomon.

The high-profile insider trading case that the SEC had been promising for years finally broke in May 1986. The arrest of Dennis B. Levine, an investment banker in Drexel Burnham Lambert's New York offices, set in motion a chain of events that riveted public attention on Wall Street and the SEC. Working in conjunction with the ambitious U.S. attorney in New York, Rudolph Giuliani, Shad's enforcement division uncovered a conspiracy in which Levine had earned $12.6 million in profits on the sale of inside information. The SEC chief had reason to be satisfied with his first high-profile insider trading bust, as Levine proved willing and able to incriminate his co-conspirators in exchange for leniency. Levine's testimony provided damning evidence against Ivan Boesky, a Wall Street arbitrageur who specialized in purchasing blocks of shares of corporations targeted for takeover. The connection opened the investigation that made Shad's SEC the number one U.S. crime-fighting organization in the 1980s.

Boesky provided an appropriate symbol of Wall Street malfeasance. He made his living by imposing his $3 billion in stock purchasing power between corporations and prospective corporate raiders, driving up prices for his shares by greenmail or delivering blocks of shares to takeover specialists. Inside information enhanced the profitability of his scheme. Working with Levine and informants at other top banks,

Boesky accumulated illegal profits in excess of $203 million in 1985 alone.[48]

The Boesky investigation was the most important case that the SEC had handled in decades, and Chairman Shad was determined to prosecute the arbitrageur without destabilizing the broader financial markets in which Boesky played a decisive role. These were nerve-racking days for Shad. He put on weight, often went without much sleep, and smoked more than usual. Subordinates became used to Shad's repeated, almost neurotic phone calls to glean any hint of new information about recent developments. The slightest misstep could send Shad into a frenzy.

When the moment finally came to move against Boesky, Shad authorized agents from the SEC's enforcement agency to notify Boesky of his impending arrest. Shad also permitted Boesky to sell off parts of his current stockholdings to raise $100 million in fines, fearful that the publicity would "have had a drastic effect on the market" to the point that the SEC could not collect its share of Boesky's ill-gotten gains.[49] The decision attracted a fresh deluge of criticism of Shad's business-friendly outlook, especially after prosecutors reached a favorable plea-bargain settlement with Boesky shortly after his dramatic arrest at 4:30 P.M. on Friday, November 14, 1986 (an event carefully planned to prevent undue panic in the stock market). Senator Howard Metzenbaum called the SEC's handling of the situation "an absolute abandonment of their responsibilities."[50] While the controversy transfixed Shad's opponents on Capitol Hill, the *Wall Street Journal*—in an editorial critical of Shad's crackdown on insider trading—observed that the appearance of leniency in the Boesky case probably signaled that "the SEC's enforcement division is after a bigger fish."[51]

It was.

Ivan Boesky's cooperation was vital to the SEC's pursuit of the biggest and most elusive suspected offender in corporate finance. Throughout Shad's tenure at the SEC, government investigators had repeatedly probed charges of illegal activities linked to the junk bond division of Drexel, ruled by Michael Milken out of an office in his native Beverly Hills. No fewer than four SEC investigations between 1981 and 1985 had targeted Milken's use of inside information, bribes, and disclosure violations to augment his personal fortune and the power of his Drexel division in the global financial market.[52] Scrutiny of Drexel and Milken responded in part to the banking establishment's widespread resentment of the upstart bank. Milken's jealous stewardship of the junk bond juggernaut was the foundation of Drexel's dominant position in the leveraged buyout field. Controlling two-thirds of the market for the high-yield securities that financed the LBO trend, Drexel rarely passed up an opportunity to throw its weight around in transactions with rival institutions.[53] With a characteristic lack of modesty, Milken promoted Drexel's contribution to economic growth and self-empowerment as a historic social achievement. "Junk bonds," he proclaimed, in a celebratory tone that further provoked his enemies, "allow entrepreneurs outside the system to get capital to realize their dreams."[54]

Ivan Boesky provided the SEC with the first usable evidence that Milken's aggrandizing dreams led Drexel to operate outside the legal system. Using testimony, documents, and covert audio recordings obtained by Boesky, the SEC began building a case against the bank and its star financier. John Shad would not be part of the final prosecution of Milken. By the time the SEC filed its complaint against Drexel in September 1988, naming the corporation, Michael Milken and his brother, and two other Drexel employees as parties to fraud and disclosure violations, Shad no longer served as SEC chairman. His tenure, the longest in the history of the agency, ended in June 1987, when he accepted President Reagan's offer of the post of U.S. ambassador to the Netherlands. Earlier that year, Shad had done a major about-face when he pushed for the biggest increase of the SEC's budget and staff in years. Shad's days as a Reaganite budget cutter were over, and he had grown tired of being the long arm of the federal law on Wall Street. It was time for a change. With his wife Patricia, then suffering from the cancer that would soon claim her life, Shad left for Europe only weeks before the market crash of October 1987.

For a time, the sojourn in Europe meant a quieter time for Shad. His days were spent in ceremonial duties and also helping to care for Patricia, who died in 1988. Inevitably, though, Shad soon missed the action. In January 1989, Shad surprised the business community by confirming reports of his pending decision to sign on as chairman of the reorganized Drexel group.[55] A widower, Shad returned to the United States that spring to engage in a new round of counseling with his former charge, Fred Joseph. "We chat about things every day," Joseph said of Shad at Drexel. "He's the guy I can bounce ideas off of."[56]

It is a measure of the hubris that Shad imbibed during his years on

Wall Street that he thought he could save the day for Drexel Burnham Lambert in 1989. His was no rubber-stamp chairmanship, and he hotly denied that his tenure was window dressing for Drexel's reform program. "That's not the kind of man I am," he said.[57] Rather than limit his activities to chairing the oversight committee in charge of compliance with the SEC settlement, Shad embraced a wide range of executive roles. He urged Joseph to build up Drexel's credentials in the field of merchant banking, saying, "[W]e have the potential of being a major principal."[58] He spent weeks in Asia trying to educate Hong Kong and Japanese banks about the benefits of leveraged buyouts and high-yield financing.[59] By the time he took office, however, the collapse of the junk bond market and the default of major Drexel clients had spelled the bank's doom.[60] When operating assets slipped below the federally mandated level, none of John Shad's former friends at the SEC were willing to negotiate an alternative arrangement. Drexel filed for bankruptcy protection on February 13, 1990, and Shad's brief tenure at the head of a major investment bank came to a painful close. An editorial commented on Shad's quixotic effort to stave off the inevitable as the act of "a man so in love with the gambling spirit that . . . he would bet on two cockroaches crossing the floor."[61] He lost his bet on Drexel, but won the satisfaction of finally playing the Wall Street game at the top.

The last hurrah of John Shad at Drexel Burnham Lambert confirmed his undying faith in American capitalism and his own ability to make it work for the best. In the twilight of his career, he observed, "I'm still as naive about the world, and as optimistic" as in 1949. Speaking of his friends from the Harvard Business School, he declared, "I look at our class, and how we've done, and I know that the system works."[62]

14

Taken Over

I n September 1980, Marvin Traub presided over the opening of Bloomingdale's most spectacular promotion ever: "Come to China," a tribute to China costing at least $2.5 million. The promotion showed every side of Traub's larger-than-life marketing approach. First, there was statesmanlike diplomacy with the communist regime in Beijing, with the goal of bringing to Bloomingdale's a set of priceless ceremonial Chinese robes that had never left the wall of the Forbidden City. One reason the Chinese government went along was that the promotion also featured some $14 million worth of Chinese-made or Chinese-oriented goods. When the promotion opened, Traub guided China's ambassador to the United States around the store, utterly at ease in his role as curator and statesman.

The China promotion also showed off the most important ingredi-ent for Traub's enduring success: his knack for what *People* magazine would call "show and sell," getting customers into Bloomingdale's and having them open their wallets. "Good marketing doesn't respond to needs," Traub would say later. "They help to create the need." As Traub saw it, the basic fact of life was that most people had most of the things they needed. "People don't need to buy another suit or dress. . . . They have enough ties in their closet. . . . A good retailer really creates the feeling that you have to have this even though you may have enough."

"Come to China" was promoted with a massive advertising blitz in newspapers and magazines, as well as news coverage of the unusual displays, which included not just the robes, but an authentic sampan in the White Plains store and a group of Chinese artisans demonstrating lace making. Of course, there was also the perennial Bloomingdale's secret weapon: word of mouth. The combination worked spectacularly. "We estimate over 11 million people have visited our stores to see the promotion," Traub said later in the fall.[1]

The China exhibit kicked off what promised to be an extraordinary decade for Marvin Traub. Fifty-five years old in 1980, Traub was at the top of his game. Thirty years after arriving at Bloomingdale's as a lowly manager, Traub completely dominated the company as CEO and chairman of the board. His base salary was in the mid-six figures, with bonus payout on top of that. While Bloomingdale's had gotten a reputation for catering to celebrities—Faye Dunaway, Barbra Streisand, and Diana Ross were among the 1.2 million holders of Bloomingdale's charge cards—Traub himself had managed to join their ranks. Photos in the society pages captured Traub's wide swath: Traub with tennis star Björn Borg, promoting a tennis clothing line at the store; Traub with Calvin Klein, one of the hottest new designers in the country; Traub and his wife Lee with Betty Ford. At Traub's office, invitations poured in for high-profile parties across the city and the country.

Four decades earlier, it would have been difficult or impossible for a department store head to have this kind of cachet. Traub's high profile was due not just to the specifics of his success at Bloomingdale's or to the cultural moment. It was due as well to the growing importance of consumer goods to the U.S. economy as a whole. By the 1980s, the extent to which the U.S. economy was driven by consumer spending was widely acknowledged by economists. Traub understood all of this very well. "The consumer has enormous power in our country," he observed. It was a power that seemed to grow ever greater over time, and "consumer confidence" now ranked among the most important of all economic indicators. Inevitably, those leading business figures who specialized in catering to the American consumer also saw their power grow.

Traub reveled in his life in the fast lane and tried to take in as much of it as he could. The passing years hadn't diminished Traub's drive one bit. "No matter what he does, whether it's running Bloomingdale's or having a dinner party, he has incredible, endless energy," his wife commented.[2] For Traub's employees, this energy could be both a boon and a burden. The great thing about working with Traub was that he engaged so deeply with the worlds of fashion and art. An overseas buying trip with Traub was like a college field trip. As one of Traub's vice presidents said: "Between meetings and buying, he guides us through galleries, museums, cottage industries or anything else that strikes his fancy. He's enthusiastic about everything."[3]

The downside of working for Traub was that he expected others to be as enthusiastic as he was and to put in the same killer hours at the office as he did. Traub would sometimes call meetings for 7:30 A.M., and many of his executives would find themselves still at the office at 8 P.M. He was known for his sharp questions and acidic comments. It was not a management style that made everyone happy. One of Traub's ex-managers commented to a reporter, "He turns over people like he turns over the merchandize. He buys the best, gets the most he can from them, then buys someone new."[4]

In contrast to the younger executives who often worked for him, who had grown up in a wealthy and secure America, Traub and his generation came from an era of depression and war in which progress could not be taken for granted. It showed in their working styles, and Traub was forthright about his relentlessness. "I have high standards for myself and I have them for the store and the people I work with," he said in 1980. "If you're going to do something well and if Bloomingdale's is going to be unique, it's going to take long hours. It would be marvelous to say that you can do it all from 9 to 5, five days a week, but in the real world that's hard to achieve."[5]

Balancing work and family had long been a constant challenge for Traub, especially when his three children were younger in the 1960s and 1970s. Lee Traub insisted that at least two or three nights a week be spent at home as a family. Lee also had another rule: that Sundays remain completely free, with no invitations or obligations. Marvin complied with these requests and tried to stay engaged with the family amid the powerful draw of work.[6] By the early 1980s, the kids had grown up and Marvin and Lee were alone. During the week, they lived in a thirty-ninth-floor apartment on the Upper East Side, not far from the store, with large glass windows and breathtaking views of Manhattan and beyond. On weekends, they retreated to their home in Greenwich, Connecticut, a custom-built house on six acres. Naturally, it was filled with Bloomingdale's furnishings.

The 1980s began with great promise for Traub and Bloomingdale's. The retail market boomed spectacularly in the first few years of the decade. The store was in an enviable position, with an unusually powerful brand name that had national resonance and could sell a wide range of products. "We do incredible business with anything that says 'Bloomingdale's,'" Traub commented in a remark that would have seemed nakedly self-aggrandizing if it weren't so manifestly true.[7] Traub's great ambition during the 1980s was to realize the full potential of the Bloomingdale's brand, exploiting numerous new markets in an America with more wealth than ever. "I'm not the kind of person who can sit by and relax," Traub said. At the beginning of the 1980s, Traub planned to break out of the northeast, where all of Bloomingdale's stores were located. His gaze was focused on Chicago, California, and the prospering new Sun Belt states. "Over the next five or 10 years Bloomingdale's is going to become a national business," Traub said in 1980.[8]

Traub would be true to his word. During the new campaign of expansion, he would open branches in Texas, Washington, D.C., Boca Raton, Florida, and 13 other locations during the 1980s. The branches benefited from some of the same merchandising flair that characterized the flagship store, with celebrity tours, special classes, and fancy in-store restaurants. National sales increased 48 percent from 1980 to 1985. Bloomingdale's By Mail, the catalog business, was booming so much that it had problems maintaining enough inventory to meet demand. Still, the 59th Street store continued to generate the lion's share of the excitement and over a third of all Bloomingdale's revenues.[9]

As Traub focused his energies on managing an expanded Bloomingdale's, the sharks were circling. The 1980s was the era of takeovers, and no company was safe from predators. Sometimes hostile takeovers grew out of long-plotted business strategies; other times they were the product of a billionaire's impulsive whim. According to legend, a family outing at the Bloomingdale's branch in Boca Raton was the source of the first successful takeover of Bloomingdale's. In November 1987, the Canadian real estate developer Robert Campeau visited the Florida store and marveled at its compelling design and appealing merchandise. He decided on the spot that he wanted to own Bloomingdale's and its parent company, Federated Department Stores. Within weeks, Campeau had initiated bidding for a hostile takeover of the company.

Campeau's spontaneous charge at Bloomingdale's was entirely

within character. A French Canadian who had dropped out of school at the age of 14, Campeau was known as an erratic and unstable mogul. He could be devastatingly charming, but also arrogant and imperious. Over the years, he had had several emotional breakdowns. He had also married his second wife while still wed to his first.

Traub and other executives at Federated had picked up early warning signs that the company was a potential target for a takeover. The booming retail market of the 1970s and early 1980s, in which Bloomingdale's had established itself as the store to watch, gave way in mid-decade to leaner times as a consequence of costly branch expansion, higher interest rates, saturated markets, and the rise of major discount chains such as Wal-Mart.[10] Bloomingdale's had posted annual growth of 10 to 13 percent through the 1970s and remained strong during the first half of the 1980s, but trouble set in as the decade wore on, with revenues going flat. Federated's other stores proved even less successful. Federated stock had already started to lose value before the stock market crash of October 1987. The company emerged from the crisis shaken, sinking to $33 from $42.50 a share. The low stock prices made Federated easy pickings for a takeover.

Campeau Corporation submitted its first bid for Federated—$47 a share, totaling $4.2 billion—on January 25, 1988. The offer created tremendous excitement, the opening salvo in what would be an extended takeover drama. Other offers were also in the works from May Department Stores and R.H. Macy Company. Federated's board of directors, which included Traub, preferred to accept a bid from one of the other retailers rather than from Campeau. Beyond his reputation as a loose cannon, Campeau's corporation was heavily leveraged.

Traub was particularly active in trying to stop Campeau's offer, even meeting with LBO king Henry Kravis. The hope of Traub and others was that another suitor could come up with a better offer than Campeau, or that lenders would realize the folly of giving Campeau so much money. Neither strategy worked. On April 1, 1988, Campeau captured Federated with an offer of $73.50 a share. For a total price of $6.5 billion, a new leader with no practical experience in retail took control of Bloomingdale's and the other Federated stores. It was one the largest hostile takeovers yet in American financial history.

Following the successful bid, Traub was among the first Federated executives to call Campeau to congratulate him. When they finally met,

Traub found that they had an immediate good rapport. Still, working with Campeau was a challenge. Campeau's lack of knowledge about retailing included a limited perception of Traub's own accomplishments. "Marvin, you may be a great merchant," Campeau said in a speech in Chicago, "but I'm going to teach you how to make a profit."[11] Traub considered Campeau at times to be off-the-wall, and he didn't appreciate it when Campeau would sometimes call him at six in the morning. But Traub accepted him as his new boss and worked to be a loyal subordinate. He arranged parties around New York to introduce people to Campeau, including a black-tie society dinner at the Met.

Ultimately, the big problem with Robert Campeau's ownership of Federated would not be his lack of experience and his eccentric personality, but rather his financial problems. To arrange financing for the restructured Campeau Corporation's combined $7.9 billion in new and old debt, the Canadian had promised to make $869 million in annual interest payments out of the proceeds of Federated earnings. "No banker, ever, and I repeat, ever came to Bloomingdale's to ask if I thought we could deliver those numbers," Traub said later.[12] In fact, even during Federated's best years, the company never cleared pretax profits of more than $680 million.[13] In the lean market of the late 1980s, punctuated by the profit-draining store wars of 1989 to 1990, the shortfall far exceeded $190 million. Within 18 months of the Campeau buyout, Federated Department Stores had filed for Chapter 11 bankruptcy protection.

Marvin Traub struggled to keep Bloomingdale's and his own career afloat through the financial crisis. Traub managed to maintain good relations with Campeau in spite of the reality that the Canadian had essentially destroyed Federated. Traub also managed to keep Bloomingdale's stocked and operating, often calling in favors from old friends like Ralph Lauren to keep shipments on schedule in spite of the bankruptcy. Using Chapter 11's provisions to terminate leases, Traub closed a number of nonperforming Bloomingdale's branches. At one point, in late 1989 and 1990, it looked like Traub could possibly buy Bloomingdale's himself, and he worked hard to pull together a group of investors to back him. The effort was a failure.

Eventually, Robert Campeau stepped aside as owner of Federated and the company was reorganized under the leadership of Alan Questrom. Traub helped to guide Bloomingdale's and its parent corporation back to financial health. But Traub's efforts to save Bloomingdale's could not protect his own position in the restructured Federated company. In 1991, amid a wave of forced resignations by department store CEOs in Federated, Allied, and other chains, Traub announced that he was stepping aside for a new number one at Bloomingdale's. He had been at the store for a total of 41 years. Although most of that time had been invigorating, Traub couldn't say the same about his last four years. "The 1987 to 1991 period was the most stressful I ever experienced."

Traub's last day at Bloomingdale's was orchestrated in a fitting manner. An elaborate ceremony staged on the first floor featured pom-pom girls and a marching band. Tears flowed from longtime employees as Traub said a few words of farewell. Finally, with the band playing, he was gone.

The era of the merchant prince was over.[14]

Jack Davis also was in for an interesting ride during the takeover wars of the 1980s.

Davis's Resorts International had scored big in the late 1970s by opening up Atlantic City. During the heady days of its monopoly on gambling in the city, it had pulled in cash at an unbelievable rate. Davis himself had become a multimillionaire. But in the early 1980s, Resorts faced major threats to its financial stability. New hotels and casinos were opening in Atlantic City—competition that soon included Bally's, Caesars, and a series of properties owned by New York real estate mogul Donald Trump. Though Resorts remained Atlantic City's premier casino operator, Trump's wife, Ivana, rightly observed that "the cheesecake is getting sliced thinner."[15]

The compulsive urge of Davis's boss, James Crosby, to buy up new property in Atlantic City compounded Resorts' problems, increasing the company's debt burden. By the mid-1980s, Resorts owned 15 percent of all the assessed real estate in Atlantic City.[16] "Resorts is a real estate company in the disguise of a casino," observed a financial analyst in 1986.[17] As casino earnings tumbled from 12 percent margins in 1984 to 1 percent in 1986, Crosby's investments looked less and less viable, dragging down the price of Resorts International stock.[18] Davis dealt with the chill of tough business times even as he worked ceaselessly to bring zip to the company's casino. His second wife, Caroline, was an enormous help in this regard. Through the 1980s, she orchestrated a series of fancy parties that became the most coveted invitations in town. One of her earliest was a Halloween party that had people talking for months. In time, her parties turned into ever more elaborate extravaganzas.

In April 1986, things changed dramatically when Crosby died. For Davis, it was the end of a partnership that had lasted over a quarter century. Crosby had at times been a difficult boss, making bad business decisions and running Resorts like a personal fiefdom. Yet the partnership had worked year in and year out, and it had made Jack Davis a very wealthy man. In the wake of Crosby's death, Davis took over as CEO amid rumors that the company was up for sale. Crosby's death coincided with the heyday of hostile takeovers and leveraged buyouts, and the company naturally drew the gaze of raiders. Davis insisted publicly that Resorts' fate would "continue to remain with the Crosby family" under his stewardship.[19] Davis also moved to "reinforce the ongoing interest of the Crosby family" by orchestrating his own replacement with Henry Murphy, a longtime member of the board who was the cousin of Davis's Harvard classmate, Thomas Murphy.[20]

While he worked publicly on behalf of the Crosbys, Davis negotiated behind the scenes with outside interests. His particular concern was to find a source of new capital for the highly leveraged company. Two major new developments were running behind schedule and over budget. The first was the $400 million renovation of Atlantic City's Steel Pier, which Resorts was remaking as an entertainment center and amusement park that Davis promised would "truly be one of the wonders of the world."[21] The second project—a towering hulk of beams and construction debris on a tremendous lot near the original Resorts casino—was the Taj Mahal casino and hotel complex. The Taj Mahal had already cost $400 million and was years away from opening. An observer noted that the completion of the Taj Mahal was critically important to the Crosby family, which saw the complex as "a last memorial to Jim Crosby."[22] In fact, the project was equally vital to Jack Davis, who later explained that he himself "gave birth to the Taj" during his tenure as president. "It was my design concept," he exclaimed. "I named it [and] I chose a theme. I designed the operation."[23] If Davis's dream project was to survive, Resorts International needed a buyer to continue the project and reorganize corporate finances.

Davis placed his bet for the future of the Taj Mahal and Resorts International on Donald Trump. In the mid-1980s, Trump enjoyed a reputation as a miracle maker, whose Midas touch could transform the most troublesome investments into gold. "The [Crosby] family believed that he was so strong financially that he would not need to sell off the company's assets to pay its debt," noted a member of Trump's organization.[24] Trump was already a player in the Atlantic City real estate and gaming markets, with his own casino, the Trump Castle, where Ivana Trump served as general manager. The Resorts takeover "was Donald's kind of deal," an opportunity to pick up prime properties at a fire-sale price. The company's assets included the Boardwalk complex, which was still considered Atlantic City's premier casino,[25] and the 1,200-room Taj Mahal, a Trump-scale project that would be a real credit to the developer's name. Davis and Trump, moreover, had become friends despite the rivalry between their casinos. During Trump's well-publicized love affair with Marla Maples, Davis had hosted the couple at his home, discreetly providing an out-of-the-way place for Maples to stay.[26] Throughout 1986, Davis worked quietly to smooth the way for a Trump buyout, perhaps even maneuvering behind the scenes to drive down the value of the stock to reduce the purchase price.[27] The effort succeeded in July 1987, when Trump bought Resorts International for $101 million. After the sale, Trump rewarded Davis with $1 million a year in salary as a consultant to Resorts.

Trump hit trouble almost immediately with his new holdings. Rocked by the financial strains of completing the Taj Mahal and other far-reaching projects, the Trump empire fell into disarray in the late 1980s. Within a year of the purchase, Resorts was up for sale again. This time the suitor was another high-profile figure, entertainer Merv Griffin. After taking control of Resorts, one of Griffin's early moves was to fire Davis from his million-dollar-a-year job. Trump had taken pains to protect his friend Davis, inserting a "platinum parachute" clause into the sale contract that kept Davis on the payroll for at least two years, and Griffin's actions prompted Davis to file a breach-of-contract lawsuit.[28]

The lawsuit went nowhere, but no matter: Davis had plenty of money and very little to do, which he found was not such a bad combination. He and Caroline decided it was time to wind down a bit, and they spent the next two years traveling around the world including an extended stay in Bora Bora in Tahiti. "We did everything we ever wanted to do." They returned in 1990 when Trump regained control of the Taj Mahal in a property swap with Griffin and named Davis as president of the Taj. It was a nice way to return to Atlantic City for Davis, taking over at the helm of the project that he had worked to see realized for many years. Caroline's party-throwing skills were also put to use, and this time she was on the payroll.

The new casino's 3,000 slot machines and other games went into action in April 1990. Though revenues rolled in at the rate of $1.5 million per day during the early months, management problems persisted, resulting in the dismissal of two Taj Mahal presidents before the end of July. Davis's own tenure at the helm of Trump's gargantuan complex was also short, and he announced his resignation in May 1991. His split with Trump and the casino he had brought to the boardwalk was amicable, and his outlook on the episode remained upbeat. "Everything worked out fine," Davis concluded, predicting that his own career in Atlantic City would continue.[29]

When Davis left the Taj Mahal, he was 66 years old. He'd been in the gambling business since the mid-1960s. At this point in his life it would have been easy to call it quits and focus on spending money and having fun. But Jack Davis found it wasn't easy to just walk away from the gambling industry. He was too good at what he did, and he enjoyed his work far too much. Within two years, Davis would be named CEO of another major casino company.

The game continued.

Epilogue:
The Long Twilight

S tanley Greenfield had to steal time away from his new Internet business. Bill Ruane found room in his quiet days of studying stocks. Joe Amaturo took time away from managing his media company, headquartered in Fort Lauderdale. Marvin Traub was busy with a bustling consulting firm, but he put the most energy into the event as the program chairman.

The 50th reunion of the class of 1949 had to be done right.

Traub was a natural producer for the event, slated for the first weekend of June 1999. A decade had passed since Traub had held sway as Bloomingdale's impresario. During the 1990s, he'd led a lower-profile life as a retailing consultant. Gone were the days when he orchestrated extravaganzas on Bloomingdale's large showroom floors. Now, pushing 75, he worked in a comfortable office on Madison Avenue quietly counseling a variety of clients on how to bring some magic to their businesses. But Traub hadn't lost his own touch for making things happen, and the 50th reunion was the kind of event he considered worthy of his talents. Plenty of other die-hard class members stood ready to make the reunion a success. Beyond Stan Greenfield and Bill Ruane and Joe Amaturo, there were volunteers for different committees: Jim Burke and Tom Murphy helped out, as did Gray Garland, George Berman, Roger Sonnabend, Ernie Henderson, and others.

Like Traub, many of the men involved in planning the reunion led extremely busy lives, even in their mid-70s. A number were still actively involved in running businesses, caught up in the day-to-day whirl of decision making. A few had tried to retire, only to return to work. Other 49ers had made a clear break from work and yet still found themselves in constant motion as they focused their energies in the world of charity—museums, hospitals, famine relief organizations. It was difficult for a group of men raised during the Great Depression and used to hard work to simply stop doing things.

Beyond work or charity, family was another thing that kept the 49ers busy in their 70s. Remarkably, the vast majority of the 49ers had never divorced. As they gathered for their 50th reunion, most were still married to the same wives with whom they had shared the past half century. The 49ers typically attributed this fact to the more traditional values that they had been raised with, in an America not yet hit by the sexual revolution. Yet even by the standards of their generation, the 49ers were exceptionally stable in their marriages. "There's a rootedness that they have that's impressive," the pollster Daniel Yankelovich had once commented about the 49ers.

The stable marriages among the 49ers didn't mean that their lives had been free of family turmoil and tragedy over the years. Peter McColough lost two of his five children, one to a heart attack, the other to kidney disease. James Craig's eldest son committed suicide in the late 1960s. Hank Halmers's youngest son committed suicide at the age of 15, after being molested by a choirmaster while a choir boy. Lee Landes's son was killed by a drunken driver at the age of 26. William Henschel's son, a U.S. Marine serving in Vietnam, was left completely disabled after being badly wounded during the Tet offensive. Several class members, including Jack Davis, had wives who suffered from severe mental illness and claimed their own lives. One 49er's wife was murdered. For all the successes after Harvard, and the class's famous luck, the decades had not always been easy.

The weekend of the reunion was suffused with a powerful sense of nostalgia. Over a quarter of the class had passed away, and everyone who attended the reunion knew a few who were gone, either as longtime friends, one-time roommates, or just passing acquaintances. By far the most prominent 49er who didn't make it to the 50th reunion was John Shad, whose many years of hard living and heavy smoking finally took their toll in July 1994. Shad died after heart surgery, just a month after he had joined his old classmates in celebrating the 45th reunion in

Boston. "I don't feel old," Shad had told a television reporter at the reunion. "I really don't."

Besides John Shad, nearly 80 members of the class of 1949 had died in the decade following the 40th reunion. Others had had very close calls with death. "Let us give thanks that we have been sustained and privileged to reach this day," Stanley Greenfield wrote in a tribute for the 50th reunion. In 1992, Greenfield had undergone quadruple bypass heart surgery. "Let us give thanks for the fortitude to have borne the trials and tragedies that are part of every human life."

A half century gone by. Many of the 49ers had a common question for each other: "Where did the time go?" The class members were generally a content lot, and so the question was not asked as a lament but more as a genuine mystery. One moment you're in your 50s or early 60s. Next thing you know you're halfway through your eighth decade of life. How did that happen?

The last time the class had come together in a big way was in 1990, for the 40th reunion. That event was held at the tail end of the booming 1980s, and many of the class members were still in the public eye. John Shad was in the middle of his salvage operation at Drexel; Marvin Traub was attempting to save Bloomingdale's; Tom Murphy presided over Cap Cities/ABC; Jim Burke had only recently given up active management of Johnson & Johnson. The 40th reunion had featured so many high-profile movers and shakers that *Fortune* magazine had sent a reporter to cover the event and dubbed it "The CEO's Ball."

But even in 1990, as the class was toasted for its power, there had been a sense among many 49ers that the twilight years were coming on. "Despite what everyone says, somewhere around 60 or so you see life is finite," Jim Burke had commented at the time. "There are certain things you want to do—and you'd better do them while you can."[1] Peering into this new, final stage of life conjured up regret for some 49ers who didn't make it as big as they had hoped. Henry Brandt, for example, reflected that it was not bad being a senior vice president of Shearson Lehman Hutton and a multimillionaire, but it wasn't the big time. "It's not the same as being head of Cap Cities/ABC," Brandt said. "You never read about me." Brandt also had a more mundane complaint in 1990: He had sold 1,500 shares of Berkshire Hathaway, Warren Buffett's company, before it became one of the most legendary stocks on Wall Street.

For other class members who felt that they had made missteps or failed to achieve their potential, the 40th reunion had been a sobering moment to confront the dwindling time left to realize any unfulfilled hopes. The specter of true old age was everywhere apparent in the class. One 49er arrived at the reunion in a wheelchair, the victim of a recent stroke. He could smile and make eye contact, but he couldn't speak a single coherent word.

Now, in 1999, even more time had run through the clock for the 49ers.

The 1990s had seen 49ers take many different paths. For nearly all, it was a period to wind down. Many 49ers reveled in lives of leisure after decades of driving work. Enduring friendships among class members were nurtured on vacations that grew longer now that there was not much point in rushing back to the office. Every December, The Group—including Tom Murphy, Jack Muller, Peter McColough, Jim Burke and others—still gathered with their families in Vail for "Operation Snowflake." Over 50 people were sometimes part of the gatherings, as the ranks of grandchildren swelled. Beyond the annual ski vacation in Vail, there were other rites of leisure that 49ers pursued with one another. Peter McColough and Frank Mayers had begun a tradition of taking bicycling trips in Europe every September, sometimes with other 49ers. The trips took them through France, Italy, and the British Isles. They also compelled both men to get in good cycling shape every summer to prepare for days where they'd cover more than 30 miles on a bike. McColough, who had made a point of long vacations even at the height of his career with Xerox, also kept in shape for a variety of other outdoors activities that he pursued year around, including whitewater rafting, trekking in the Himalayas, and hiking in the Grand Tetons. He gave little thought during the 1990s to the world of business or to politics, another of his old interests. Finally, Peter McColough was on a permanent vacation.

For Tom Murphy, the 1990s featured all the best parts of life: a crowning business triumph and then a new chance to give something back to society through a cause that deeply moved him.

The late 1980s had been difficult for Murphy. His initial years of running ABC saw major losses at the huge media company, and something very usual for Murphy: criticism of his business acumen. "Nobody expected Tom Murphy to turn ABC around overnight," *Forbes* magazine sniped in 1987, "but the progress to date is distinctly disappointing."[2] By 1989, however, a major turnaround at ABC had finally begun. Slowly, Murphy's formula of cost cutting and smart management began to produce results. Propelled by a new generation of hits produced by ABC programming director Brandon Stoddard, the network's golden days returned. ABC struck the perfect note with its reorganized schedule in the late 1980s and early 1990s, winning young adult viewers with hit shows such as *Moonlighting, thirtysomething,* and *The Wonder Years.* Advertising revenues increased accordingly. Another Murphy holding, ESPN, emerged as the industry-leading cable network, reaching 70 million homes in 130 countries.[3] Overall, by the mid–1990s, Cap Cities/ABC administered the country's most powerful and profitable string of local television stations and the largest national radio network. Ten years after the takeover, ratings were high, earnings were up, and stock prices were astronomical. In 1994, the stock had risen to an astounding $675 a share.

The rapid capitalization of Cap Cities/ABC, combined with Buffett's gorilla's share of the outstanding stock, provided a measure of protection against a hostile takeover in an era of predatory business. Analysts estimated in 1994 that a prospective buyer would have to come up with $12 to $19 billion to grab Cap Cities.[4] But with more than $600 million in annual cash flow and high-performance assets, Murphy's conglomerate was irresistibly attractive. And Murphy himself felt the old familiar pressure to keep the business growing. In particular, Murphy hoped to find ways to improve the in-house production of television content.[5] Ten years into the ABC venture, Murphy found himself poised on the brink of a momentous decision—to buy or sell. Nearing the age of 70, his inclination was to sell.

Dan Burke's retirement in 1994 was another factor that made Murphy think more about getting out. Burke and Murphy had worked hand in glove for more than 20 years, playing off each other's strengths. It was a tremendously successful partnership. Warren Buffett had once said that having Murphy and Burke in the same company was like having Babe Ruth and Lou Gehrig in the same lineup. By the time he hit 65, however, Burke was ready to slow down in life and move on to other interests. Burke's retirement was significant enough to merit an article in the *Wall Street Journal,* which called the Burke/Murphy partnership "one of the longest running and most-respected management teams in broadcasting history."[6] With Burke gone, Murphy took on the job of actively running Cap Cities/ABC. Murphy still saw Burke regularly—both men lived in Rye, New York, and they socialized regularly together—but business without him just wasn't the same.

The sale of Cap Cities/ABC began in July 1995 with a walk on Wildflower Street in Sun Valley, Idaho, where some of the nation's top business executives and financiers had gathered for a high-powered conference put together by investment banker Herbert Allen. Many of the biggest movers and shakers of the era were there, schmoozing amid the spectacular views and crisp mountain air: Sumner Redstone, Edgar Bronfman, Bill Gates, Michael Eisner. It was a testament to how high Murphy has risen in life that he was an obvious, natural invitee to the gathering. Deal making was in the air during the event, and Murphy was open to offers. Spotting Murphy on his way to play golf with Warren Buffett, Disney CEO Michael Eisner called out a proposition. "Hey, Tom," said Eisner, "don't you think it's time for our companies to get together?" Murphy had been talking on and off to Eisner for years about a possible merger—always with Warren Buffett in the conversation. Murphy's reply to Eisner was anything but casual. "Sounds good," Murphy said. "Let's go talk to Buffett."[7]

A few days later, the principals met in New York and finalized the deal in less than two and a half hours. The Walt Disney Company agreed to purchase Capital Cities/ABC for stock and cash valued at $19 billion. Both sides saw the deal as a natural fit. "Every part of your company is working. Every part of my company is working," Eisner told Murphy.[8] The deal brought together what Eisner called "the two premier family entertainment companies in America."[9]

Murphy stayed on temporarily as the chief executive at Capital Cities/ABC, which retained its name and substantial autonomy in operations. Then in 1996 he finally retired. In one of his few material indulgences in life, Murphy had recently bought a condo in Florida—the first second home he had ever owned—and it had fine golfing nearby. For a while, Murphy spent much of his free time on the golf course, trying to improve his handicap. He didn't improve easily and soon found himself bored. Service on several corporate boards helped occupy his time, but then Murphy came upon an opportunity that was utterly different than anything he had done before: In July 1998, he became chairman of the board of trustees of an international relief organization, Save the Children, that operates in 40 countries. Soon, Murphy was back in the swing of things. His travels for the organization took him to the Middle East, to Central America, and to Vietnam. It was some of the most satisfying work of his life.

Jim Burke also turned to nonprofit work in the 1990s. When he retired as CEO from Johnson & Johnson in 1989, Burke was still extremely energetic. He burned off some of his energy through ocean sailing in a 60-foot yacht, and he tried to do the various things in life that had been crowded out during three decades on the corporate fast track. Yet, like Murphy, Jim Burke was not the kind of guy who could be content relaxing and spending down his multi-million-dollar fortune. So he focused his attention—and considerable reputation—on helping several nonprofit organizations. Burke's highest-profile venture was as chairman of the Partnership for a Drug-Free America.

Burke was drawn to the problem of drugs because he knew firsthand about the challenges of addiction. His first wife had been an alcoholic, and one of his children had had problems with drugs. Burke himself had started smoking cigarettes at the age of 12, and he had found it impossible to quit for 30 years, despite many attempts. Burke was keenly interested in the devastating toll of alcohol and cigarettes in American society. In the 1970s and 1980s, major public health campaigns had been waged to reduce tobacco use, which Burke considered "the most dangerous of all substances." Some of these efforts were backed by the Robert Wood Johnson Foundation, where Burke sat on the board.

As the problem of illegal drugs spread in American society, Burke saw an opportunity to use his marketing background to address the problem. "Advertising is the most efficient way to change attitudes there is," he believed. Getting involved with the Partnership at the suggestion of his brother Dan, Burke poured his formidable energies into the organization. In the course of the 1990s, the Partnership pried loose more than $2 billion in pro bono advertising aimed at preventing drug abuse. Burke's leadership of the organization placed him near the center of one of the most heated social debates in American society. There would be appearances on *Nightline,* CNN, and other television shows, as well as speeches around the country. Burke's role in the drug war won him both tremendous praise—President Clinton would award him the Medal of Freedom for his work—and criticism from those who saw the antidrug ads as counterproductive and the whole war on drugs as misguided. Burke took it all in stride. "I'm not really working," he said in 1998. "I'm having a good time."[10]

Beyond the Partnership for a Drug-Free America, Burke remained active on the board of directors of International Business Machines Corporation, Prudential, Inc., and the United Negro College Fund. He also served as chairman of the Business Enterprise Trust, a group that honors people in business who demonstrate courage, integrity, and social vision. In his mid-70s, Jim Burke was more active and engaged with the world than some of his classmates had been at the height of their careers. The busy pace suited him. "I haven't found retirement difficult at all," Burke commented, some years after leaving Johnson & Johnson. "In fact, it's hard for me to find anything wrong in my life."[11]

The 50th reunion of the class of 1949 was akin to the finish line in the long race between class members to scale the highest heights. Judged by their gravitas within corporate America, Tom Murphy and Jim Burke were easily the two most successful members of the class. But judged by another, very straightforward criteria—personal wealth—there were others who bested them.

Well before 1999, Lester Crown had won the race for richest member of the class. Crown alone among the 49ers who regularly made the *Forbes* list of the 400 richest Americans, and by 1999 *Forbes* was estimating his wealth, along with that of his family, at $2.9 billion. Inevitably, Crown's appearance on the list generated press attention in Chicago, where Crown was one of the wealthiest men in the city. Crown found this publicity unsettling, and he also disputed *Forbes'* methodology, saying that his money was so tied up in various family trusts and assets that it was absurd to call Crown himself a billionaire. "You would be more embarrassed than words could tell if you knew what my own net worth was, no matter what the family net worth was," Crown had once told *Forbes.*[12]

Whatever Lester Crown's true personal wealth, one thing was indisputable: It increased significantly during the 1990s. The death of his father, Henry, in 1990 at the age of 94 elevated Lester to the position of family patriarch and main guardian of the Crown fortune. Crown remained as head of Material Service and as chairman of the executive committee of the board of directors. As his investments in General Dynamics and elsewhere gained value in the stock market boom of the 1990s, Crown rose higher on the *Forbes* list: moving to the position of sixtieth richest man in America by 2001. The rise in Crown's wealth in the 1990s did not mean that everything always went well with his business activities. One highly publicized setback for Crown occurred when he took a major stake in Maytag, only to see the company experience hard times and the stock plummet.

The inevitable ups and downs of business didn't much faze Lester Crown as he entered his 70s. Although Crown was the final decision maker in the family, the next generation was increasingly bearing the daily stresses of running the Crown empire during the 1990s. Several of Lester Crown's children moved into key positions, and younger nephews and nieces also were active. Important matters were hashed out by the family through a roundtable forum, which involved group discussion among more than a dozen Crown family members. In the early 1990s, the third generation of Crowns occasionally had meetings to which Lester and other older family members were not invited. The torch was being passed.

A growing involvement in philanthropy also helped direct Lester Crown's energy away from the day-to-day activities of business. Crown's interests were extensive, seeming to widen as time passed. He sat on the boards of a half dozen organizations, including the Aspen Institute and the Jerusalem Foundation. At Northwestern University, where he was a board member, Crown created the Crown Family Center for Jewish Studies and endowed a series of professorships. In October 2000, the Crown family awarded $2 million to create the Lester Crown University Professorship in Ethics. As his philanthropic career blossomed, Crown took satisfaction in moving into the role of a respected elder in both Chicago and broader establishment circles.

No amount of success or money would buy Jack Davis a respected position within the establishment during his twilight years, but that was fine by him. In 1999, Davis occupied the same position within the class of 1949 that he had held for several decades: the guy with the most unusual career.

The 1990s had seen Davis's last hurrah in the gambling business. In 1994, at a time when most men his age were thinking about retiring, Davis took on a major new challenge when he became CEO of Capital Gaming International. Capital Gaming had big ventures under way, including gambling on Indian reservations in New England and river-boat casinos in Louisiana and Mississippi. In Davis, the board members saw an industry veteran who could lead them to a promised land of vast profits. The company put big money on Davis's reputation as a winning executive, offering him one of the highest salaries in the industry and an attractive package of stock options. Things did not work out as planned. Davis and Capital Gaming encountered a series of setbacks on ballot initiatives and financing, and the company's prospects steadily worsened.[13] In 1996, Davis left his position as CEO and decided to live full time in Aspen. It was a relaxed community for most of the year, but with plenty of activity during the winter, including many old friends passing through. There wasn't a casino within hundreds of miles of Aspen. Davis's gambling days were over.

Like Davis, Roger Sonnabend also occupied an unusual niche within the class that remained unchanged even as the 50th reunion rolled around. Sonnabend was the class radical. Since the late 1960s, he had distinguished himself as the 49er who was most apt to talk of social justice and also to do something about it. In his early 70s, Sonnabend still wore a neatly trimmed goatee and mustache. The passing years had treated him well; he was a spry man, alert and slim. He kept young by staying in motion, shuttling between different homes and spending time with his six children and eight grandchildren. There were also visits to his far-flung luxury hotels—including those in Peru, Egypt, Bermuda, and Tuscany.

Sonnabend's relationship with his fellow 49ers was as curious as ever as the years passed. On the one hand, Sonnabend took part in all the reunions. He had hosted the 45th reunion at the Royal Sonesta Hotel in Boston, and he was a member of the planning committee that put together the 50th reunion. On the other hand, Sonnabend was prone to be a bit contemptuous of his classmates and their values. At the 40th reunion, in 1990, Sonnabend had commented that "This class represents a segment of society that is very much in favor today but does not contribute adequately to society's problems."[14] Sonnabend liked to proudly remind his classmates that he once had a place on Richard Nixon's enemies list. And he never stopped insisting that "what is best for America is best for business."[15]

Unlike some of his classmates, Sonnabend had never been forced to retire—it was one of the benefits of owning one's own company—and so he continued working into his mid-70s as CEO of Sonesta International Hotels. During the 1980s and 1990s, the company had gone through major changes. These changes had taken Sonesta in the opposite direction of many companies—from a major corporation back to a smaller family business. The shift in direction began in the 1970s, after a period of intense expansion, when Roger Sonnabend and his two brothers had come to own only 8.5 percent of the company.[16] It was not a situation that they liked. "Do we really want to run a large public company where we have a minority interest and where our involvement is more as dealmakers and financiers?" Roger asked his brothers. "We decided that what we'd rather do is to operate and control our hotels," he recalled.[17]

Sonnabend set out to rebuild Sonesta as a family business, consolidating properties and buying up stock. In the 1970s and 1980s, he sold off half of the chain's hotels and all of the manufacturing subsidiaries. The Sonnabend shareholders made a tender offer in 1978, buying up 60 percent of the stock.[18] Sonesta International remained a publicly traded company, but the family's leading role as owners and operators became its most distinguishing feature. The reorganization transformed the management and aesthetic profile of the chain as profoundly as it did the company's finances. The hotels that remained in the chain conformed to a new ideal that sought to win the allegiance of luxury vacation travelers. No longer would Sonesta attempt to compete for business travelers in urban markets.[19]

As the business evolved in the 1990s, Sonesta held to the basic vision that Sonesta should specialize in small and intimate hotels. Resisting various temptations to expand and rejecting buyout offers, Sonesta consisted of two-dozen upscale properties by 2000. The hotels continue to emphasize the corporation's social responsibilities, encouraging employees to devote time to public service and promoting a "green program" of recycling, energy conservation, and environmental awareness. It also had one of the largest corporate art programs in America.

By the 1990s, Roger Sonnabend's own outspoken career in public service was winding down. "Aside from some financial support," he acknowledged in 1999, "I leave most participation in community, business, educational, and other nonprofit organizations to the next generation." That generation includes his daughter Stephanie Sonnabend, who assumed the responsibilities of corporate president in 1996, and the children of his brothers, who also serve in executive roles in the family business. Sonnabend is confident that his children and nephews can continue the family tradition, saying, "I leave it to them to change the world."[20]

It was easy for Roger Sonnabend to stand out at the 50th reunion as the big class radical because one obvious competitor for that distinction missed the reunion: Jack O'Connell. In the 1960s, at the same time that Sonnabend was discovering the liberal within himself, O'Connell had become a filmmaker of the counterculture. Even though none of his films ever made much money, O'Connell never stopped pursuing his career as an independent filmmaker. This uphill struggle was made even more difficult in 1979 as a result of a brutal mugging that left him with severe brain injuries. It was a long road to recovery. O'Connell literally had to learn to respeak the English language. Day after day, for hours on end, O'Connell sat in his Manhattan apartment with a dictionary learning to pronounce words he had once used with ease. It was not until the early 1990s that O'Connell felt completely back to normal.

Once recovered, O'Connell threw himself into the work of trying to make his small film company, Astron Films Corporation, a success. Several of O'Connell's films were shown in revivals, and O'Connell was respected in the alternative film world as an early pioneer of independent filmmaking. O'Connell's most important legacy was his role in helping to revolutionize how films were financed, when he used a limited partnership to finance *Greenwich Village Story*. In subsequent years, this innovation and other, more Byzantine, tax shelters enabled film producers to raise huge amounts of money that would otherwise have been unavailable. He worked hard to leverage this reputation into video and cable deals for his films that would bring in a profit. O'Connell's official reason for missing the reunion was that he was too busy rushing back and forth between Paris, New York, and Los Angeles on business.

As always, money was tight for O'Connell. At the age of 79, O'Connell lived in the same one-bedroom apartment in Chelsea that he had lived in for 34 years, with a spacious terrace and soaring views of the city. While money was always tight for O'Connell, age had barely slowed him down, and he still worked long hours marketing his early films and trying to get new projects off the ground, including one about his experiences during World War II.

Stanley Greenfield would never have dreamed of missing the 50th reunion. He enthusiastically helped plan the event, serving as a one-man publicity committee. Like many other 49ers, Greenfield had become enormously nostalgic about his comrades from Harvard as the years passed, and he seized every chance he got to spend time with them.

Greenfield had gone through a number of major changes over the years. During the early decades of his career, for nearly 20 years, he had worked at Ziff-Davis Publishing Company. It was fun and diverse work, and, among other things, Greenfield had been a pioneer in the creation of new product-oriented magazines like *Stereo Review* and *Popular Photography* that helped feed the consumer boom of the 1960s. Greenfield had been happy at Ziff-Davis and especially grateful to CEO Bill Ziff for his support during Greenfield's struggle with depression—a struggle he overcame after 20 years, thanks in part to lithium carbonate. In the early 1970s, though, Greenfield found himself eased out of Ziff-Davis.

The next decade would be a period of twists and turns for Greenfield. For a while, he was president and publisher of *Playbill*—the theater publication. After *Playbill,* Greenfield took on a number of other projects until he was invited back to Ziff-Davis as a consultant in 1984. He stayed in that position until 1994, when Ziff-Davis sold the company. Again adrift, Greenfield struck out on his own with a small Internet start-up company called Dial-A-Book, which provided book chapters as content for web sites. Greenfield labored intensely on the project at the same time that the Internet was growing red hot. Soon, he had a small but successful company on his hands.

As an Internet entrepreneur in his 70s, Greenfield was an unusual figure in an industry dominated almost entirely by young people. He found that he seldom met anyone in the course of his work that wasn't at least 30 years his junior. The generational isolation didn't bother Greenfield one bit, and he found his new career immensely rewarding. "I find that one of the benefits of being an entrepreneur at this stage of life," he said in 1999, "is that you cannot be eased out."

If Stanley Greenfield wanted to work forever, retirement came naturally to Peter McColough. By the time the 50th reunion rolled around,

McColough had been retired for well over a decade. He had ended his role as CEO of Xerox in 1982, remaining as chairman until 1987, when he also gave up that position. Nearly three decades after joining the company when it was still called Haloid, he was finally a free man. Even at the height of his career, McColough had taken an extraordinary amount of vacation—traveling, sailing, reading. Now, with all the time in the world, McColough was in his element. He avoided serving on boards and becoming involved with too many philanthropies. Winters were spent at a home in Palm Beach, and the rest of the year he lived in Greenwich, Connecticut.

Even as McColough fell out of the public eye, debate about his role at Xerox increased with passing years. As the computer revolution transformed America, there was great fascination with Xerox's early work in the field—and why that work didn't allow it to dominate the high-tech field. A number of books came out that chronicled the company's rise and fall and rise again. One account was scathingly titled *Fumbling the Future,* and it lambasted McColough for devoting too much time to public service and allowing Xerox to lose its competitive edge. Other historians shot back with accounts that emphasized how visionary McColough had been for setting up Xerox PARC.

McColough himself didn't seem to worry much about his place in history. He generally didn't comment on the books written about Xerox, and he didn't write any of his own retrospectives on his time with Xerox. To the degree that he did voice his views about his accomplishments, they were typically modest. McColough believed that with or without Xerox, the information revolution would have gone charging ahead. Others had a different view of his contribution. "The father of the Mac is Xerox. The father of Windows is Xerox," said Microsoft's Bill Gates, who succeeded McColough as the most visible visionary in the information technology industry of the 1980s and 1990s.[21] To Gates and others, Peter McColough was an enduring icon.

Like McColough, Bill Ruane was not the kind of guy who would be comfortable talking about any kind of personal legacy. For one thing, Ruane was way too humble and modest for such talk. For another, he was among those 49ers who never thought seriously about retirement. Even in his mid 70s, as the 50th reunion rolled around, Ruane still saw his life and career as a work in progress. Certainly the year 1999, with

Ruane's Sequoia Fund in meltdown, would not have been the best time to take stock of his accomplishments.

The 1980s and 1990s had been interesting decades for Ruane. By the 1980s, Ruane was already into his fourth decade of investing. He was a generation or two older than the majority of people working on Wall Street, his suits were a bit conservative for the time, and his hair was going gray. In his basic values, Ruane was nothing like the predators that prowled New York during the decade—a type of financier typified by Gordon Gekko, the character in Oliver Stone's movie *Wall Street* who proclaims that "greed is good." "Greed's built a lot," Ruane once acknowledged, when someone asked about Gordon Gekko's proclamation. But it was the wrong motivation. "There's a lot of guys who have made a lot of money . . . well, they've cut corners. I wouldn't want to live their lives. . . . I wouldn't want to live with them."

At the beginning of the 1980s, Ruane took advantage of low market prices to shop for bargains. Buying only when prices were low and selling as soon as price-to-earnings ratios climbed into the double digits, Ruane's formula continued to pay off. In the bleak investment year 1982, Ruane & Cunniff's $243 million in investments posted a 6.6 percent gain, making it the best performer by a wide margin in a survey of 157 money management companies.[22] The performance attracted considerable attention from eager investors, who poured money into the Sequoia Fund and Ruane & Cunniff's private accounts. Among the investors were members of the class of 1949 who were clued in to Ruane's success through the alumni grapevine.

After accepting $67.4 million in new business in 1982—an amount that increased the firm's total assets by 50 percent—Ruane and his partner shocked the investment community by closing the fund and the firm to additional sales. "The decision to discontinue sales to new investors," they told shareholders, "reflects management's belief that unrestrained growth might impair investment flexibility." In particular, they worried that excess cash might dilute the high standards applied in the value-investing technique. With the Sequoia Fund at $280 million and private accounts at $230 million, they had as much money as they could responsibly handle. "If I had a million dollars to manage, I'd do a hell of a lot better," Cunniff declared.[23]

The Sequoia Fund didn't always prosper through the 1980s. In

1984, the fund had a good year when it gained 18.5 percent at the same time the Dow and Standard & Poor's indexes posted 1.3 and 6.1 percent gains, respectively.[24] But other years weren't conducive to Ruane's value-investing philosophy. Speculation surrounding the takeover boom that gripped Wall Street in the mid-1980s inflated the prices of stocks that might otherwise have been attractive to Ruane. In a move that would have been unthinkable to other investors, Ruane kept substantial percentages of the fund's assets in cash at different points in the 1980s.[25] The strong cash position cost Sequoia big gains during the stock market boom of 1982 to 1987. For three consecutive years, the fund fell substantially below the increases on the Dow and S&P.

Sequoia bounced back during the first part of the 1990s, reaffirming its place among the star performers of Wall Street. The fund soared through the decade, right up until 1999 when its success was derailed by the tech stock craze. Establishing a strong stake in tech stocks ran against everything Ruane believed. As he saw it, most of the hot companies of the moment had no demonstrable long-term value. And so, even as Nasdaq vacuumed money away from old-economy stocks, and even as those who didn't go into Nasdaq paid a huge penalty, Ruane hung tough to his core philosophy. The result was that the Sequoia Fund took one of the biggest hits in its history, losing 23 percent of its value in 1999.

Ruane was in good company with his 1999 stock market losses. Warren Buffett's Berkshire Hathaway was also way down. In fact, the severity of the Sequoia Fund's loss was due to the fact that it held a major stake in Berkshire Hathaway. Ruane didn't complain to Buffett about the way that Berkshire dragged down Sequoia. If anything, the longtime friendship between the two was psychologically more important in 1999 than ever because both men were out of step with the times. Ruane didn't talk much of his friendship with Buffett; it was a private thing and he didn't want to seem as though he was playing up his connection to one of America's richest and best-known businessmen. But those who knew Ruane also knew that he talked frequently with Buffett and considered the Omaha investor to be a genius. The friendship helped both men get through the hard times of late 1999 and early 2000.

After the Nasdaq crash of spring 2000, Ruane allowed himself a bit of gloating now and again. He savored the fact that in an economy that had grown tired of smoke and mirrors, value investing was suddenly back. Most satisfying of all was the 2000 performance of the Sequoia Fund. By year's end, the fund had posted a 20 percent gain—29 points ahead of the S&P 500. The year 2000 also saw the fund celebrate its 30th anniversary. Viewed over the period of three decades, the Sequoia Fund was especially impressive. Investors who put in $10,000 in 1970 and held their position would have seen their money grow to $1.3 million by 2000.

At the dawn of the new century, with his life's work spectacularly vindicated, Bill Ruane had no intention of retiring. He enjoyed the routine of his life: quiet days analyzing stocks in his room in the Sherry-Netherland Hotel, weekends in Connecticut with his wife Joy, and active vacations together with one of his closest friends, fellow 49er Joe Amaturo. It was a life well lived. "No one will ever say I haven't taken time to smell the roses," Ruane commented. Nor would anyone say about Bill Ruane that he had lived a life entirely absorbed with making money and having fun. In his later years, with a vast fortune to draw upon, Ruane had increasingly turned to making the world a better place. Mental illness and inner-city poverty were his two main concerns, and Ruane could be extremely generous when something inspired him. For example, he donated $8 million to a project aimed at preventing suicide among teenagers.

Like so many of his fellow 49ers, Bill Ruane was deeply grateful for all that life had given him. He was grateful to the federal government for making business school possible through the GI Bill; he was grateful to those on Wall Street who had taken a chance on him in his early years and to value-investing guru Benjamin Graham for showing him the light; he was grateful to the clients who had believed in him when he started the Sequoia Fund; and he was endlessly grateful to the friends he had made at Harvard Business School who remained, year after year, among the closest and dearest people in his world. "To say that life has been good to me . . . would be an understatement," Ruane observed.

Marvin Traub was also an eternally grateful person. Often, through much of his life, he had felt grateful simply to be alive. The German machine gunners who cut him down in France in 1944 came very close to extinguishing his life. "That is as close as one can come," Traub said later, "and it makes one appreciate life after that." For years after Traub emerged from his grueling rehabilitation, he would sometimes stop to savor the bare fact of existence. In the 50 years following business school, Traub did his best to live a full and rich existence. Blooming-dale's was the chapter that made him famous, and when that chapter was finally closed, Traub might well have gone quietly into retirement. But retirement was not an option that Traub seriously considered.

Traub began his second career a week after leaving Federated Department Stores in 1992. The new vehicle for his work energies was his own consulting firm, Marvin Traub Associates. (Traub also joined the investment banking firm of Financo, Inc., as a senior advisor in 1994.) Pitching himself as a consultant was easy for Traub given his unparalleled track record in retailing, and soon his fledging firm had a slew of major clients: American Express, Jones New York, Ralph Lauren, Lacoste, Saks Fifth Avenue. Traub also branched out overseas, picking up clients in Germany, Paris, London, China, and Hong Kong. Across the globe, business leaders had heard of Bloomingdale's and knew of Marvin Traub. They proved more than ready to pay for advice from the retailing wizard himself. Traub burnished his reputation by publishing a book on his experiences at Bloomingdale's, *Like No Other Store*. The book revealed Traub's retailing secrets and unloaded plenty of criticism of the management failures that had driven Bloomingdale's into bankruptcy.

At the close of the 1990s, as the new millennium approached, Traub was actively engaged in work, with a hectic travel schedule, and he was as current as ever on many of the latest trends in business. He became involved in several Internet businesses and stayed close to the action in fashion and retailing as the new and glitzy boom reached its peak in 1999. Still, Traub knew that he was from another era. Putting together the 50th reunion of the class of 1949, brought up powerful feelings of nostalgia for Traub. In a book of profiles for the reunion, class members were asked to share their thoughts and reflections. Traub set down over a thousands words. He wrote: "The Class of 1949 has had its time and been exemplary in the incredible evolution from the wartime years of the 1940s to the affluent society of today with its greater understanding of human rights, civil liberties, and the compatibility of nations."

Like most of the 49ers, Traub was humble about his accomplishments. He hadn't saved the world with retailing and he didn't imagine that he was the greatest business leader of his day. Traub was as horrified as others when once, at a 1991 fete, Ralph Lauren had called him "the greatest genius of the twentieth century." Instead, Traub saw himself as a participant in five critical decades that had transformed America. He had done his part to help produce the great wealth of the postwar era and in turn had supported others who tried to ensure that this wealth was the basis of a better and more just society.

"We have a long way to go as a nation and society," Traub said, "but I truly believe we are far better than we were 50 years ago."

To say Americans were better off at the dawn of the new century than they were in 1949 was a supreme understatement, of course. In 2000, America had a $10 trillion economy, and average Americans were three times wealthier than they had been in 1949. Americans were better educated, better housed, healthier, and living longer than ever before. Poverty had been cut in half over the decades, and the earnings gap between men and women, as well as between blacks and whites, had dramatically narrowed. These changes were testament to how the social revolutions that swept America in the second half of the twentieth century worked in tandem with the wealth-creation machine of the postwar economy.

Certainly, some things got worse during the postwar years—or, more to the point, things did not get as good as they should have given all the new wealth generated in American society. The 1970s saw the breakdown of a social contract in which those who worked hard were guaranteed steadily rising wages and access to affordable housing and health care. A new inequality took hold in the 1980s and 1990s, and one of America's best features—its egalitarianism—was forced into retreat during this period.

George McManmon is a 49er who sees the failings of America's economic system every day. In 1983, McManmon was shocked to learn that a friend of his who had been crushed by a trash truck on Christmas Day had been homeless. McManmon soon learned that there were many other homeless people near where he lived in Fairfax county in northern Virginia, and so he founded an organization to help feed them and provide them with shelter. The group, called Lazarus at the Gate, grew during the 1990s and came to feed 1,400 people a day. McManmon works like a demon at the job, for which he receives no salary. It is difficult to keep up with the misery and hunger of what McManmon notes is "one of the wealthiest counties" in America. If he weren't now so used to the presence of poverty amid plenty, it would break his heart.

The 49ers were never ones to deny the imperfections of capitalism. Many of them had been appalled at the excesses of the 1980s and they found themselves again deeply disappointed in the late 1990s and early twenty-first century as a new era of greed swept America, producing huge scandals at companies like Enron, WorldCom, and Tyco. "Frankly, it's disgusting," Peter McColough said of the behavior of top corporate leaders. "We were brought up to believe that it was less important to make money than to build a company that you were proud of. We weren't interested in amassing outrageous fortunes or building mansions. People find that hard to understand today." Many 49ers had a difficulty comprehending why, exactly, the drive for great personal wealth had become such a corrupting force in business. "I never wanted a yacht, or any of that kind of stuff," commented Tom Murphy, whose aggressiveness in the corporate world had been legendary. "I used to say that if I ever made $250,000, I'm going to buy a Cadillac. Well, I have a Cadillac. . . . We were a different generation."

American capitalism is not a static system. It can be shaped to bring out people's best, or their absolute worst. It can serve the great American principles of fairness and egalitarianism, or ruthlessly subvert these principles. To the 49ers, what makes the critical difference are the people who run the system and, more important, the values that inform their beliefs and guide their actions. In this respect, the 49ers like to think that they set an example for others to follow.

Acknowledgments

Writing a book about a business school class that included 700 members and whose careers spanned five decades has been a challenging undertaking. For the purposes of creating a manageable narrative, I chose to focus on only a handful of class members who worked in business sectors that saw particularly dynamic developments during the past half century. Where possible, I highlighted the experiences of additional class members, and I have faithfully tried to capture the class's overall experience in, and impact upon, the business world during the postwar era. Yet inevitably, I was unable to discuss or even mention the important and exciting careers of many, many class members.

This book could not have been written without the help and encouragement of others. Airie Stuart at John Wiley & Sons helped develop this project from the beginning and brought a strong and insightful editorial vision to the book. Others at Wiley who have worked to ensure the success of this project include Laurie Harting, Michelle Patterson, Emily Conway, and Jessie Noyes. At Forbes, Jim Michaels brought to this project not just extraordinary knowledge of business history and a special passion for the topic of this book, but also many keen editorial suggestions. Additional help at Forbes was provided by Harriett Miller, Barbara Strauch, and the staff at the Forbes library, including Ann Mintz, Naomi Prall, and Natalie Cannestra. Chris Furry proved a patient and astute copy editor of the book. Andrew Stuart, my literary agent, has been a great advisor and friend, helping to develop both this and other projects.

LeeAnna Keith, my research assistant for this book, was the kind of ally and partner that most book writers can only dream of. A talented and accomplished historian, LeeAnna imposed order on a vast and intimidating research enterprise. She tracked down huge amounts of information on the individuals and companies profiled in this book, as well as extensive analyses of the economic and business trends that shaped postwar America. She's a total superstar!

Beyond drawing heavily on secondary source material, this book is based on numerous interviews with class members. Forbes conducted a major oral history project focusing on the Harvard Business School class of 1949, which greatly enriched my research. In addition, a number of class members shared their memories with me and provided other help for this book, including Joe Amaturo, George Berman, Jim Burke, James Chalmers, James Craig, Howard Davis, Jack Davis, Stanley Greenfield, Ernest Henderson, Earle Jones, Peter McColough, Jack Muller, Tom Murphy, Jack O'Connell, Bill Ruane, Roger Sonnabend, and George Wilkerson. Marvin Traub deserves special thanks for his help with many aspects of this book.

Finally, I am deeply indebted to Wendy Paris, who not only supported me personally during the writing of this book, but also drew on her keen grasp of language and character to offer important advice on the final manuscript. This would have been a lonely journey without her.

David Callahan
New York City

Notes

INTRODUCTION

1. Tim Quinson, "Sequoia Fund Investors Should Note Changes," *Chicago Sun-Times,* June 25, 1998, p. 60.
2. Ian McDonald, "Are These Values Managers in a Slump or a Coma?" *TheStreet.com,* February 28, 2000.
3. Ilana Polyak, "Timber!! Once-Mighty Sequoia Has Fallen on Hard Times Lately," *Investment News,* September 20, 1999, p. 11.
4. Marilyn Wellemeyer, "The Class the Dollars Fell On," *Fortune,* May 1974, p. 225.

CHAPTER 1

1. Marilyn Wellemeyer, "The Class the Dollars Fell On," *Fortune,* May 1974, p. 227.
2. Stratford P. Sherman, "You're Invited to the CEO's Ball," *Fortune,* January 15, 1990, p. 140.
3. Bob Tamarkin, "The Ordeal of Lester Crown," *New York Times,* December 7, 1986, p. 41; Margaret Carroll, "Crown Jewels," *Chicago Tribune,* February 3, 1988, p. 7.
4. "Executives: Rocking the Boat," *Newsweek,* May 19, 1967, p. 85.
5. Jeffrey Zaslow, " 'New Nepotism' Calls for Junior to Earn Stripes Away from Home," *The Wall Street Journal,* January 14, 1986, p. 9.
6. "Men on the Move: The Sonnabend Brothers," *Boston,* January 1963, p. 2.
7. H. John Steinbreder, "Taking Chances at J&J," *Fortune,* June 6, 1988, p. 60.

261

8. Steven Prokesch, "A Leader in Crisis: James Edward Burke," *New York Times,* February 19, 1986, p. B6.

9. Marvin Traub and Tom Teicholtz, *Like No Other Store: The Bloomingdale's Legend and the Revolution in American Marketing* (New York: Times Books/Random House, 1993), p. 21.

10. Stratford P. Sherman, "Capital Cities' Capital Coup," *Fortune,* April 15, 1985, p. 51.

11. Marc Frons, "Low Profile, High Power: Tom Murphy's Quiet Rise to the Top," *Business Week,* April 1, 1985, p. 77.

12. Mark Stevens, *Sudden Death: The Rise and Fall of E.F. Hutton* (New York: Nal Books, 1989), p. 54.

13. Gene Smith, "Personality: A Series of Promotions to the Top Post," *New York Times,* May 26, 1968, p. 3.

CHAPTER 2

1. "At Harvard University—Down to the Business of Learning Business," *Newsweek,* November 22, 1954, p. 86.

2. Jeffrey L. Cruikshank, *A Delicate Experiment: The Harvard Business School, 1908–1945* (Boston: Harvard Business School Press, 1987), p. 55.

3. Donald K. David, "Introduction," in Malcolm P. McNair, ed., *The Case Method at the Harvard Business School* (New York: McGraw-Hill, 1954), p. 3.

4. Donald R. Schoen and Philip A. Sprague, "The Case Method as Seen by Recent Graduates," in Ibid., p. 80.

5. James A. Bowie, *American Schools of Business* (London: Sir Isaac Pittman & Sons, Ltd., 1932), p. 14.

6. Carter A. Daniel, *MBA: The First Century* (Lewisberg: Bucknell University Press, 1998), p. 129.

7. Andrea Gabor, *The Capitalist Philosophers: The Geniuses of Modern Business—Their Lives, Times, and Ideas* (New York: Times Business, 2000), p. 131; Deborah Shapley, *Promise and Power: The Life and Times of Robert McNamara* (Boston: Little, Brown & Co, 1993), p. 35.

8. Melvin T. Copeland, *And Mark the End of an Era: The Story of the Harvard Business School* (Boston: Little, Brown & Co, 1958), p. 124.

9. "Business Is Rallied to Fight Communism," *New York Times,* September 11, 1949, p. 21.

10. Martin Bower, ed., *The Development of Executive Leadership* (Cambridge: Harvard University Press, 1949), p. v.

11. Daniel, *MBA: The First Century,* p. 138.

12. Copeland, *And Mark the End of an Era: The Story of the Harvard Business School,* p. 121.

13. James Michaels, "Kindred Spirits," *Forbes,* October 18, 1999, p. 134.

14. Laurence Shames, *The Big Time: The Harvard Business School's Most Successful Class and How It Shaped America* (New York: Harper & Row, 1986), p. 87.

15. McNair, ed., *The Case Method at the Harvard Business School,* pp. 27, 35.

16. Cruikshank, *A Delicate Experiment: The Harvard Business School, 1908–1945,* p. 270.

17. John A. Byrne, *The Whiz Kids: The Founding Fathers of American Business—And the Legacy They Left Us* (New York: Doubleday, 1993), p. 8.

18. Cruikshank, *A Delicate Experiment: The Harvard Business School, 1908–1945,* p. 272.

19. Shames, *The Big Time: The Harvard Business School's Most Successful Class and How It Shaped America,* p. 21.

20. Marilyn Wellemeyer, "The Class the Dollars Fell On," *Fortune,* May 1974, p. 227.

21. Clarence Brown Oral History, Forbes Oral History Collection.

22. Shames, *The Big Time: The Harvard Business School's Most Successful Class and How It Shaped America,* p. 25.

23. Wellemeyer, "The Class the Dollars Fell On," p. 227.

24. "B-School Reports," *Business Week,* May 9, 1953, p. 65.

25. Roger Sonnabend Oral History, Forbes Oral History Collection.

26. Duncan Norton-Taylor, "The Business Schools: Pass or Flunk?" *Fortune,* June 1954, p. 240.

27. Wellemeyer, "The Class the Dollars Fell On," p. 227.

28. Peter Fuhrman, "A Teacher Who Made a Difference," *Forbes,* July 13, 1987, p. 362.

29. Malcolm P. McNair, "Tough-Mindedness and the Case Method," in McNair, ed., *The Case Method at the Harvard Business School,* p. 15.

30. "Harvard MBAs of '49 Assess Their 20 Years," *Business Week,* June 14, 1969, p. 62.

31. Wellemeyer, "The Class the Dollars Fell On," p. 340.

32. Tamar Lewin, "World's a Stage for '49 Class," *New York Times,* April 4, 1986, p. D3.

CHAPTER 3

1. Peter F. Drucker, "The Graduate Business Schools," *Fortune,* August 1950, p. 117.

2. "Ivory Hunting on the Charles," *Fortune,* January 1948, p. 116.

3. Shames, *Big Time: Harvard Business School's Most Successful Class and How It Shaped America,* p. 106.

4. David Lidman, "X Not an Unknown Factor to C. Peter McColough," *New York Times,* March 9, 1963, p. 12.

5. Gene Smith, "Personality: A Series of Promotions to the Top Post," *New York Times,* May 26, 1968, III, p. 3.

6. Lidman, "X Not an Unknown Factor to C. Peter McColough," p. 9.

7. Janice Jorgenson, ed., *Encyclopedia of Consumer Brands,* vol. 3, *Durable Goods* (Detroit: St. James Press, 1994), p. 633.

8. Smith, "Personality: A Series of Promotions to the Top Post," III, p. 3.

9. Marilyn Wellemeyer, "The Class the Dollars Fell On," *Fortune* 89, May 1974, p. 342.

10. Walt Hawver, *Capital Cities/ABC, The Early Years: 1954–1986* (*How the Minnow Came to Swallow the Whale*) (Radnor, PA: Chilton Book Company, 1994), p. 16–18.

11. F. Leslie Smith, *Perspectives on Radio and Television: Telecommunication in the United States* (New York: Harper and Row, 1985), p. 73–74.

12. Sammy R. Danna, Ph.D., "Technical History of Television" (Copyright Sammy R. Danna, Ph.D., 1998), p. 22.

13. "Hall of Fame: Thomas Sawyer Murphy," *Fortune,* April 5, 1993, p. 112.

14. Hawver, Capital Cities/ABC, The Early Years: 1954–1986, pp. 18–19.

15. Ibid., pp. 13–14.

16. "Frank Smith, 56, Radio-TV Leader," *New York Times,* August 8, 1966, p. 27.

17. "From Cripple Creek to Capital Cities," *Forbes,* October 1, 1976, p. 52.

18. "Frank Smith, 56, Radio-TV Leader (Obituary)," p. 27.

19. Thomas S. Murphy interviewed by Rita Koselka, Forbes Magazine Collection.

20. Allan Sloan and Thomas Baker, "Murphy's Law," *Forbes,* March 16, 1981, p. 70.

21. "Hall of Fame: Thomas Sawyer Murphy," p. 112.

22. *Statistical Abstract of the United States, 1960* (Washington: Government Printing Office, 1960), p. 859.

23. "Tom Murphy's Pleasant Cash Problem," *Forbes,* October 1, 1976, p. 14.

24. Thomas S. Murphy, interviewed by Rita Koselka, Forbes Magazine Collection.

25. "Men on the Move: The Sonnabend Brothers," *Boston,* January 1963, reprint, p. 2.

26. Thomas P. Murphy, "Sonnabend's Sackful," *Fortune,* September 1958, pp. 133–134.

Chapter 4

1. Marvin Traub, *Like No Other Store: The Bloomingdale's Legend and the Revolution in Marketing* (New York: Crown, 1993), pp. 47–49.

2. H. John Steinbreder, "Taking Chances at J&J," *Fortune,* June 6, 1988, p. 60.

3. "The Superstars of Selling," *Sales & Marketing Management,* March 1991, p. 48.

4. Steinbreder, "Taking Chances at J&J," p. 60.

5. Karen Damato, "Loner Sequoia Can't Keep Gawkers Away," *The Wall Street Journal,* February 9, 1996, p. C25.

6. Edward Chancellor, *Devil Take the Hindmost: A History of Financial Speculation* (New York: Farrar, Strauss and Giroux, 1999), p. 235.

7. "The Money Men: Look at All Those Beautiful, Scantily Clad Girls Out There!" *Forbes,* November 1, 1974, p. 43.

8. Dolly Setton, "The Disciples," *Forbes,* October 12, 1998, p. 110.

9. Andrew Kilpatrick, *Of Permanent Value: The Story of Warren Buffett* (Birmingham, AL: APKE, 1994), p. 35.

10. "The Money Men: Fighting the Tape," *Forbes,* April 1, 1973, p. 48.

11. Ibid., p. 42.

12. "SEC's Chairman: Wall Street-Wise," *Nation's Business,* November 1983, p. 30.

13. "The $14,000-a-Year Man," *Fortune,* June 1959, p. 118.

14. Mark Stevens, *Sudden Death: The Rise and Fall of E.F. Hutton* (New York: Nal Books, 1989), p. 54.

15. "SEC's Chairman: Wall Street-Wise," *Nation's Business,* November 1983, p. 30.

16. Bob Tamarkin, "The Ordeal of Lester Crown," *New York Times,* December 7, 1986, p. 41.

17. Andrew Hermann, "Tycoon Henry Crown Dies: Huge Fortune Matched 'Lofty Achievements,'" *Chicago Sun-Times,* August 15, 1990, p. 5.

18. "The Crowning Touch," *Forbes,* December 8, 1980, p. 82.

19. Hermann, "Tycoon Henry Crown Dies: Huge Fortune Matched 'Lofty Achievements,'" p. 5.

20. Lawrence Shames, *Big Time: Harvard Business Schools Most Successful Class and How It Shaped America* (New York: Harper & Row, 1986), p. 62.

CHAPTER 5

1. *Class of 1949: Fiftieth Reunion Profile* (Cambridge, MA: Harvard Business School, 1999), p. 191.

2. Thomas Horton, *"What Works for Me": 16 CEOs Talk About Their Careers and Commitments* (New York: Random House, 1986), p. 15,

3. Ibid., pp. 26–27.

4. U.S. Census Bureau, *Statistical Abstract of the United States* (Washington, DC: Government Printing Office, 1999), p. 581.

5. Adele Hast, *International Directory of Company Histories,* vol. 3 (Detroit: St. James Press, 1991), p. 36.

6. "The 88 Ventures of Johnson & Johnson," *Forbes,* June 1, 1972, p. 24.

7. Daniel F. Cuff, "Chief of Johnson & Johnson To Step Down in Revamping," *New York Times,* October 25, 1988, p. D 1.

8. *Statistical Abstract of the United States,* 1960, p. 763; 1971, p. 669.

9. Tina Grant, ed., *International Directory of Company Histories,* vol. 12 (Detroit: St. James Press, 1996), p. 36.

10. Penny Gill, "NRF Salutes Marvin Traub: 'Mr. Bloomingdales,' " *Stores,* January 1991, p. 19.

11. Traub Oral History, Forbes Library.

12. Jesse Kornbluth, "The Department Store as Theater," *New York Times Magazine,* April 29, 1979, p. 30.

13. Marylin Bender, "Bloomingdale's and Its Customers— Dancing Chic to Chic," *New York Times,* September 8, 1974, p. III 2.

14. Kornbluth, "Department Store as Theater," p. 30.

15. Marvin Traub, *Like No Other Store: The Bloomingdale's Legend and the Revolution in American Marketing* (New York: Crown, 1993), p. 107.

16. Ibid., pp. 101–102.

17. Jeffrey A. Trachtenberg, *Ralph Lauren: The Man Behind the Mystique* (Boston: Little, Brown, & Co., 1988), p. 55.

18. Traub, *Like No Other Store,* p. 210.

19. Bill Davidson, "The Mafia: Shadow of Evil on an Island in the Sun," *Saturday Evening Post,* February 25, 1967, pp. 30–33.

20. Richard Oulahan and William Lambert, "The Scandal in the Bahamas," *Life,* February 3, 1967, p. 63.

21. Mahon, "Paradise Regained: How Resorts International Got Its Start," p. 5.

22. Ibid., p. 8.

23. Howard Kohn, "Strange Bedfellows: The Hughes-Nixon-Lansky Connection: The Secret Alliances of the CIA from World War II to Watergate," *Rolling Stone,* May 20, 1974, p. 82.

24. Mahon, "Paradise Regained: How Resorts International Got Its Start," pp. 25–27.

25. "Resorts Queried on Fund," *The Washington Post,* January 26, 1979, p. 13.

26. Mahon, "Paradise Regained: How Resorts International Got Its Start," p. 27.

27. Kohn, "Strange Bedfellows: The Hughes-Nixon-Lansky Connection: The Secret Alliances of the CIA from World War II to Watergate," p. 85.

28. Gigi Mahon, "Speculation or Gamble? Resorts International Is Wall Street's Own Floating Crap Game," *Barron's,* September 26, 1977, 18.

29. *Statistical Abstract of the United States, 1971,* p. 744–745.

30. "All in the Family," *Forbes* 158, July 29, 1996, 68.

31. "Executives: Rocking the Boat," *Newsweek* 77, May 19, 1969, p. 86.

32. Ibid., p. 87.

33. Roger P. Sonnabend, "The American Businessman: A Modern Revolutionary," *Vital Speeches of the Day* 34, August 1, 1968, p. 626.

34. "Executives: Rocking the Boat," p. 86.

35. Sonnabend, "The American Businessman: A Modern Revolutionary," p. 624.

36. Ibid., p. 628.

Chapter 6

1. "Out Again, In Again," *Forbes,* March 15, 1970.

2. "General Dynamics Calls Rest of Preferred Issue for April 15 Redemption," *The Wall Street Journal,* April 1, 1966.

3. George Berman Oral History Interview, p. 1–20.

4. Lawrence Shames, *The Big Time: Harvard Business School's Most Successful Class and How It Shaped America* (New York: Harper & Row, 1986), p. 55.

5. Alfred R. Zipser, "Recession Spurs Photocopiers," *New York Times,* June 27, 1958, p. 38; Janice Jorgenson, ed., *Encyclopedia of Consumer Brands,* vol. 3, *Durable Goods* (Detroit: St. James Press, 1994), p. 633.

6. Jorgenson, ed., *Encyclopedia of Consumer Brands,* p. 633.

7. Adele Hast, ed., *International Directory of Company Histories,* vol. 3 (Chicago & London: St. James Press, 1991), p. 172.

8. Jorgenson, ed., *Encyclopedia of Consumer Brands,* p. 633.

9. David A. Kearns and David A. Nadler, *Prophets in the Dark: How Xerox Reinvented Itself and Beat Back the Japanese* (New York: Harper-Business, 1992), p. 36.

10. Robert E. Bedingfield, "Personality: Original Mind in Copying Field" *New York Times,* December 10, 1961, III, p. 3.

11. Richard Hammer, "There Isn't Any Profit Squeeze at Xerox," *Fortune* 66, July 1962, p. 48.

12. David Lidman, "X Not an Unknown Factor to C. Peter McColough," *New York Times,* March 9, 1963, p. 9.

13. Hammer, "There Isn't Any Profit Squeeze at Xerox," p. 48.

14. Vartanig G. Varta, "Xerox Votes Five-to-One Split and Doubles Rate of Dividend," *New York Times,* November 8, 1963, p. 41.

15. Lidman, "X Not an Unknown Factor to C. Peter McColough," p. 9.

16. Douglas K. Smith and Robert C. Alexander, *Fumbling the Future: How Xerox Invented, Then Ignored, The First Personal Computer* (Lincoln, NE: iUniverse.com, 1999), p. 29.

17. "The Advantage of Starting Young," *Forbes,* July 1, 1971, p. 33.

18. Kearns and Nadler, *Prophets in the Dark: How Xerox Reinvented Itself and Beat Back the Japanese,* p. 44.

19. "Why Xerox's Money Machine Slows Down," *Business Week,* April 5, 1976, p. 60.

20. "Looking for Trouble," *Malaysian Business,* May 16, 2000.

21. Smith and Alexander, *Fumbling the Future: How Xerox Invented, Then Ignored, The First Personal Computer,* p. 29.

22. Kearns and Nadler, *Prophets in the Dark: How Xerox Reinvented Itself and Beat Back the Japanese,* p. 44.

23. Gene Smith, "Personality: A Series of Promotions to the Top Post," *New York Times,* May 26, 1968, III, p. 3.

24. "People and Business," *New York Times,* August 7, 1973, p. 52.

CHAPTER 7

1. "The Money Men: Fighting the Tape," *Forbes,* April 1, 1973, p. 48.

2. "The Money Men: Look at All Those Beautiful, Scantily Clad Girls Out There!" *Forbes,* November 1, 1974, p. 42.

3. Kerry Hannon, "How Sequoia Grows: A Winning Portfolio for Copycats," *U.S. News and World Report,* July 8, 1996, p. 62.

4. James Sterngold, *Burning Down the House: How Greed, Deceit, and Bitter Revenge Destroyed E.F. Hutton* (New York: Summit Books, 1990), p. 39.

5. Mark Stevens, *Sudden Death: The Rise and Fall of E.F. Hutton* (New York: Nal Books, 1989), p. 60.

6. Stevens, *Sudden Death: The Rise and Fall of E.F. Hutton,* p. 54.

7. Robert Metz, "Market Place," *New York Times,* October 24, 1969, p. 66.

8. "E.F. Hutton & Co. Names 2 to Major Executive Posts," *New York Times,* January 7, 1970, p. 66.

PART 3

1. Robert Reinhold, "'49ers, Richer and Grayer, Revisit Harvard Business School," *New York Times,* June 3, 1974, p. 47.
2. Tamar Lewin, "World's a Stage for '49 Class," *New York Times,* April 4, 1986, p. D1.
3. Marilyn Wellemeyer, "The Class the Dollars Fell On," *Fortune,* May 1974, p. 80.
4. Ibid., p. 78.
5. Ibid.

CHAPTER 8

1. Juliet Schor, *The Overspent American* (New York: Basic Books, 1998), p. 17.
2. Bernadine Morris, "The Store is 100 Years Old, and, Oh, the Styles It's Seen," October 4, 1972, p. 52.
3. Gill Penny, "NRF Salutes Marvin Traub: 'Mr. Bloomingdales,' " *Stores,* January 1991, p. 19.
4. Jesse Kornbluth, "The Department Store as Theater," New York Times Magazine, April 29, 1979, p. 72.
5. Ibid., p. 30.
6. Penny, "NRF Salutes Marvin Traub," p. 19.
7. Walter McQuade, "Making a Drama Out of Shopping," *The Wall Street Journal,* March 24, 1980, p. 107.
8. Marvin Traub, *Like No Other Store: The Bloomingdale's Legend and the Revolution in American Marketing* (New York: Crown, 1993), p. 122.
9. Ibid., p. 262.
10. Murray Schumach, "Bloomingdale's Is 100 and Is Still Looking Up," *New York Times,* September 7, 1972, A45.
11. Ibid.
12. "Where the 'Beautiful People' Find Fashion," *Business Week,* September 2, 1972, p. 44.
13. Bender, "Bloomingdale's and Its Customers," p. 1.

14. Marylin Bender, "Bloomingdale's and Its Customers—Dancing Chic to Chic," *New York Times,* September 8, 1974, p. C1.

15. Kornbluth, "The Department Store as Theater," p. 72.

16. Traub, *Like No Other Store,* p. 150.

17. Ibid.

18. Bender, "Bloomingdale's and Its Customers," p. 2.

19. "Where the Beautiful People Find Fashion," p. 44.

20. Isadore Barmash, "The Race for the Carriage Trade," *New York Times,* September 23, 1979, p. 1.

21. Ibid.

22. Penny, "NRF Salutes Marvin Traub," p. 19.

23. Wellemeyer, "The Class the Dollars Fell On," p. 81.

24. Thomas R. Horton, *"What Works for Me": 16 CEOs Talk About Their Careers and Commitments* (New York: Random House, 1987), p. 27.

25. Ibid., p. 30.

26. "Prescription for Growth," *Forbes,* June 26, 1978, p. 4.

27. Ibid.

28. Smith, "A Long Way from Baby," p. 64.

29. "Prescription for Growth," *Forbes,* June 26, 1978, p. 97.

30. "At Johnson & Johnson, A Mistake Can Be a Badge of Honor," *Business Week,* September 26, 1988, p. 127.

31. Thomas Moore, "The Fight to Save Tylenol," *Fortune* 106, November 29, 1982, p. 45.

32. "Prescription for Growth," p. 97.

CHAPTER 9

1. Marilyn Wellemeyer, "Reassessment Time for Forty-Niners," *Fortune,* May 21, 1979, p. 118.

2. Phyllis Berman, "An Offer You Can't Refuse," *Forbes,* November 13, 1978, p. 110.

3. Wellemeyer, "Reassessment Time for the Forty-Niners," p. 118.

4. Douglas K. Smith and Robert C. Alexander, *Fumbling the Future: How Xerox Invented, Then Ignored, The First Personal Computer* (Lincoln, NE: iUniverse.com, 1999), p. 131.

5. Ibid., p. 131.

6. Wellemeyer, "Reassessment Time," p. 118.

7. David A. Kearns and David A. Nadler, *Prophets in the Dark: How Xerox Reinvented Itself and Beat Back the Japanese* (New York: Harper-Business, 1992), pp. 46–47.

8. Uttal, "Xerox Is Trying Too Hard," p. 85.

9. Ibid.

10. Andrew Pollack, "Xerox: New Chief's Challenge," *New York Times,* May 17, 1982, p. D1.

11. Frank Rose, *West of Eden: The End of Innocence at Apple Computing* (New York: Viking Press, 1989), pp. 43–44.

12. Kearns and Nadler, *Prophets in the Dark: How Xerox Reinvented Itself and Beat Back the Japanese,* pp. 96–97; "What Xerox Salvaged from Its Big Mistake," *Business Week,* August 4, 1975, p. 65.

13. Rose, *West of Eden: The End of Innocence at Apple Computing,* p. 48.

14. Ibid., p. 47.

15. Stephen Manes and Paul Andrews, *Gates: How Microsoft's Mogul Reinvented an Industry and Made Himself the Richest Man in America* (New York: Touchstone Books, 1993), pp. 106–107; Rose, *West of Eden: The End of Innocence at Apple Computing,* p. 46.

16. Michael S. Malone, *Infinite Loop: How the World's Most Insanely Great Computer Company Went Insane* (New York: Doubleday, 1999), p. 233.

17. Manes and Andrews, *Gates: How Microsoft's Mogul Reinvented an Industry and Made Himself the Richest Man in America,* p. 165.

18. Andrew Pollack, "Xerox Stalks the Automated Office," *New York Times,* May 3, 1981, III, p. 4.

19. Kearns and Nadler, *Prophets in the Dark: How Xerox Reinvented Itself and Beat Back the Japanese,* p. 102.

20. Smith and Alexander, *Fumbling the Future: How Xerox Invented, Then Ignored, The First Personal Computer,* p. 122.

21. Kearns and Nadler, *Prophets in the Dark: How Xerox Reinvented Itself and Beat Back the Japanese,* p. 88.

22. "The Advantage of Starting Young," *Forbes,* July 1, 1971, p. 33.

23. Marc Frons, "Low Profile, High Power: Tom Murphy's Quiet Rise to the Top," *Business Week,* April 1, 1985, p. 77.

24. Ibid.

25. Christine Foster, "Couples," *Forbes,* December 2, 1996, p. 18.

26. Walt Hawver, *Capital Cities/ABC, The Early Years: 1954–1986* (*How the Minnow Came to Swallow the Whale*) (Radnor, PA: Chilton Book Company, 1994), pp. 106, 132.

27. U.S. Census Bureau, *Statistical Abstract of the United States, 1980* (Washington: Government Printing Office, 1980), p. 597.

28. Hawver, *Capital Cities/ABC, The Early Years: 1954–1986* (*How the Minnow Came to Swallow the Whale*), pp. 133–136.

29. Frons, "Low Profile, High Power: Tom Murphy's Quiet Rise to the Top," *Business Week,* p. 77.

30. "Capital Cities Is Likely to Firmly Control ABC in a Smooth Transition Following Their Merger," *The Wall Street Journal,* March 20, 1985, p. 4.

31. "A Star Is Born: The Cap Cities/ABC Megamerger Opens the Door to More Media Takeovers," *Business Week,* April 1, 1985, pp. 76–80.

32. Stratford P. Sherman, "Capital Cities' Capital Coup," *Fortune* 111, April 15, 1985, p. 52.

33. "Capital Cities' Reputation with Unions Contrasts Adoring View of Wall Street," *The Wall Street Journal,* March 21, 1985, p. 8.

34. "Why Cap Cities Is Sitting Pretty," p. 121.

35. Allan Sloan and Thomas Baker, "Murphy's Law," *Forbes,* March 16, 1981, p. 67.

36. "Why So High?" *Financial World* 154, April 13–16, 1985, p. 36.

37. "Capital Cities' Reputation with Unions Contrasts Adoring View of Wall Street," p. 8.

38. Sloan and Baker, "Murphy's Law," *Forbes,* p. 66.

39. "Why Cap Cities Is Sitting Pretty," p. 121.

40. Frons, "Low Profile, High Power," p. 77.

41. Robert M. Reed and Maxine K. Reed, *The Encyclopedia of Television, Cable & Video* (New York: Van Nostrand and Reinhold, 1992), p. 389.

42. Hawver, *Capital Cities/ABC, The Early Years: 1954–1986* (*How the Minnow Came to Swallow the Whale*), p. 262.

43. "The People's Airwaves," *Forbes,* October 2, 1978, p. 134.

44. "Tom Murphy's Pleasant Cash Problem," *Forbes,* October 1, 1976, p. 50.

45. Bob Tamarkin, "The Ordeal of Lester Crown," *New York Times,* December 7, 1986, p. 41.

46. "Out Again, In Again," *Forbes,* June 15, 1970.

47. Tamarkin, "The Ordeal of Lester Crown," p. 41.

48. Wayne Biddle, "Lester Crown Blames the System," *New York Times,* June 16, 1985, p. III.1.

49. Quoted in Roger Franklin, *The Defender: The Story of General Dynamics* (New York: Harper & Row, 1986), p. 226.

50. Tamarkin, "The Ordeal of Lester Crown," p. 41.

51. Subcommittee on Oversight and Investigations, Committee on Energy and Commerce. Federal Securities.

52. "Happy Ending? Thanks to David Lewis, Henry Crown's 15-Year Love-Hate Affair with General Dynamics May Yet Have a Happy Ending," *Forbes,* July 1, 1974.

53. Ibid; "General Dynamics Sees Record Profit Again This Year on Increase in Sales," *The Wall Street Journal,* March 30, 1976; Clare M. Reckert, "General Dynamics Profit Up by 12.4% to a Record," *New York Times,* August 6, 1976.

54. Matthew L. Wald, "General Dynamics Loses $359 Million in Accord," *New York Times,* June 10, 1978.

55. Howard Rudnitsky, "The Crowning Touch," *Forbes,* December 8, 1980, p. 83.

56. Ibid.

57. Wellemeyer, "The Class the Dollars Fell On," p. 225.

CHAPTER 10

1. Peter Mattiace, Associated Press, May 31, 1978.

2. Gigi Mahon, "Betting on the Boardwalk: Resorts International Needs Atlantic City to Change Its Look," *Barron's,* October 3, 1977, p. 5.

3. Gigi Mahon, "Speculation or Gamble? Resorts International is Wall Street's Own Floating Crap Game," *Barron's,* September 26, 1977, p. 3.

4. U.S. Census Bureau, *Statistical Abstract of the United States, 1980* (Washington: Government Printing Office, 1980), p. 248.

5. Tina Grant, ed., *International Directory of Company Histories,* vol. 12 (Detroit: St. James Press, 1996), p. 418.

6. Peter Mattiace, Associated Press, May 29, 1979.

7. Ibid.

8. Gigi Mahon, "Landing on the Boardwalk," *Barron's,* November 20, 1978, p. 23.

9. "Atlantic City's Midas," *Washington Post Magazine,* May 27, 1979, p. 5.

10. Ibid.

11. Peter Mattiace, Associated Press Reports, December 19, 1978.

12. "Resorts Queried on Fund," *The Washington Post,* January 26, 1979, p. A12.

13. Harry Anderson and Pamela Abramson, "Gambling: Aces for Resorts," *Newsweek,* March 12, 1979, p. 75.

14. Peter Mattiace, Associated Press, August 2, 1979.

15. Marilyn Wellemeyer, "Reassessment Time for Forty Niners," *Fortune,* May 21, 1979, p. 118.

16. Laurence Shames, *Big Time: Harvard Business School's Most Successful Class and How It Shaped America* (New York: Harper & Row, 1986), p. 117.

17. Robert J. Flaherty, "Will the Fish Bite Again at the Same Old Bait," *Forbes,* September 18, 1978, p. 41.

18. Harvard Business School, *Bulletin,* September/October 1969.

19. Flaherty, "Will the Fish Bite Again At the Same Old Bait," p. 41.

20. Ibid.

21. Ibid.

22. Ibid.

23. *Harvard Business School Class of 1949: Thirtieth Reunion Profile* (Cambridge: Harvard Business School, 1979).

CHAPTER 11

1. *Harvard Business School Class of 1949, 30th Reunion Profile* (Cambridge, MA: Harvard Business School, 1979).

2. "Fighting the Tape," *Forbes,* April 1, 1973, p. 48.

3. Ibid., p. 48.

4. John Dennis Brown, *101 Years on Wall Street: An Investors' Almanac* (Englewood Cliffs, NJ: Prentice Hall, 1991), p. 92.

5. Marshall E. Blume, Jeremy J. Siegel, and Dan Rottenberg, *Revolution on Wall Street: The Rise and Decline of the New York Stock Exchange* (New York: W.W. Norton & Company, 1993), p. 57.

6. Brown, *101 Years on Wall Street: An Investors' Almanac,* p. 95.

7. John Steele Gordon, *The Great Game: The Emergence of Wall Street as a World Power, 1653–2000* (New York: Scribner, 1999), p. 274.

8. Kerry Hannon, "How Sequoia Grows: A Winning Portfolio for Copycats," *U.S. News & World Report,* July 8, 1996, p. 62.

9. "The Money Men: Look at All Those Beautiful, Scantily Clad Girls Out There!" *Forbes,* November 1, 1974, p. 42.

10. Robert Metz, "Market Place: Mutual Funds Back on Firm Footing in '76," *New York Times,* January 5, 1977, p. D2.

11. "The Money Men: The Tortoise and the Hare," *Forbes,* February 1, 1977, p. 56.

12. Ibid., p. 87.

13. Richard Phalon, "Personal Investing: Three Mutual Funds See Good Buys," *New York Times,* June 4, 1977, p. 26.

14. Blume, Siegel, and Rottenberg, *Revolution on Wall Street: The Rise and Decline of the New York Stock Exchange,* p. 107.

15. Robert J. Shiller, *Irrational Exuberance* (Princeton: Princeton University Press, 2000), p. 36.

16. Courtney M. Slater and Cornelia J. Strawser, *Business Statistics of the United States* (Lanham, MD: Bernan Press, 1999), pp. 368–369.

17. Mark Stevens, *Sudden Death: The Rise and Fall of E.F. Hutton* (New York: NAL Books, 1989), p. 57.

18. Stevens, *Sudden Death: The Rise and Fall of E.F. Hutton* (New York: NAL Books, 1989), p. 59.

19. Ibid., p. 60.

20. Ibid., p. 62.

21. Ibid., p. 62; James Sterngold, *Burning Down the House: How Greed, Deceit, and Bitter Revenge Destroyed E.F. Hutton* (New York: Summit Books, 1990), pp. 51–56.

22. Stevens, *Sudden Death: The Rise and Fall of E.F. Hutton,* p. 64.

23. Robert J. Cole, "As No. 2 Talks, Many Listen," *New York Times,* September 28, 1975, p. III.7.

24. Sterngold, *Burning Down the House: How Greed, Deceit, and Bitter Revenge Destroyed E.F. Hutton,* p. 65.

25. Stevens, *Sudden Death: The Rise and Fall of E.F. Hutton,* p. 59.

26. Ibid., p. 60.

27. Felix Belair Jr., "Javits Is Opposed to Nixon Slate for Foreign-Investment Agency," *New York Times,* July 11, 1970, p. 29.

28. "Getty in E.F. Hutton Testimonial," *New York Times,* July 17, 1972, p. 46.

29. "Let's Hear It For E.F. Hutton," *Forbes,* November 13, 1978, p. 196.

30. "A Hard Sell Strategy at Hutton," *Business Week,* January 19, 1981, p. 110.

PART 4

1. Tamar Lewin, "World's a Stage for '49 Class," *New York Times,* April 4, 1986, p. D1.

2. Alex Kuczynski, "100 Candles for a Darling of Society and Charity," *New York Times,* March 30, 2002, p. B1.

3. Laurence Shames, *Big Time: The Harvard Business School's Most Successful Class and How It Shaped America* (New York: Harper and Row, 1986), p. 194.

4. Shames, p. 204.

CHAPTER 12

1. Lee Smith, "J&J Comes a Long Way from Baby," *Fortune,* June 1, 1981, p. 61.

2. Ibid., p. 44.

3. Daniel F. Cuff, "Chief of Johnson & Johnson to Step Down in Revamping," *New York Times,* October 25, 1988, p. D1.

4. Thomas Moore, "The Fight to Save Tylenol," *Fortune,* November 29, 1982, p. 44.

5. Ibid., p. 44.

6. Ibid., p. 44.

7. Ibid., p. 47.

8. "Tylenol's 'Miracle' Comeback," *Time,* October 17, 1983, p. 67.

9. Ibid., p. 67.

10. "After Its Recover, New Headaches for Tylenol," *Business Week,* May 14, 1984, p. 137.

11. "Tylenol's 'Miracle' Comeback," p. 67.

12. N. R. Kleinfeld, "Tylenol's Rapid Comeback," *New York Times,* September 17, 1983, p. 33.

13. Tamar Lewin, "Business Ethics' New Appeal," *New York Times,* December 11, 1983, p. B4.

14. Gail Collins, "Tylenol Again Top Pain Reliever After Trauma of Cyanide Deaths," United Press International, August 5, 1983.

15. "Johnson & Johnson: Needing an Antidote," *Economist,* December 1983, p. 78.

16. "Clean Teeth and a Clear Conscience," *Economist,* January 31, 1987, p. 58.

17. Rick Atkinson, "Waking Up to the New Tylenol Nightmare," *The Washington Post,* February 23, 1986, p. A1.

18. Atkinson, "Waking Up to the New Tylenol Nightmare," p. A1.

19. "The Tylenol Rescue: J&J Rushes to Limit the Corporate Damage," *Newsweek,* March 3, 1986, p. 52.

20. Michael Norman, "FBI Finds No Tampering with Packaging of Tyelnol," *New York Times,* February 19, 1986, p. B6.

21. "Tylenol Rescue," p. 52.

22. Karin Laub, "Burke Says J&J Has Not Been Defeated," Associated Press, February 18, 1986.

23. Steven Prokesch, "A Lender in Crisis: James Edward Burke," *New York Times,* February 19, 1986, p. B6.

24. Marlene Aig, "Grief Stricken Mom of Tylenol Victim Says Capsule Ban Too Late," Associated Press, February 18, 1986.

25. "Switching to Caplets," *Fortune,* March 17, 1986, p. 8.

26. "The Tylenol Rescue," p. 52.

27. "Tylenol Not 'True Crisis' Says Herbert Schmertz," O'Dwyer's PR Services Report, December 1989.

28. Shames, *The Big Time,* p. 170.

29. Marlene Aig, "Family Sues Drug Manufacturer Over Death," Associated Press, February 20, 1987.

30. James Brady, "The Big Men Behind the Big Move," *Advertising Age,* March 25, 1985, p. 3.

31. "A Star Is Born—The Cap Cities Megamerger Opens the Door to More Media Takeovers," *Business Week,* April 1, 1985, p. 74.

32. Marc Frons, "Low Profile, High Power: Tom Murphy's Quiet Rise to the Top," *Business Week,* April 1, 1985, p. 77.

33. "Repeating a Class Act," *Financial World,* April 15, 1986, p. 111.

34. Geraldine Fabrikant, "Not Ready for Prime Time?" *New York Times Magazine,* April 12, 1987, p. 30.

35. "Why Cap Cities is Sitting Pretty," *Business Week,* March 21, 1983, p. 121.

36. Frons, "Low Profile, High Power: Tom Murphy's Quiet Rise to the Top," p. 77.

37. "Tom Murphy's Pleasant Cash Problem," *Forbes,* October 1, 1976, p. 50.

38. *Television and Cable Factbook, 2000, Number 68, Cable Volume 2* (Washington: Warren Communications, 2000), p. F-1.

39. Fabrikant, "Not Ready for Prime Time?" p. 30.

40. Walt Hawver, *Capital Cities/ABC, The Early Years: 1954–1986* (*How the Minnow Came to Swallow the Whale*) (Radnor, PA: Chilton Book Company, 1994).

41. "A Star Is Born—The Cap Cities Megamerger Opens the Door to More Media Takeovers," p. 75.

42. Hawver, *Capital Cities/ABC, The Early Years: 1954–1986,* p. 316.

43. "Wall Street, Broadcast Industry React Favorably to Capital Cities–ABC Merger," *The Wall Street Journal,* March 19, 1985, p. 3.

44. "A Star Is Born—The Cap Cities Megamerger Opens the Door to More Media Takeovers," p. 75.

45. Subrata N. Chakravarty, "We Bought, We Leveraged, We Improved," *Forbes,* November 7, 1994, p. 198.

46. "Big Media, Big Money," *Newsweek* 105, April 1, 1985, p. 59.

47. "Capital Cities Is Likely to Firmly Control ABC in a Smooth Transition Following Their Merger," *The Wall Street Journal,* March 20, 1985, p. 4.

48. Pamela G. Hollie, "An Empire Builder Without Usual Ego," *New York Times,* March 20, 1985, p. D1.

49. "Big Media, Big Money," p. 52.

50. Thomas Moore, "Culture Shock Rattles the TV Networks," *Fortune* 113, April 14, 1986, p. 26.

51. Cathy Trost, "Capital Cities' Reputation With Unions Contrasts Adoring View of Wall Street," March 21, 1985, p. 33.

52. "Why So High?" *Financial World,* April 3–16, 1985, p. 36.

53. "Big Media, Big Money," p. 59.

54. Ibid., p. 59.

55. James Brady, "The Big Men Behind Big Move," *Advertising Age,* March 25, 1986, p. 3.

56. Jonathan Alter, "Taking the Knife to ABC," *Newsweek,* April 7, 1985, p. 58.

57. Dennis Kneale, "Duo at Capital Cities Scores a Hit, But Can Network Be Part of It?" *The Wall Street Journal,* February 20, 1990, p. A1.

58. Ken Auletta, "The Network Takeovers: Why ABC?" *New York Times Magazine,* July 28, 1991, p. 22.

59. Kneale, "Duo At Capital Cities Scores a Hit," p. A6.

60. Fabrikant, "Not Ready for Prime Time?" p. 30.

61. Allan Sloan and Thomas Baker, "Murphy's Law," *Forbes,* March 16, 1981, p. 66; Subrata N. Chakravarty, "An Exception to Murphy's Law," *Forbes,* August 10, 1987, p. 36.

62. "Thomas S. Murphy [Executives to Watch]," *Business Week,* April 15, 1988, p. 83.

63. Fabrikant, "Not Ready for Prime Time?" p. 36.

CHAPTER 13

1. Margaret Carroll, "Crown Jewels According to Forbes," *Chicago Tribune,* February 3, 1988, p. 7.

2. Richard I. Kirkland, Jr., "Should You Leave It All to the Children?" *Fortune,* September 29, 1986, p. 18.

3. Howard Rudintsky, "The Crowning Touch," *Forbes,* December 8, 1980, p. 78; "The Crown Family Empire," *Business Week,* March 31, 1986, pp. 50–51.

4. Bob Tamarkin, "The Ordeal of Lester Crown," *New York Times Magazine,* December 7, 1983, p. 41.

5. " 'Insider' Trading by General Dynamics in Its Own Stock Is Alleged in SEC Suit," *The Wall Street Journal,* February 28, 1980.

6. "General Dynamics: The Tangled Tale of Taki Veliotis," *Business Week,* June 25, 1984, p. 120.

7. Ibid.

8. Allan Dodds Frank, "The One That Got Away," *Forbes,* January 16, 1984, pp. 32–33.

9. Tamarkin, "The Ordeal of Lester Crown," p. 41.

10. Ford S. Worthy, "Mr. Clean Charts a New Course at General Dynamics," *Fortune,* April 28, 1986, p. 71.

11. "General Dynamics Under Fire," *Business Week,* March 25, 1985, p. 71.

12. Worthy, "Mr. Clean Charts a New Course at General Dynamics," p. 71.

13. Wayne Biddle, "Lester Crown Blames the System," *New York Times,* June 16, 1986, p. C1.

14. Tamarkin, "The Ordeal of Lester Crown," p. 41.

15. Kenneth Dreyfack and Judith Dobrzynski, "The Crown Family Empire," *Business Week,* March 31, 1986, p. 50.

16. *Hearings Before the Subcommittee on Oversight and Investigations of the Committee on Energy and Commerce,* House of Representatives, 99th Congress, 1st Session, Serial No. 99-93 (Washington: Government Printing Office, 1986), p. 373.

17. Bill Keller, "Pentagon Acts on Dynamics Director," *New York Times,* September 27, 1985, p. D1.

18. Kenneth Dreyfack, "Inside the Dynasty that Controls General Dynamics," *Business Week,* March 25, 1985, p. 74.

19. Tamarkin, "The Ordeal of Lester Crown," p. 41.

20. Ibid.

21. Gregory Gordon, "General Dynamics Official Allowed to Retain Security Clearance," United Press International, March 20, 1987.

22. Biddle, "Lester Crown Blames the System," III, p. 1.

23. Tamarkin, "The Ordeal of Lester Crown," p. 41.

24. Biddle, "Lester Crown Blames the System," III, p. 1.

25. "The Crown Family Empire," *Business Week,* March 31, 1986, p. 55.

26. Tamarkin, "The Ordeal of Lester Crown," p. 41.

27. "SEC's Chairman: Wall Street-Wise," *Nation's Business,* November 1983, p. 95.

28. Gretchen Morgenson, "The Leaky Umbrella That Is the SEC," *Money* 14, November 1984, p. 230.

29. Jeff Gerth, "Shad: Ease Regulations," *New York Times,* April 7, 1981, p. D6.

30. "A Newfound Harmony with Washington," *Business Week,* December 21, 1981, p. 79.

31. Richard L. Hudson, "The Deregulator," *The Wall Street Journal,* January 12, 1984, p. 1.

32. "Serving Up Shad for the SEC," *Newsweek,* March 9, 1981, p. 68.

33. Hudson, "The Deregulator," p. 1.

34. Bruce Ingersoll, "Inundated Agency: Busy SEC Must Let Many Cases, Filings Go Uninvestigated," *The Wall Street Journal,* December 16, 1985, p. 23.

35. Kenneth B. Noble, "Behind the Dispute Over the SEC," *New York Times,* April 21, 1982, p. D13.

36. Marshall E. Blume, Jeremy J. Siegel, and Dan Rottenberg, *Revolution on Wall Street: The Rise and Decline of the New York Stock Exchange* (New York: W.W. Norton & Co., 1993), p. 154.

37. Ingersoll, "Inundated Agency," p. 1.

38. Glenn Yago, *Junk Bonds: How High Yield Securities Restructured Corporate America* (New York: Oxford University Press, 1991), p. 24.

39. Chancellor, *Devil Take the Hindmost: A History of Financial Speculation,* p. 258.

40. Paul S. Boyer, *Promises to Keep: The United States Since World War II* (Boston: Houghton Mifflin Company, 1999), p. 421.

41. John S. R. Shad, "The Leveraging of America," *The Wall Street Journal,* June 8, 1984.

42. "S.E.C. Chief Plans Insider Trade Curb," *New York Times,* October 26, 1981, p. D1.

43. Chancellor, *Devil Take the Hindmost: A History of Financial Speculation,* p. 263.

44. Bruce Ingersoll, "SEC Should Be Empowered to Regulate U.S. Securities, Some in House Suggest," *The Wall Street Journal,* March 22, 1985.

45. Clemens P. Work, "The SEC Enters an Era of Sweeping Changes" *U.S. News & World Report* 97, October 29, 1984, pp. 83–84.

46. "The SEC Swats at Insider Trading," *Business Week,* April 19, 1982, p. 96.

47. G. David Wallace and Stan Crock, "Speaking Softly and Carrying No Stick," *Business Week,* September 23, 1985, p. 34.

48. Priscilla Ann Smith and Beatrice E. Garcia, "Boesky Apparently Reaped at Least $203 Million in Illicit Profits with Levine's Inside Information," *The Wall Street Journal,* November 24, 1986, p. 2.

49. Bruce Ingersoll, "Shad Defends SEC Move to Allow Boesky to Sell Holdings Before Probe Disclosure," *The Wall Street Journal,* November 24, 1986, p. 2.

50. Ibid.

51. "Mr. Shad's Disclosure Problem," *The Wall Street Journal,* December 5, 1986, p. 30.

52. Thomas E. Rice, "Burden of Proof: SEC's Failed Probes of Milken in the Past Show Difficulty of Its Mission," *The Wall Street Journal*, January 25, 1989.

53. Chancellor, *Devil Take the Hindmost: A History of Financial Speculation*, p. 259.

54. Yago, *Junk Bonds: How High Yield Securities Restructured Corporate America*, p. 25.

55. "Wanted: A Mr. Clean for Drexel Burnham," *Newsweek* 113, January 23, 1989, p. 42.

56. Kurt Eichenwald, "Drexel's Uncertain Future," *New York Times*, October 15, 1989, III, p. 11.

57. Steve Swartz, "Shad Says He Won't Do Window Dressing: Ex-SEC Chief Intends to Be Active Chairman of Drexel," *The Wall Street Journal*, April 17, 1989.

58. Ibid.

59. Brett Duval Fromson, "The Last Days of Drexel Burnham," *Fortune*, May 21, 1990.

60. Chancellor, *Devil Take the Hindmost: A History of Financial Speculation*, p. 280.

61. "Editorial: Securities Exchange," *The Nation*, May 8, 1989, p. 613.

62. Tamar Lewin, "World's a Stage for '49 Class," *New York Times*, April 4, 1986, pp. D1–3.

CHAPTER 14

1. Shirley Curlman, "At Yuletime, or Anytime, Bloomingdale's Chairman Marvin Traub is a Master of Show and Sell," *People*, December 22, 1980, p. 42.

2. Ibid., p. 47.

3. Ibid., p. 47.

4. Ibid., p. 44.

5. Ibid., p. 47.

6. Ibid., p. 47.

7. "Right on Target," *New Yorker*, June 23, 1986, p. 21.

8. Curlman, "At Yuletime, or Anytime, Bloomingdale's Chairman Marvin Traub Is a Master of Show and Sell," p. 47.

9. Grant, *International Directory of Company Histories*, p. 36.

10. "Talking Business with Irwin Cohen of Touche, Ross," *New York Times,* December 16, 1980, p. D2.

11. David Moin, "Traub Talks Back," *Women's Wear Daily,* November 1, 1993, p. 4.

12. Moin, "Traub Talks Back," *Women's Wear Daily,* p. 4.

13. Loomis, "The Biggest, Looniest Deal Ever," p. 2.

14. Isadore Barmash, "In Retail, It's Perilous at the Top," *New York Times,* May 17, 1991, p. D1.

15. Maggie Mahar, "Here Come the High Rollers, and Atlantic City Will Never Be the Same," *Barron's,* April 13, 1981, p. 6.

16. Ibid., p. 7.

17. Susan Duffy Benway, "Sideshow on the Boardwalk: Starring Resorts and the Wheeler-Dealers," *Barron's,* April 14, 1986, p. 28.

18. "All in the Family," *Forbes* 138, August 11, 1986, p. 110.

19. Benway, "Sideshow on the Boardwalk: Starring Resorts and the Wheeler-Dealers," p. 28.

20. "Resorts Appoints President as Chief," *New York Times,* April 16, 1986, p. D2.

21. "Resorts May Sell Part of Land Empire," *The Record,* June 18, 1986, p. A14.

22. John R. O'Donnell, *Trumped! The Inside Story of the Real Donald Trump—His Cunning Rise and His Spectacular Fall* (New York: Simon and Schuster, 1991), p. 98.

23. "Casino Veteran Pulling Up Stakes as President of the Taj Mahal," *The Star-Ledger,* May 1, 1991.

24. O'Donnell, *Trumped! The Inside Story of the Real Donald Trump—His Cunning Rise and His Spectacular Fall,* p. 98.

25. Mahar, "Here Come the High Rollers, and Atlantic City Will Never Be the Same," *Barron's,* p. 6.

26. O'Donnell, *Trumped! The Inside Story of the Real Donald Trump—His Cunning Rise and His Spectacular Fall,* p. 91.

27. "Trump's Resorts Bid 'Crucial,' " *Newsday,* February 23, 1988, p. 47.

28. Henry Stern, "Another Management Change at Trump Taj Mahal," *Associated Press,* July 31, 1990; Patrick McGeehan, "Trump Shuffles Taj Bosses—Again," *The Record,* August 1, 1990, p. E1.

29. Iris Taylor, "Casino Veteran Pulling Up Stakes as President of the Taj Mahal," *The Star-Ledger,* May 1, 1991.

EPILOGUE

1. Stratford P. Sherman, "You're Invited to the CEO's Ball," *Fortune,* January 15, 1990, p. 140.

2. Subrata N. Chakravarty, "An Exception to Murphy's Law?" *Forbes,* August 10, 1987, p. 36.

3. Jonathan Welsh, "Sharp Contrast: Why Did ABC Prosper While CBS-TV Blinked?" *The Wall Street Journal,* August 2, 1995, p. A8.

4. Subrata N. Chakavarty, "We Bought, We Leveraged, We Improved," *Forbes,* November 7, 1994, p. 197.

5. "Buy? Or Build?" *Forbes,* November 7, 1994, p. 202.

6. Elizabeth Jensen, "Burke's Retirement from Capital Cities Dismantles Partnership with Murphy," *Wall Street Journal,* February 9, 1994, p. B9.

7. Johnnie L. Roberts, "The Men Behind the Megadeals," *Newsweek* 126, August 14, 1996, p. 22.

8. Bernard Weintraub, "For Disney Chairman, a Deal Quenches a Personal Thirst," *New York Times,* August 1, 1995, p. A1.

9. Geraldine Fabrikant, "Walt Disney to Acquire ABC in $19 Billion Deal, to Build Giant for Entertainment," *New York Times,* August 1, 1995, p. A1.

10. Joseph Weber, "Dive Bomber in the War on Drugs," *Business Week,* November 23, 1998, p. 8.

11. Linda Grant, "You've Got the Stock Options, Now Get a Life," *Fortune,* June 24, 1996, p. 60.

12. Harold Seneker, "Lester Crown (and family)," *Forbes,* October 23, 1989, p. 160.

13. "Why Is Jack Davis Smiling?" *Forbes,* December 19, 1994, p. 84.

14. Strafford Sherman, "You're Invited to the CEO's Ball," *Fortune,* January 15, 1990, p. 140.

15. Roger P. Sonnabend, "Why I'm Voting for McGovern," *Nation's Business* 60, October 1972, p. 32.

16. "Sonesta President to Quit: Roger Sonnabend Is Named," *The Wall Street Journal,* August 31, 1977, p. 15.

17. David Ghitelman, Christine Levite, and Kate Rounds, "Hotel Dynasties," *Meetings and Conventions,* February 1989, p. 50.

18. "The Family Company After Going Public," *New England Business,* August 4, 1986, p. 55.

19. "CEO Interview—Sonesta International Hotels Corporation," *The Wall Street Journal,* July 18, 1994, p. 1

20. *Harvard Business School Fiftieth Reunion Profile* (Cambridge, MA: Alumni Program Office, Harvard University, 1999), p. 182.

21. Jim Carlton, *Apple: The Inside Story of Intrigue, Egomania, and Business Blunders* (New York: Times Business, 1997), p. 54.

22. Robert Metz, "Market Place: Cautious Way to Pick Stock," *New York Times,* April 12, 1982, p. D6.

23. Richard Phalon, "Embarrassment of Riches," *Forbes,* April 11, 1983, p. 200.

24. *Sequoia Fund, Inc., Annual Report,* December 31, 1984.

25. Laura R. Walbert, "Hell, NO, We Won't Buy," *Forbes,* November 4, 1985, p. 256.

Index